A GUIDE TO
MILITARY ART

—

CHARLES LYALL'S
BRITISH ARMY,
1642 TO 1812

A GUIDE TO MILITARY ART

—

CHARLES LYALL'S BRITISH ARMY, 1642 TO 1812

RAY WESTLAKE

The Naval & Military Press

Published by

The Naval & Military Press Ltd
Unit 5 Riverside
Bellbrook Industrial Estate
Uckfield, East Sussex
TN22 1QQ
England

Tel: +44 (0) 1825 749494

www.naval-military-press.com

ACKNOWLEDGEMENTS

My thanks to the Anne SK Brown Military Collection and its curator Peter Harrington for their generous help and permission to use these images. Also to a friend of some thirty-five years, Alan Seymour, whose skills around the internet are second to none. Important to any author is the support received at home, this in my case coming continuously from my guide in all things, Mrs Claire Westlake. And finally, to Chris and Gary Buckland of the wonderful Naval & Military Press for their continued faith in these 'Guides.'

INTRODUCTION

Who was Charles Lyall? Having dismissed the much written about and documented Charles James Lyall (1845-1920)—prominent member of the Indian Civil Service, authority on Eastern languages, author, poet, fellow of the British Academy, vice president of the Royal Asiatic Society and much, much more—simply on the strength of 'painter' not being mentioned in any of his lengthy and plentiful biographies, I then turned to his father. Also named Charles, he was a London banker and partner in the firm of Lyall, Matheson & Co but again, no mention of him being an artist, either professional or amateur. There was also a Sir Charles Lyall, 1st Baronet, but again, an achiever of much, but not in the world of brushes, easel, paint or canvas.

The next attempt to find an artist Charles Lyall took me to a Charles Matthew Lyall who was born in Westminster on 14 May 1832. His baptism took place at the church of Our Lady of Assumption and St Gregory, Bavarian Chapel in Warwick Street, Soho on 24 June and he would marry Frances Augusta Wallace in Somers Town on 24 July 1880. His death, at 42 Clifton Hill, St John's Wood, NW London was on 3 May 1911, his burial at St Mary's Roman Catholic Cemetery, Kensal Green—grave No 3384. Census records for this Charles Lyall, by the way, show his profession as 'vocalist'.

Now on the track of a singer, purely by chance I stumbled across the *Illustrated London News* for 13 December 1876 in which, tucked away in the classified advertisement section, I found mention of the *Universal Dance Album* for 1877. A delight, I'm sure, in which for a one shilling investment you would get twenty-eight pages of music—quadrilles, waltzes, gallops, polkas and country dances—'with superbly illustrated frontispiece drawn by Charles Lyall.'

Next, the *Repertoire International de la Presse Musicale* ('RIPM') website where, under 'Illustrations of the Week', reference is made to the nineteenth-century British musical journal, *The Musical World* in which could be found a series of illustrations 'by the English tenor Charles Lyall.' There are six, all neatly signed 'C Lyall', the 'C' and 'L' intertwined in exactly the same manner as the 'CL' initials in the bottom left-hand corners of the Charles Lyall watercolours featured in this Guide.

The 120 plates in this book have been taken from the many thousands held by the Anne SK Brown Military Collection, Brown University Library, Rhode Island, USA and represent good examples of the work of Charles Lyall—opera singer and artist. I have recorded them according to Charles Lyall's caption dates.

INDEX

1 – TRAIN OF ARTILLERY, 1642

For this painting Charles Lyall has consulted two possible sources. On page five of *The History of the Dress of the Royal Regiment of Artillery* by Captain RJ MacDonald there is an almost identical image to Lyall's in black and white which comes with the following text: 'This drawing depicts an artilleryman during the reign of Charles I, and is the earliest period about which authentic information can be obtained.' The author then goes on to say, 'The principal authority is a very rare old work in the R.A. Library, Woolwich, entitled "Ye Gunner's Glasse, 1642," by William Eldred, sometimes Master Gunner of Dover Castle. The frontispiece in this work consists of a portrait of the author [Master Gunner Eldred] in the dress of the period. It is a woodcut, and is coloured—coat blue, facings scarlet, lace yellow; but at what date this colouring was done it is impossible to say.' Both Captain MacDonald's and Lyall's images show a linstock and a pair of callipers (or compasses) for gauging the shot, being held firmly in both hands.

1642.

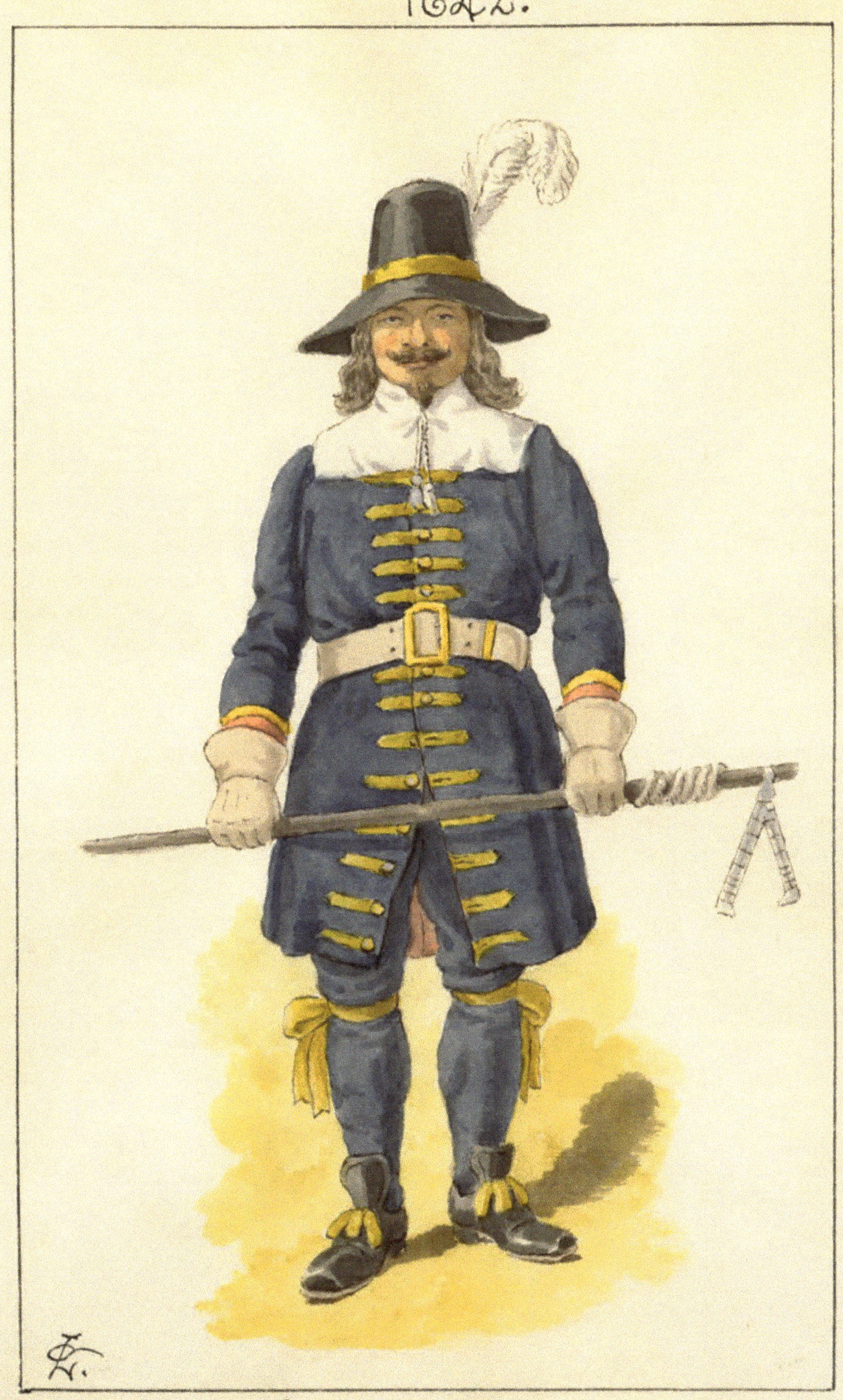

Train of Artillery.

2 – MONCK'S COLDSTREAMERS, MUSQUETEER 1650

A single figure holding a musket over his left shoulder. The right hand grasps a musket rest, the left a smouldering match. A steel breastplate is worn over a buff coat, below which are baggy red breeches and red hose tied with blue ribbons. A sword hangs from the left side, and a cartridge box attached to two red and white cords ending in tassels from the right. A large white ruff is worn and a broad-brimmed black hat with white feathers placed all around. In 1650, General George Monck (sometimes written as Monk), 1st Duke of Albemarle, had been given command of two regiments of the New Model Army. Concentrating his men at the town of Coldstream on the north bank of the River Tweed in Berwickshire, Monck later moved to London where he awaited Charles II's return to England. Here, records recall, he ceremonially laid down all weapons as a Parliamentary force, then took them up again as a regiment of the King. Monck's Regiment in 1660 was styled as The Lord General's Regiment of Foot and as Coldstream Regiment of Foot Guards ten years after that.

1650.

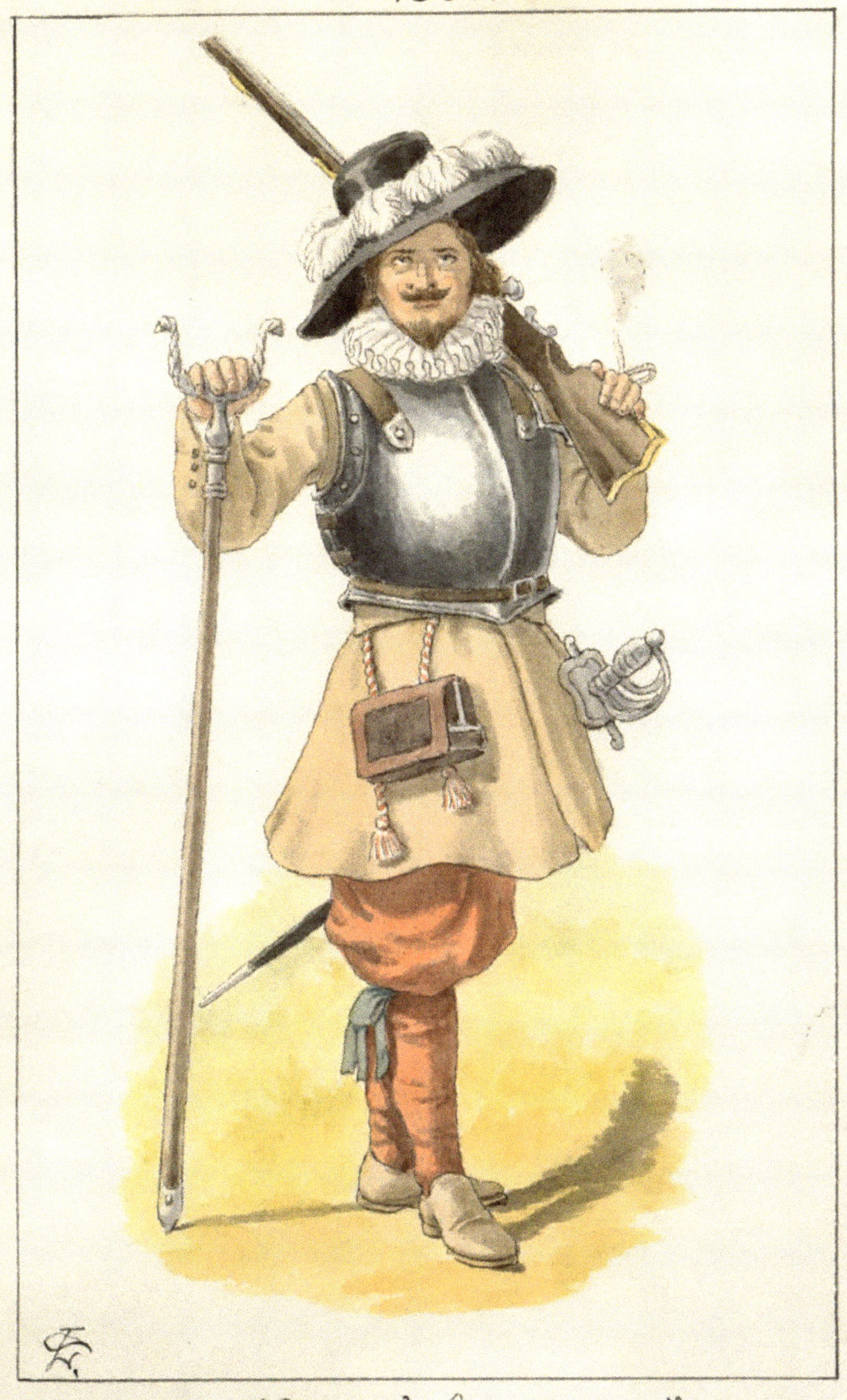

"Monck's Coldstreamers"
"Musqueteer"

3 – COLDSTREAM GUARDS OFFICER, 1660

We have learnt from Plate 2 how Monck's Regiment had been raised in 1650 and ten years after that had taken on the title of the Lord General's Regiment of Foot. The decade had seen the introduction of a long scarlet coat, falling to just above the knee, with wide gold lace down the front and around the bottom where it also provides a pointed edging to narrow slits at each side. The regiment's green facings are seen here on the cuff, this colour only surviving a further ten years until blue was introduced in 1670. The buff leather sword-belt, with its heavy brass fittings, is approximately five inches wide.

1660.

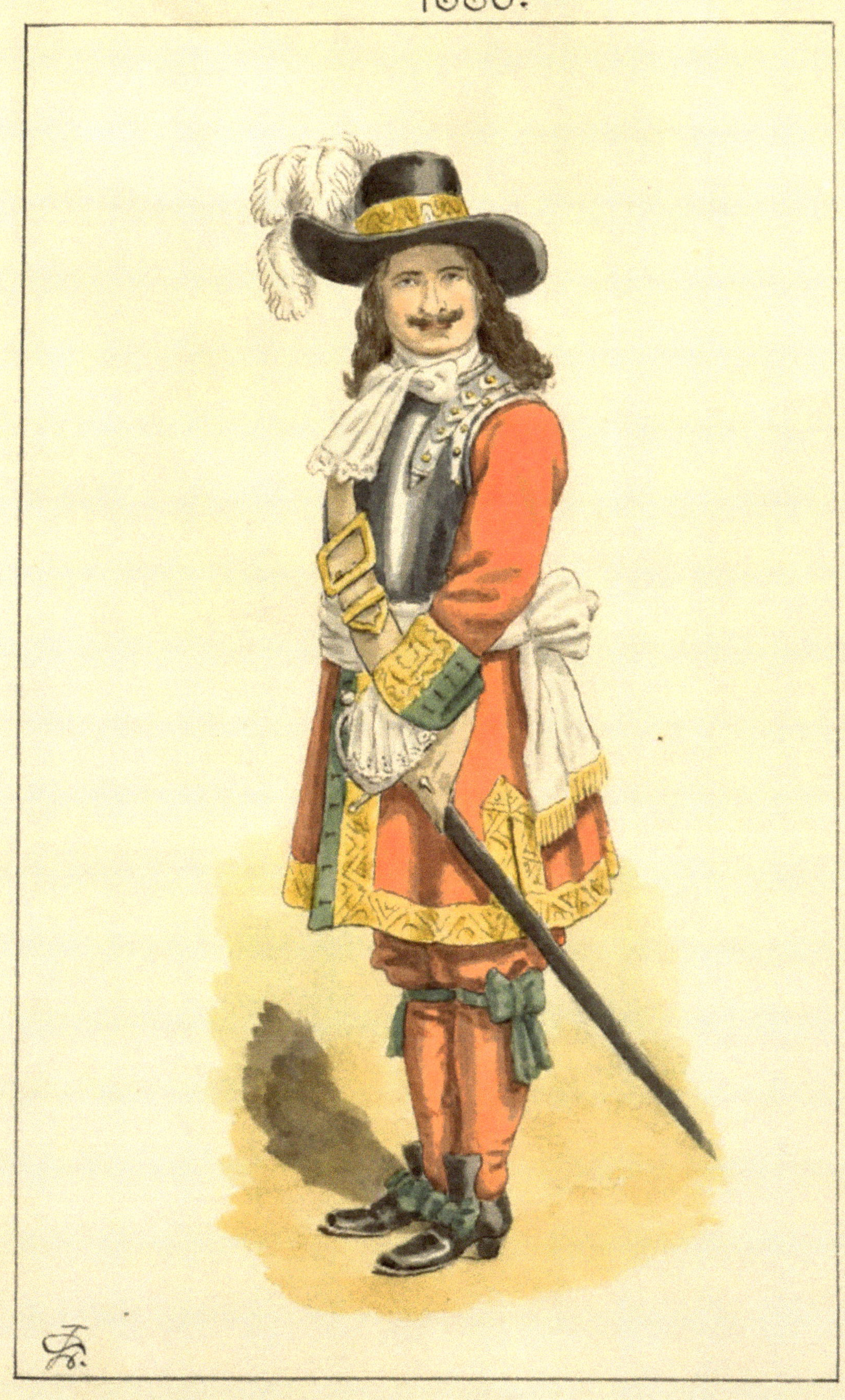

Coldstream Guards.
Officer.

4 – TRAIN OF ARTILLERY, 1660-1702

Charles Lyall entitles his watercolour as 'Train of Artillery 1660-1702', and this corresponds with the caption accompanying the first colour plate in Captain RJ MacDonald's book on Royal Artillery uniform. With his wide-brimmed hat turned up on the left side and a powder-horn hanging from the shoulder via a cord, here we have a gunner holding a linstock and wearing a broad belt around his waist from which hangs a sword.

1660-1702.

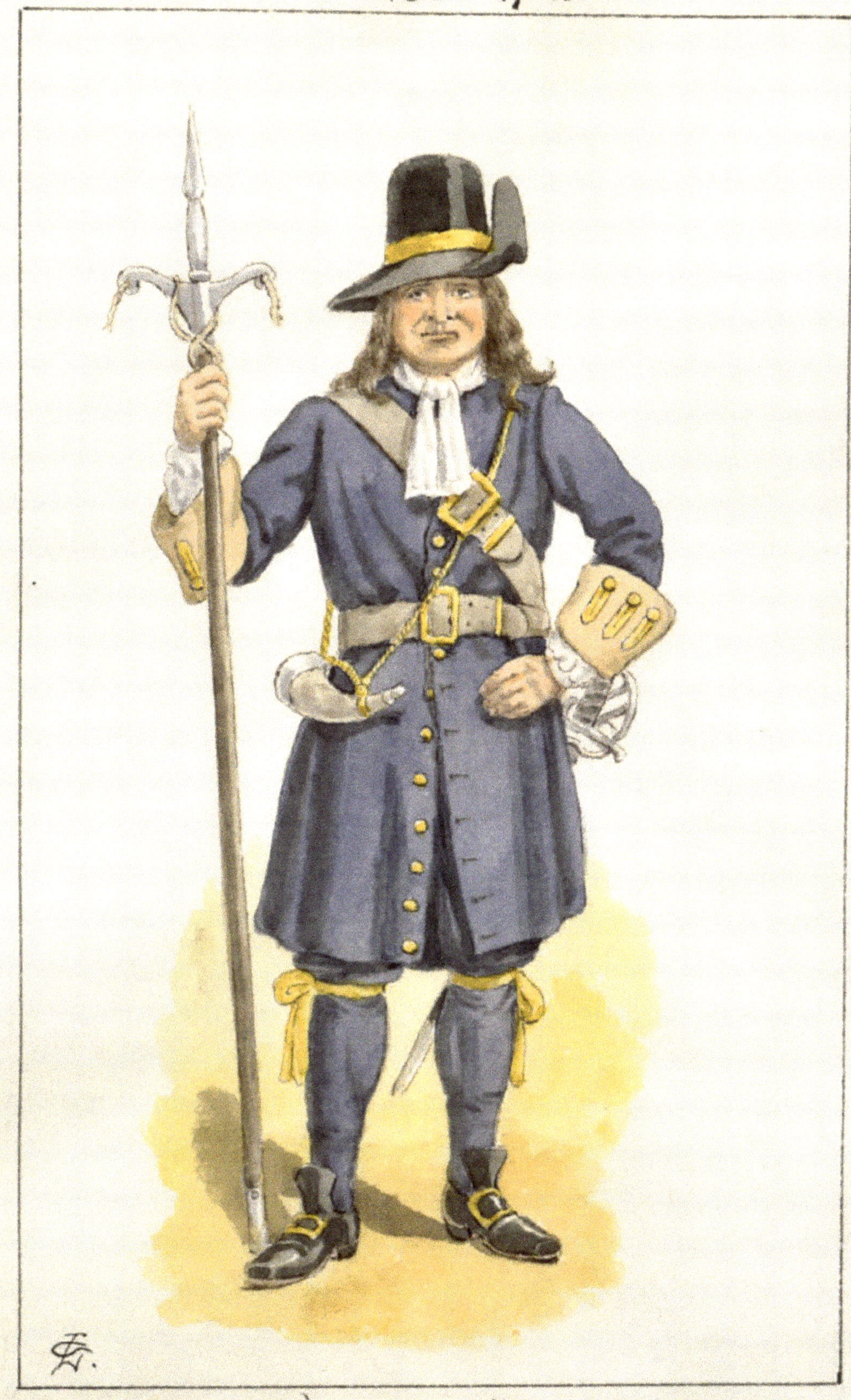

Train of Artillery

5 – TRAIN OF ARTILLERY 1660-1702, OFFICER

And from the same source as Plate 4, we have Charles Lyall's version of an officer for the period 1660-1702. Accompanying his plate, Captain MacDonald's text makes an interesting point regarding the officer's hair, pointing out that it, '...was worn curled, falling on the shoulders, and generally ending in two love-locks; but during the reigns of James II and his successors down to George II, perukes [wigs] were worn, which were made of false hair to imitate long waving curls.' Also noted is how steel caps were worn inside the hats to protect the head against sabre cuts, and how the boots seen in the painting were called 'gambadoes', the wide tops '... to prevent the leg being crushed in a charge.'

1660–1702.

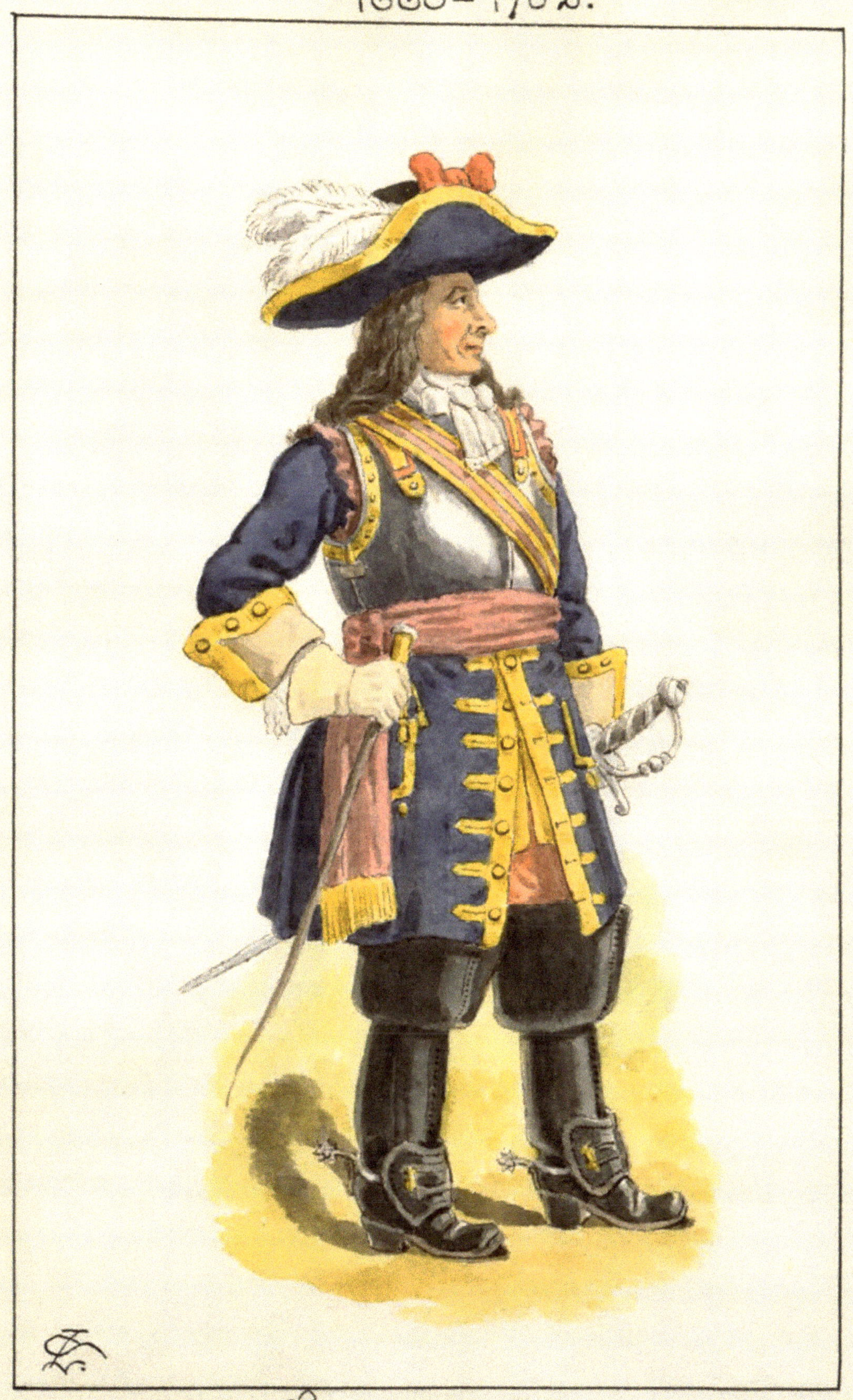

Train of Artillery.
Officer.

6 – FIRST REGIMENT OF FOOT GUARDS, 1662

The King's Royal Regiment of Guards was formed in 1660 and received the designation First Regiment of Foot Guards in 1685. It would retain this name until becoming the Grenadier Guards in 1815, an honour with regard to the regiment's defeat at Waterloo of Napoleon's Imperial Guard. But returning to 1660, it was in that year that Colonel John Russell had been commissioned by Charles II to raise a regiment of royal guards. Russell a staunch supporter of the exiled king and one of the secret band of Royalists known as 'The Sealed Knot.' Charles Lyall features a musketeer of the regiment.

(1)

1662.

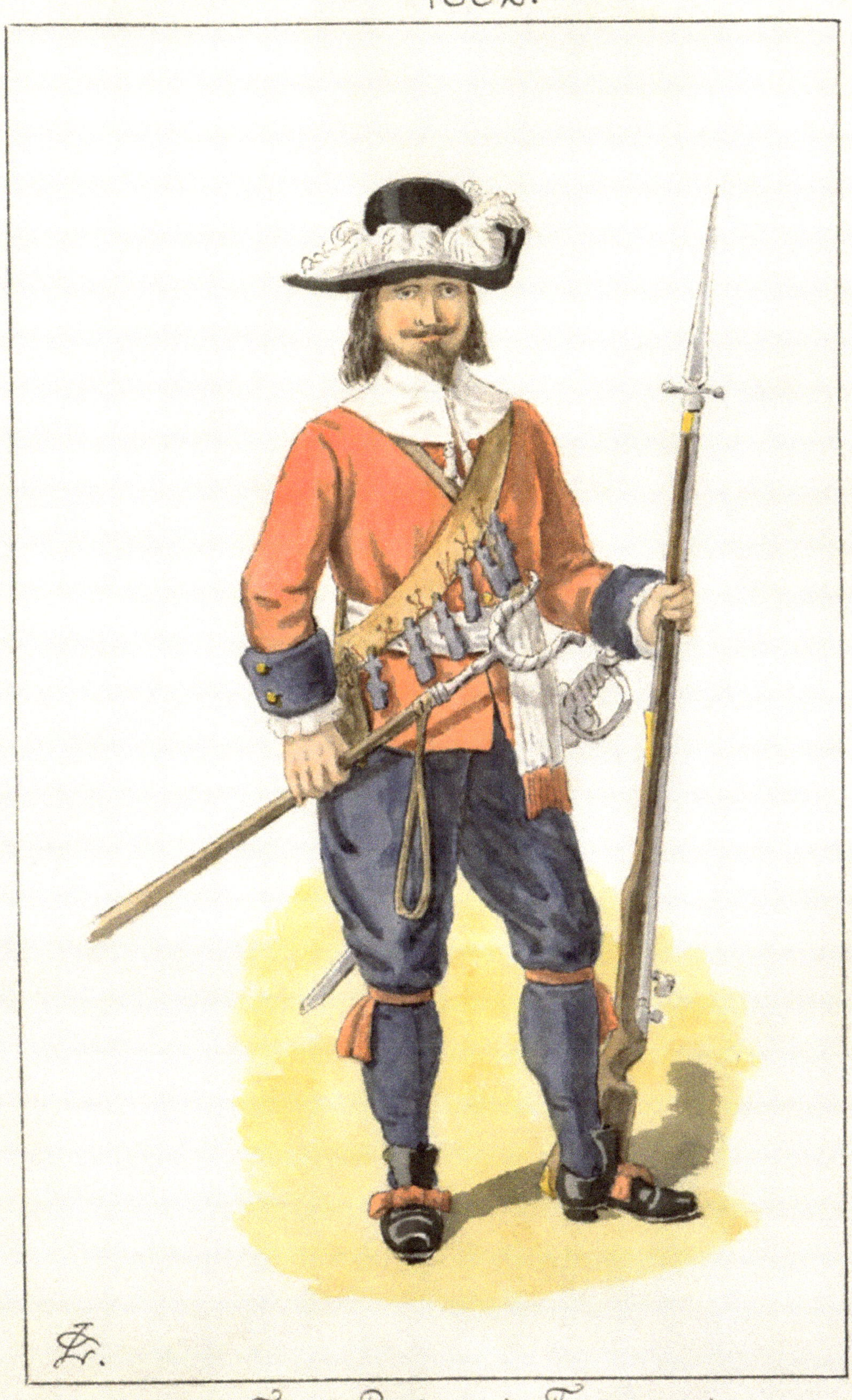

First Regiment of Foot guards.

7 – COLDSTREAM GUARDS MUSKETEER, 1669

Charles Lyall dates this painting of a musketeer as 1669, nine years into the reign of King Charles II. The title of the regiment at this time was the Lord General's Regiment of Foot Guards, its colonel being one George Monck who died on 3 January 1670, twenty years after his formation of the regiment in 1650. Here green facings are apparent in the hat band and cuffs, the coat, breeches and hose being red. Hanging from the leather bandolier are wooden cartridge charges, a bell-shaped priming flask and a black pouch containing bullets. Spare pieces of match were attached to the latter, and Lyall has been careful to show these in his image.

1669.

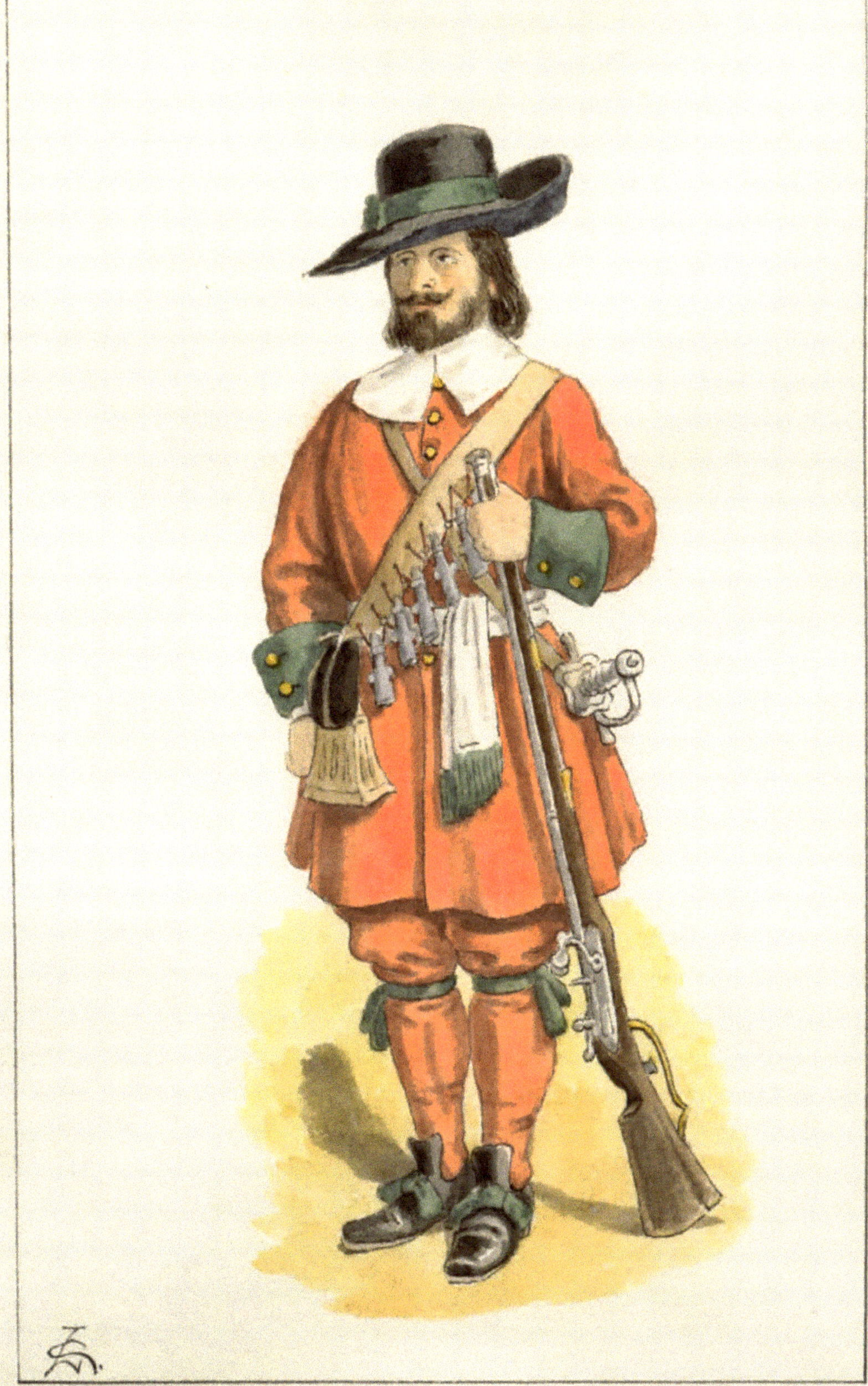

Coldstream Guards.
Musketeer.

8 – COLDSTREAM GUARDS PIKEMAN, 1669

Cecil CP Lawson notes in the first volume of his *History of the Uniforms of the British Army* how only a few years into the reign of Charles II, 'Pikes in some regiments appear to have adopted a special uniform differing from the rest of the battalion.' In some cases this was the reverse of the regiment's colours, i.e. the coat of the facing colour, the facings that of the coat. Regarding the Coldstream, Lawson draws from Cosmo, Duke of Tuscany's *Travels Through England* in which the author describes '...green coats, red cuffs, white sashes with green fringes....' 'The sash,' noted Lawson, 'was a distinguishing feature of the Pikemen's dress. His arms, the sixteen foot pike.'

1669.

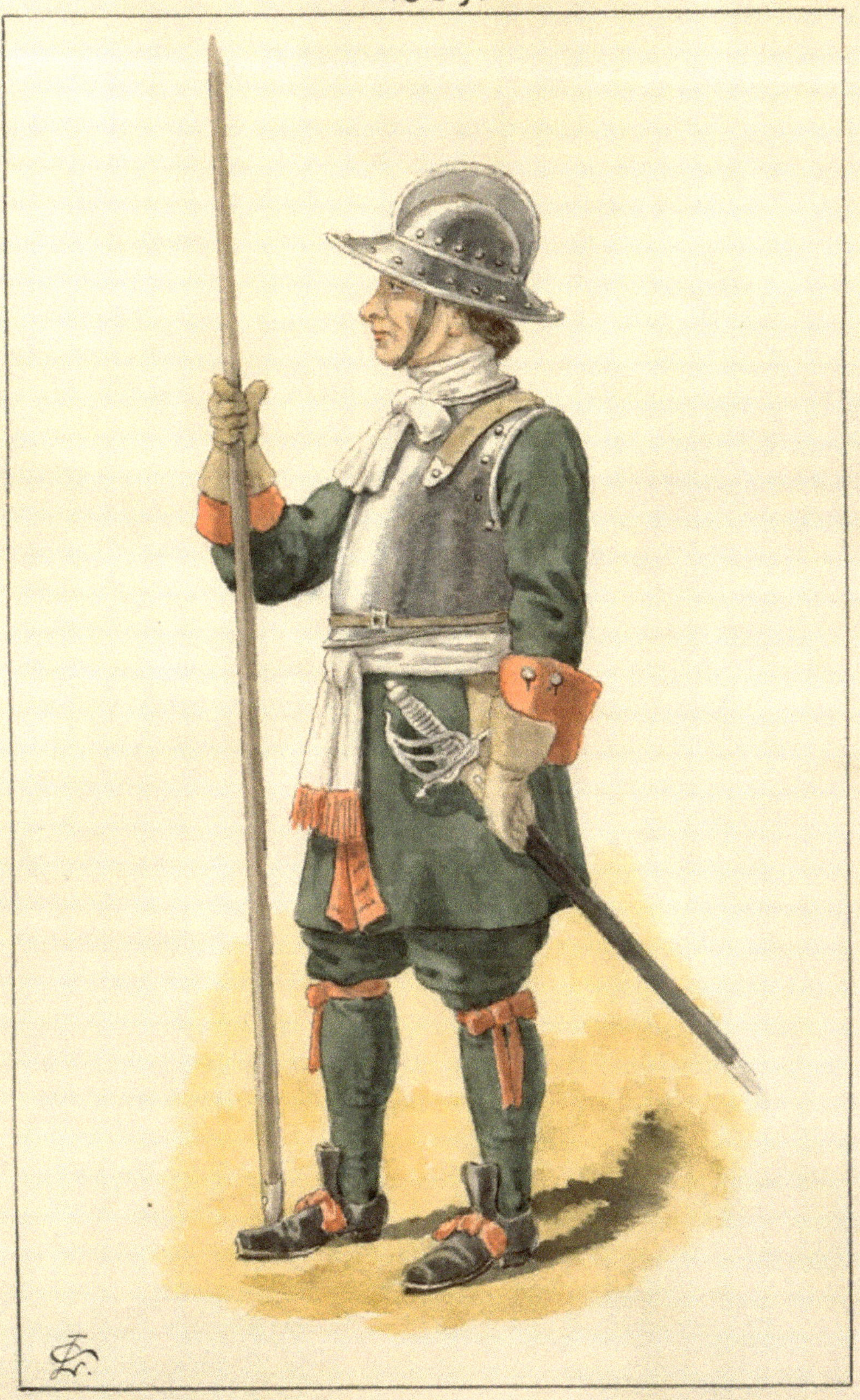

Coldstream Guards.
Pikeman.

9 – THE LORD HIGH ADMIRAL'S REGIMENT MARINES, 1669

Today's Royal Marines can trace their history back to 28 October 1664 and the formation on that date of the Duke of York and Albany's, or Lord High Admiral's Maritime Regiment of Foot, the duke at this time being the Lord High Admiral of the Navy. At Putney Heath in 1684 the regiment attended a review and was described as wearing yellow coats with red facings, red breeches and stockings and hats bound with gold lace. Charles Lyall's painting faithfully follows that information and also includes a crimson sash ending with a yellow fringe, a steel cuirass, black shoes tied with red bows and multiple white feathers in the hat. To meet the artist's date of 1669, we can add that the corps served aboard the fleet during the Dutch Wars of 1669-1680.

1669.

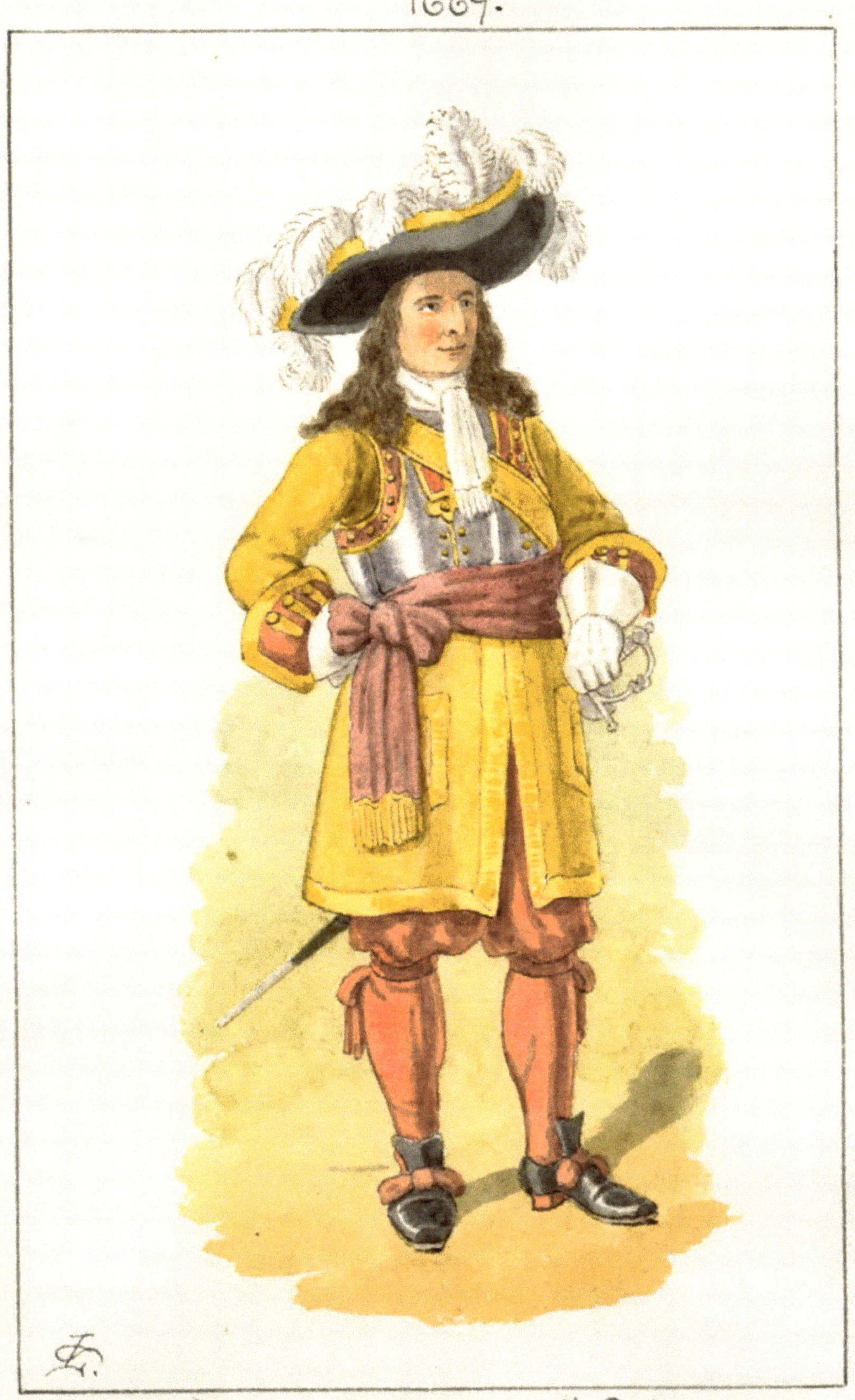

The Lord High Admiral's Reg^{t}.
Marines

10 – THE LORD HIGH ADMIRAL'S REGIMENT MARINES, 1669

We have seen in Plate 9 an officer of this corps, Charles Lyall's image this time, featuring a marine armed with a matchlock. With the yellow coat's lower four buttons undone, the artist reveals red breeches which are tied with ribbons just below the knees. Red ribbon also for the black shoes which have tongues rising up to several inches above the ankle.

1669.

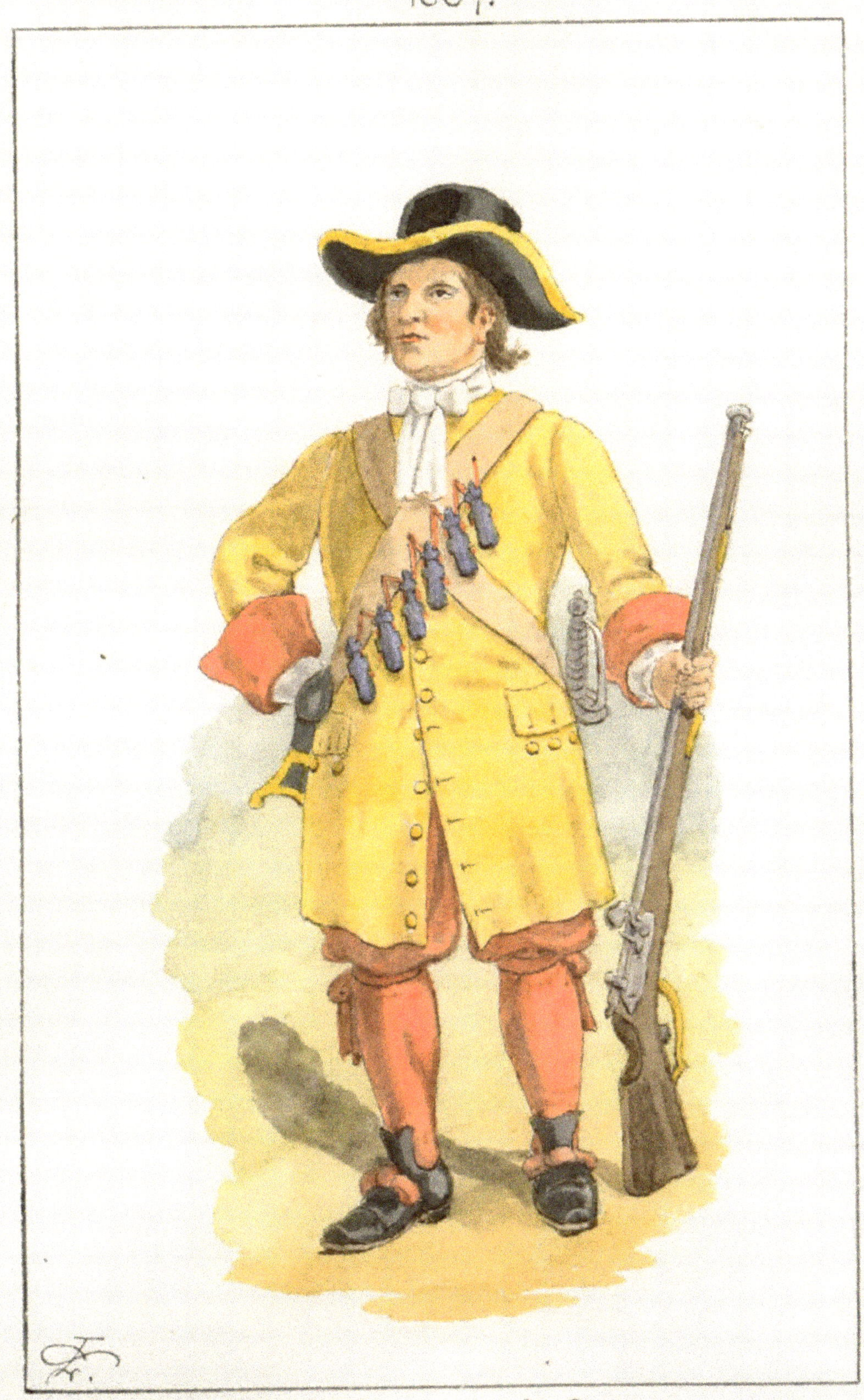

The Lord High Admiral's Regt.
Marines

11 – COLDSTREAM GUARDS GRENADIER COMPANY, 1670

With the death of George Monck, 1st Duke of Albemarle on 3 January 1670, the Lord General's Regiment of Foot Guards was renamed as the Coldstream Regiment of Foot Guards. Monck had founded the regiment in 1650. With the change in name also came a change in facing colour. The green seen in Charles Lyall's image said to have been in use until 1670 when blue was introduced. Clearly seen on the pouch at the grenadier's right side is the regimental badge of the Star of the Order of the Garter. Certainly, King Charles II had rewarded General Monck for his part in restoring him to the throne by making him a Knight of the Garter, but interestingly an article published in the *Household Brigade Magazine* for the summer of 1950 tells how the badge had not been granted to the regiment until 1695. Note the small axe worn at the side behind the pouch, and the red tassels at the ends of each button-hole loop.

1670.

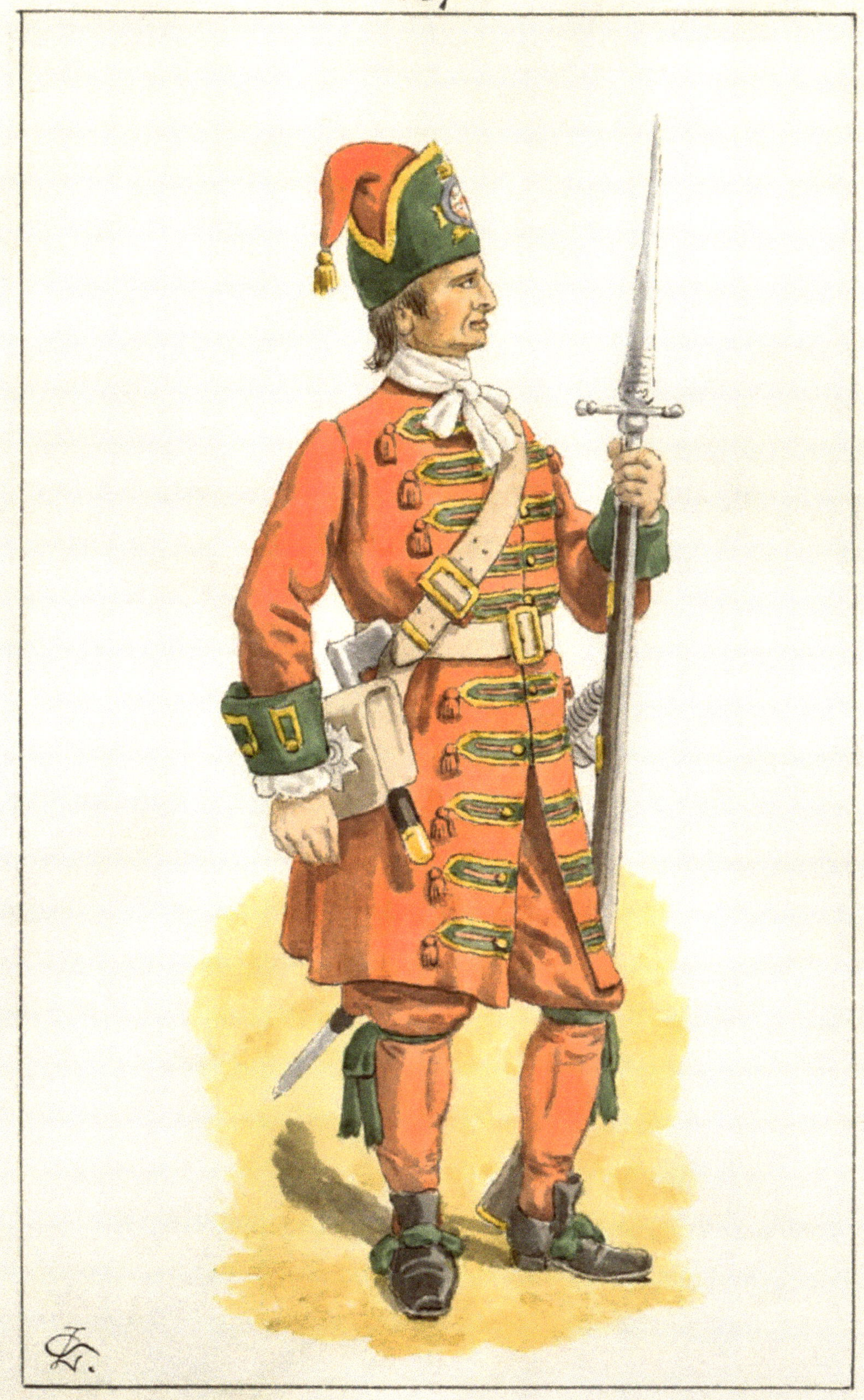

Coldstream Guards.
Grenadier Company.

12 – COLDSTREAM GUARDS DRUM MAJOR, 1670

Here we have a drum major of the year that Lieutenant-General William Craven, 1st Earl of Craven had replaced George Monck as colonel of the regiment. Monck, the founder of what in 1670 would become the Coldstream Guards, had died that year and an engraving of his funeral procession shows drummers and fifers present and a drum major wearing a uniform very much similar to that illustrated by Charles Lyall.

1670.

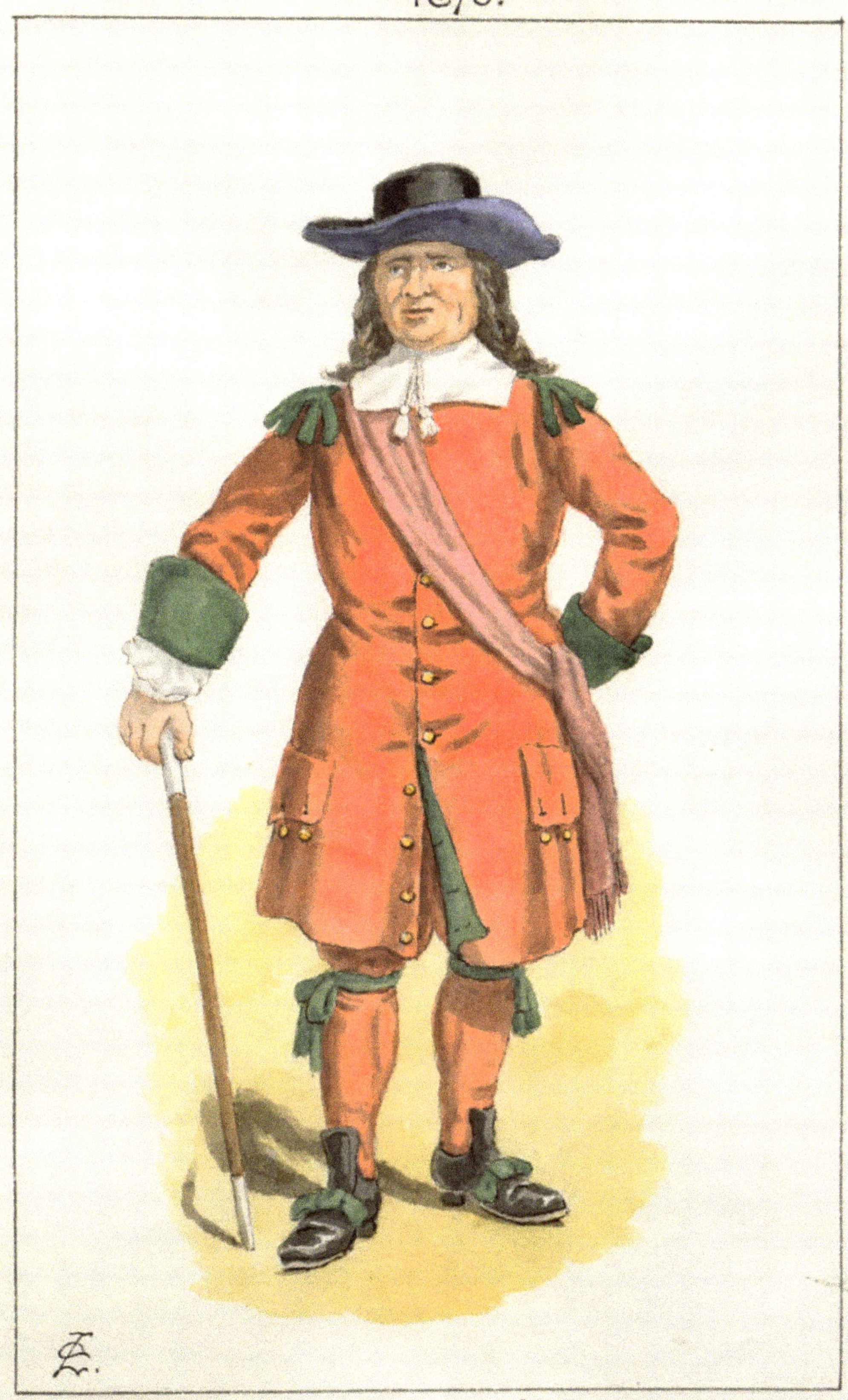

Coldstream Guards
Drum Major.

13 – LIFE GUARDS GRENADIER TROOP, 1679

When the Life Guards were formed in 1660 it comprised men that had remained loyal to Charles II—gentlemen of his court and officers on half pay, notes one source. In 1673, records Cecil CP Lawson, horse grenadiers were added to each Troop of Life Guards, these, he notes '...not composed of gentlemen but were recruited in the ordinary way.' The writer of *A History of the Uniforms of the British Army* then goes on to quote an entry in Evelyn's diary dated 5 December 1683 which reads, 'The King had now augmented his Guards with a new sort of Dragoons, who carried also grenades and were habited after the Polish manner with long peaked caps very fierce and fantastical.' Lawson also makes reference to the coats and their laced buttonholes finished with tufted ends.

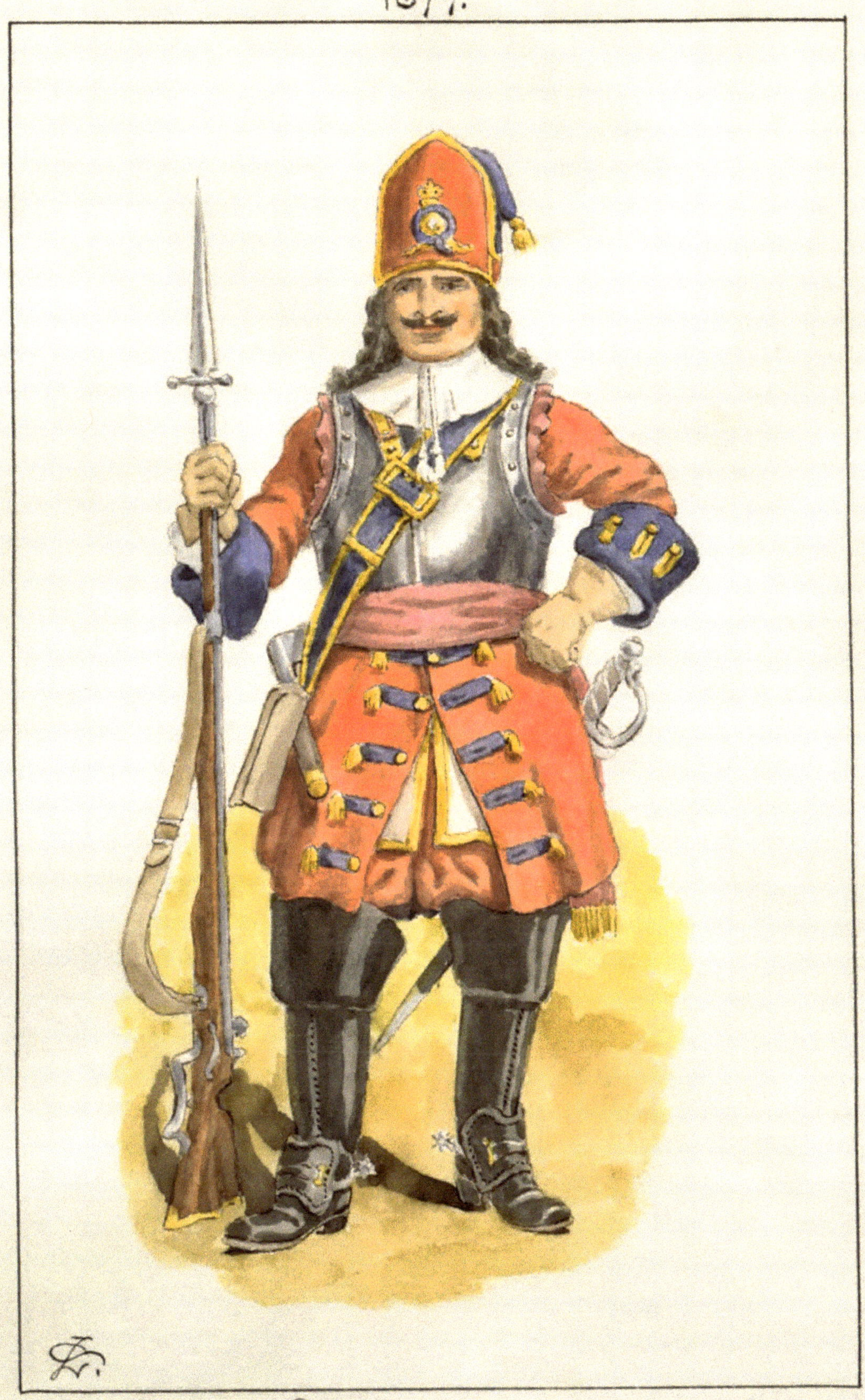

Life Guards:
Grenadier Troop.

14 – SCOTS GREYS, 1683

By a warrant dated 21 May 1678, two independent companies of dragoons were raised in Scotland under Captains John Strachan and John Inglis. For a reliable reference to early Scots Greys uniform we must thank the Rev Percy Sumner for the extensive research carried out by him in the 1930's and later published by the Society for Army Historical Research. In 1679 the companies were noted as wearing grey coats and bonnets and were armed with broadswords. The cost of coat and bonnet was £5. On now to 1683; a reference from the Register of Privy Council dated 22 February of that year records that authorisation had been given '...to import from England 2,436 ells of stone-grey cloth for clothing the Regiment of Dragoons....' Of the independent companies, these in turn would become the Royal Regiment of North British Dragoons, the 2nd Dragoons in 1751 with 'Scots Grey's finding its way into the title in 1866. Note the six cartridges hanging from the bandolier. There were in fact a further six around the back, the total number leading to the dozen being referred to as 'The twelve apostles'.

1683.

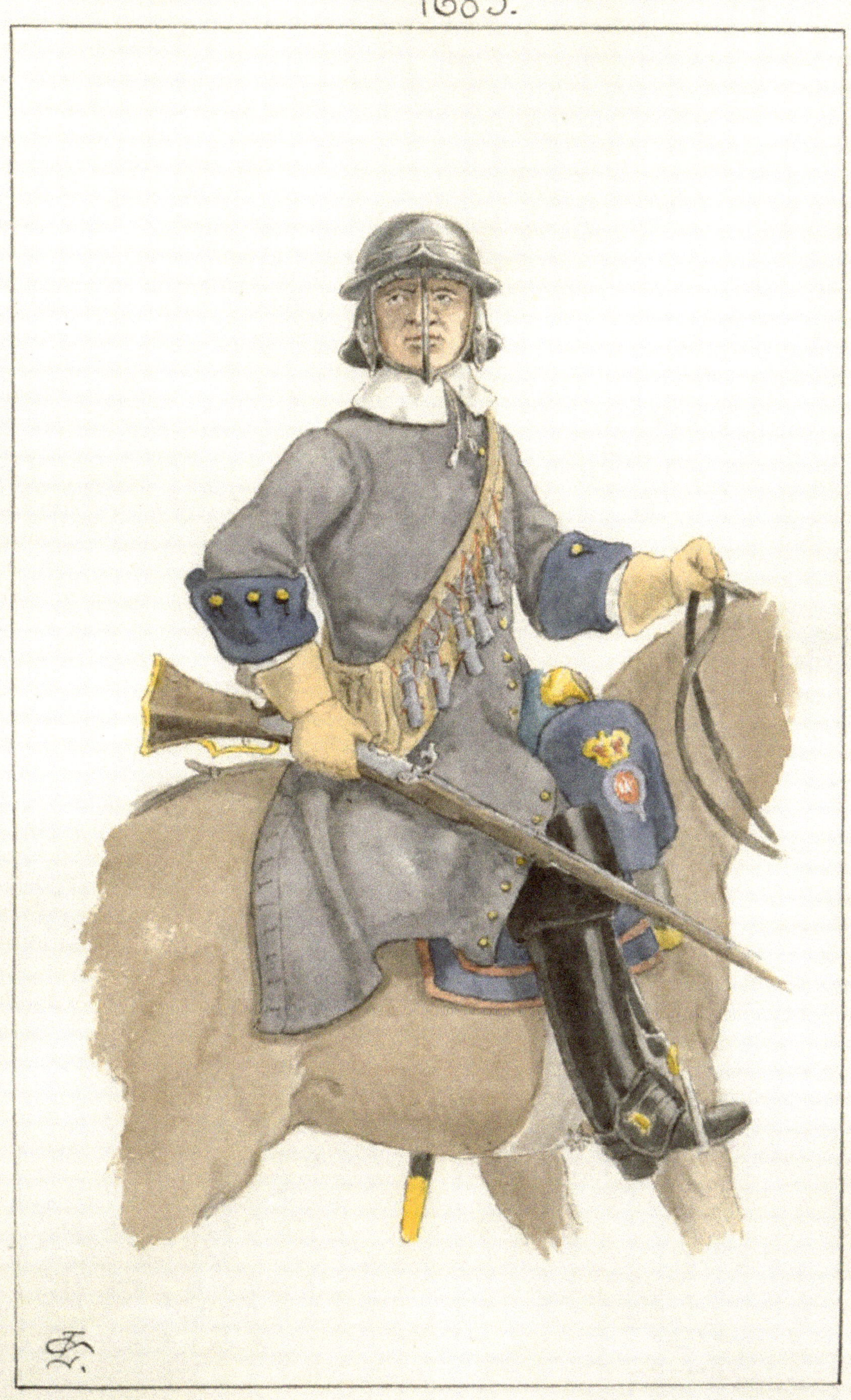

Scots Greys.

15 – DRAGOONS, 1685

Charles Lyall shows this dragoon of the first year of King James II's reign wearing a red coat with blue turnbacks and cuffs, the latter each having three buttons. There is also a narrow blue edging to the scarlet cloth wings seen protruding from under the cuirass. Blue also for the breeches which have wide scarlet stripes and gilt buttons. The horse furniture is scarlet with gold lace and fringe, the holster cap appearing to have a crown over a regimental device or cypher within the garter.

1685.

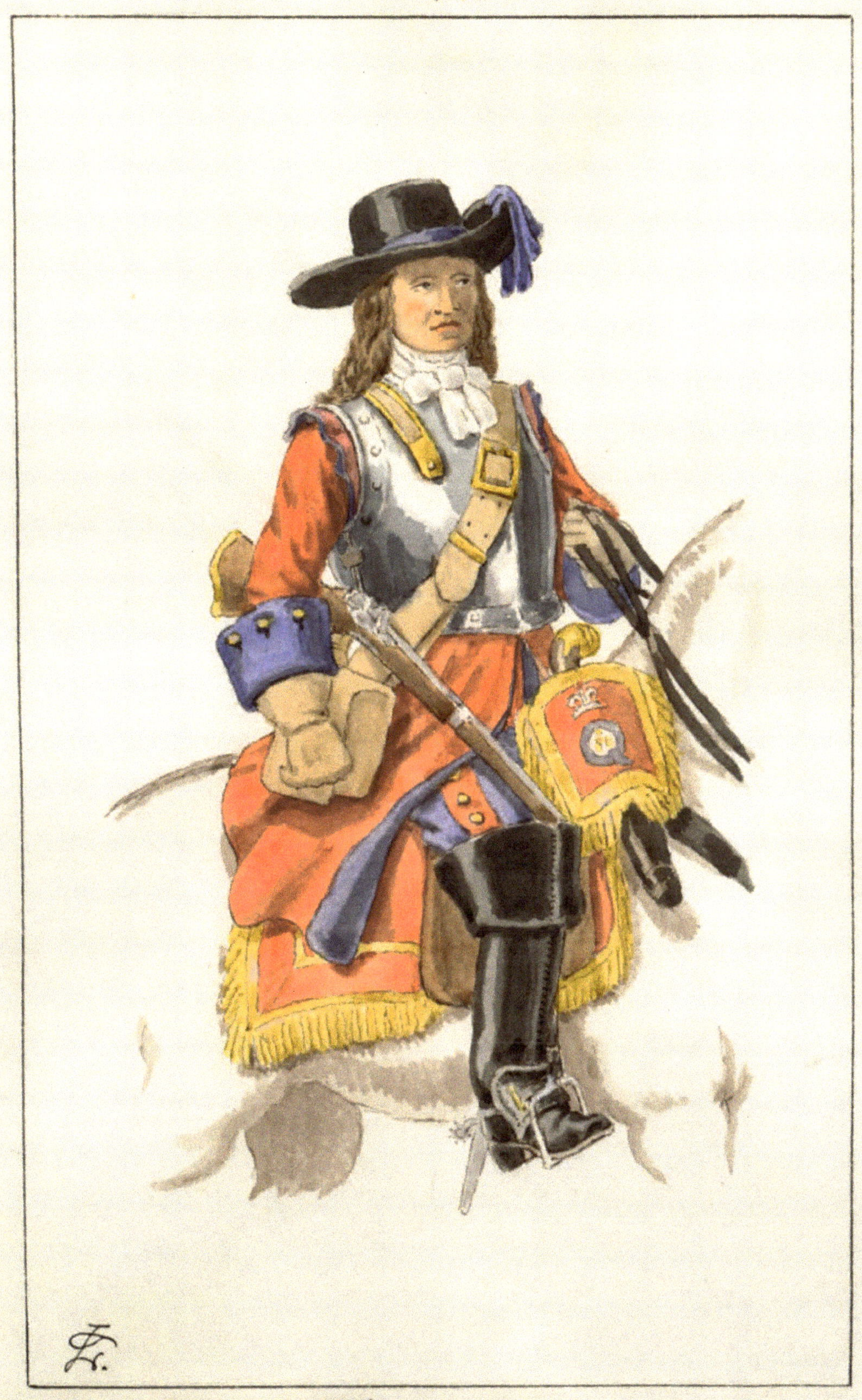

Dragoons.

16 – LIFE GUARDS OFFICER, 1685

Sixteen-eighty-five and the first year of King James II's reign. At this time the Life Guards consisted of two troops, both of them dating from 1660 and originally made up of Cavaliers who had served under Charles II. Early records suggest that the troops wore their own individual dress, but by 1669 both appeared wearing white feathers in their hats and long red coats with blue facings: gold lace for the 1st King's Troop—as seen here in Charles Lyall's painting—but none for the 3rd (later 2nd) Duke of Albemarle's. A further reference to the 1st Troop comes via WY Carman who quotes the Anglo-Irish herald and genealogist Francis Sandford who in 1685 wrote that the officers had coats of fine scarlet cloth, and 'In their hats they wore tours of white feathers.'

1685.

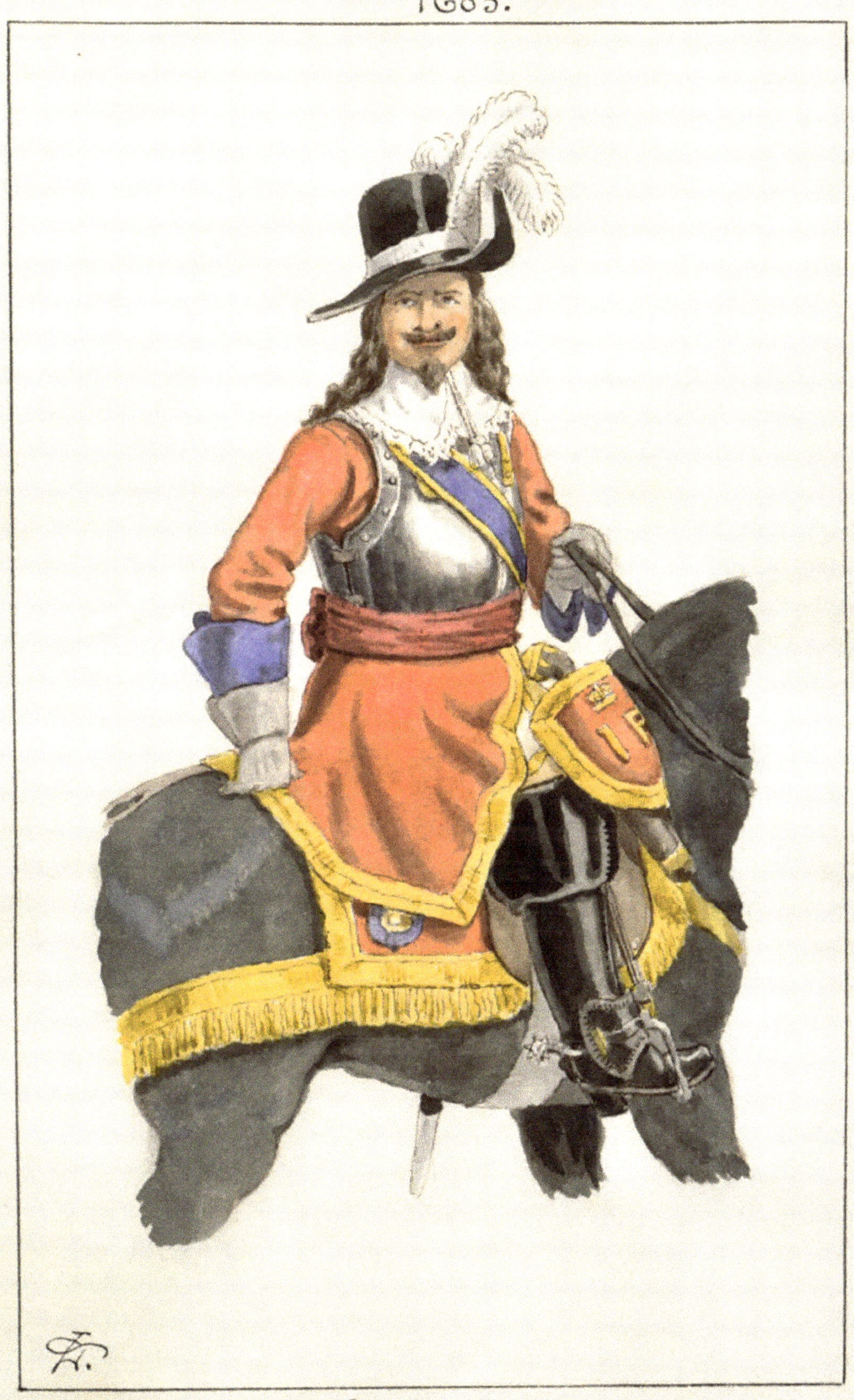

Life Guards.
Officer.

17 – 'HASTING'S' 13TH FOOT, 1685

The regiment had been raised in the southern counties of England in 1685 by the Earl of Huntingdon. Having been quartered at Buckingham and Aylesbury, its first duties included the guarding of prisoners taken after the overthrow of the Duke of Monmouth's army at Sedgemoor. At the time the uniform of the regiment was described by Cannon as, 'round hats with broad brims, the brim turned up on one side, and ornamented with yellow ribands; scarlet coats lines with yellow; yellow breeches, and grey stockings....' As we can see, Charles Lyall seems to have followed this description for his painting. Regarding the inclusion of 'Hasting's' in his caption, it would not be until 1688 that Ferdinando Hastings was given the colonelcy of the regiment that in 1751 would become the 13th of Foot.

1685.

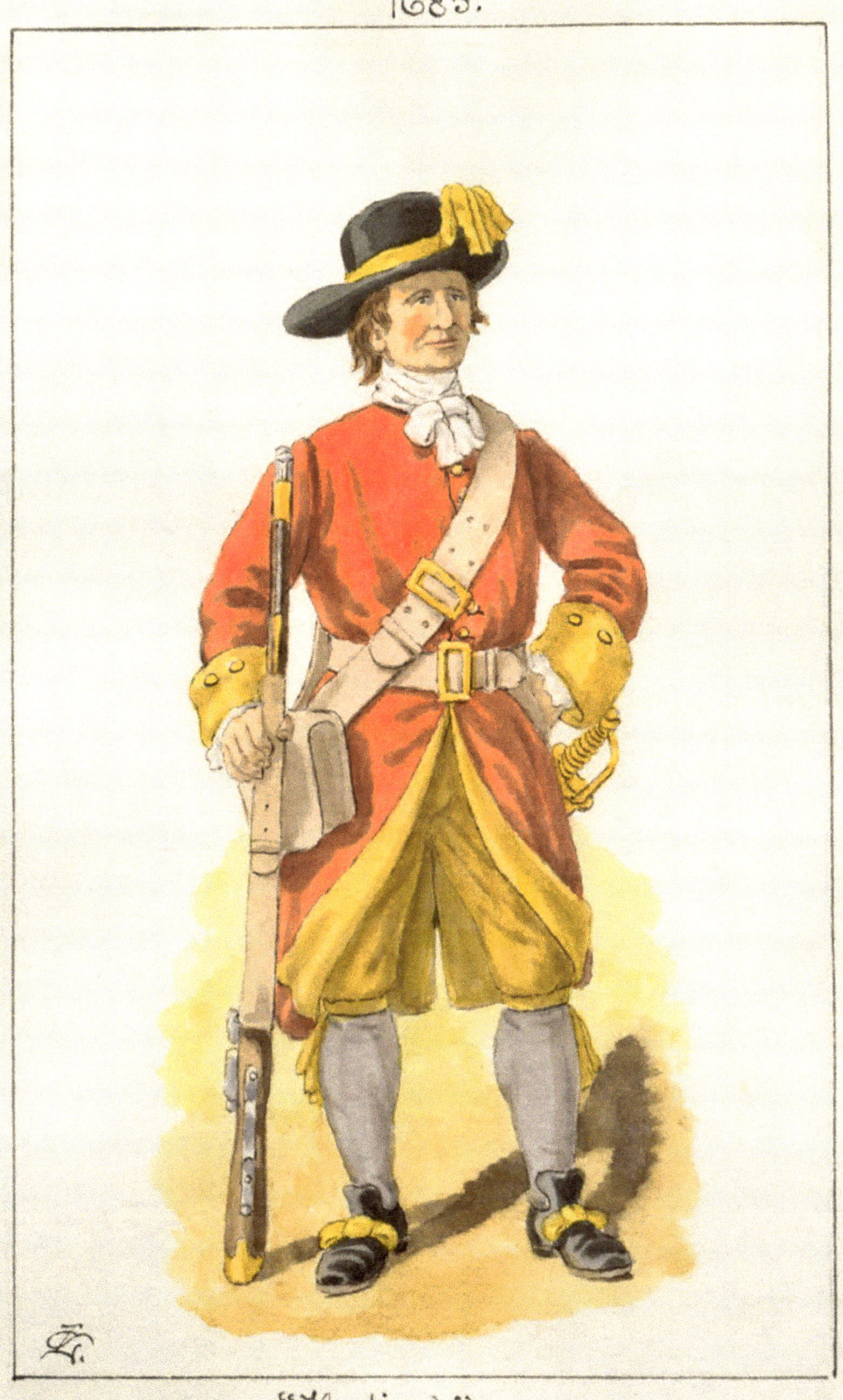

"Hasting's".
13th Foot.

18 – QUEEN'S HORSE FIRST DRAGOON GUARDS, 1687

With the cypher of James II of his yellow horse furniture, this officer of the Queen's Regiment of Horse wears a long red coat with yellow cuffs and silver lace. The regiment had been raised two years prior to Charles Lyall's caption date and within a few months of the King's accession to the throne on 6 February 1685. Historian Richard Cannon records that '...the first service performed by the Queen's Regiment of Horse appears to have been the escorting of the Duke of Monmouth and other prisoners taken at the battle of Sedgemoor from Winchester to London.' Records show that in June 1687 the regiment was encamped on Hounslow Heath, afterwards marching on 4 August to Oakingham and Reading. After taking on the title of King's Own in 1714, the regiment was designated as 1st (King's) Dragoon Guards in 1746.

1687.

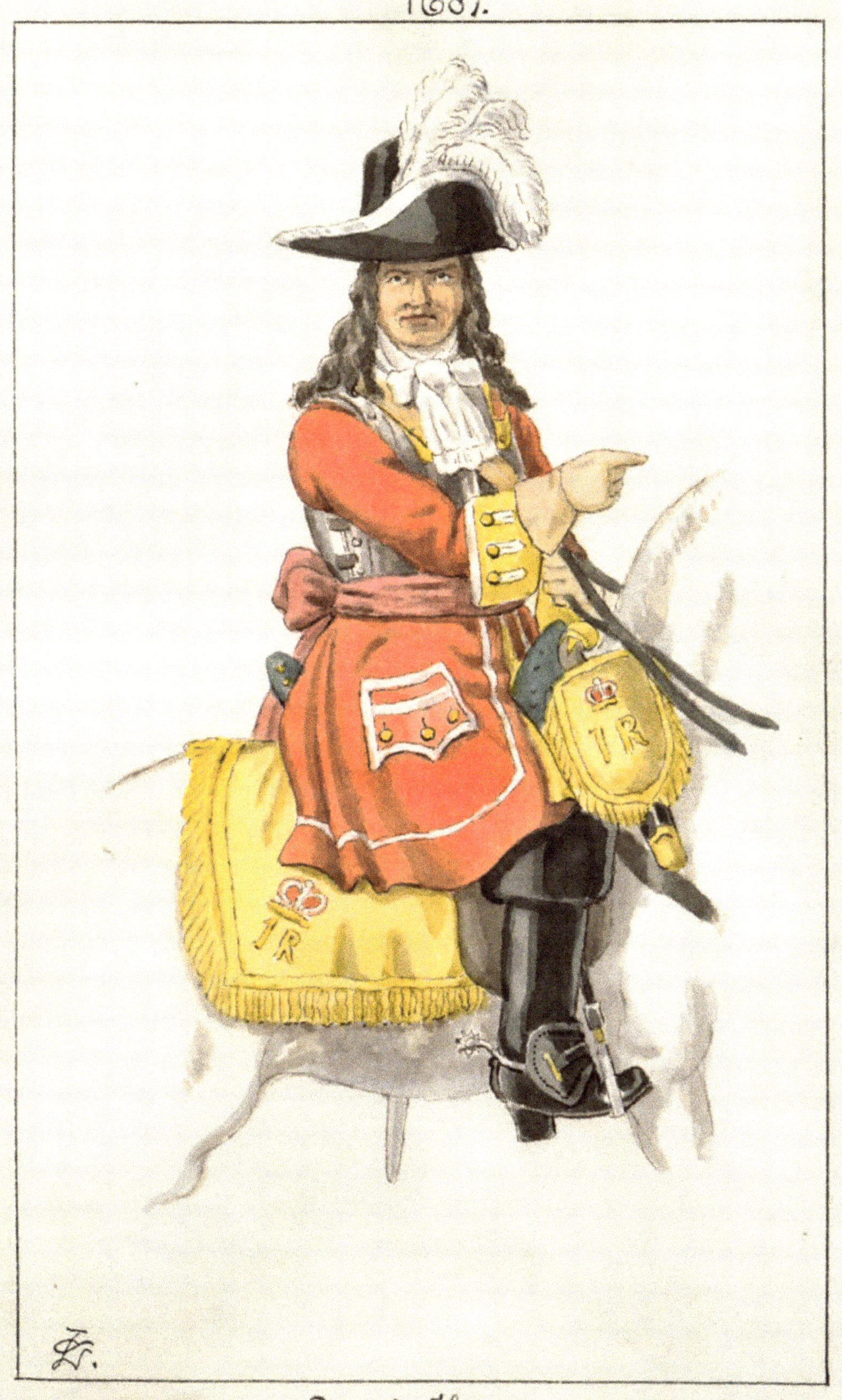

Queen's Horse.
First Dragoon Guards.

19 – 1st TANGIER REGIMENT PIKEMAN, NOW 2nd QUEEN'S, 1687

Lyall's date of 1687 places the regiment in England and in particular on Hounslow Heath as part of a body of 12,000 troops assembled in camps for an exercise and training program. By this time there had been a change in title, the Tangier Regiment having been designated as the Queen Dowager's Regiment of Foot shortly after the death of Charles II in 1685. The Queen Dowager, Catherine of Braganza, the widow of the late king. In command was Lieutenant-General Piercy Kirke whose name, together with the regiment's Paschal Lamb badge, brought about the nickname of 'Kirke's Lambs'. Sea green, seen here as the colour of a ribbon around the hat, a long waistcoat, lining to the red coat and breeches, had been worn since formation as the Tangier Regiment in 1661. The artist's inclusion of 'now 2nd Queen's' in his caption refers to the numerical designation, the 2nd (Queen's Royal) Regiment of Foot, received in 1751.

1687.

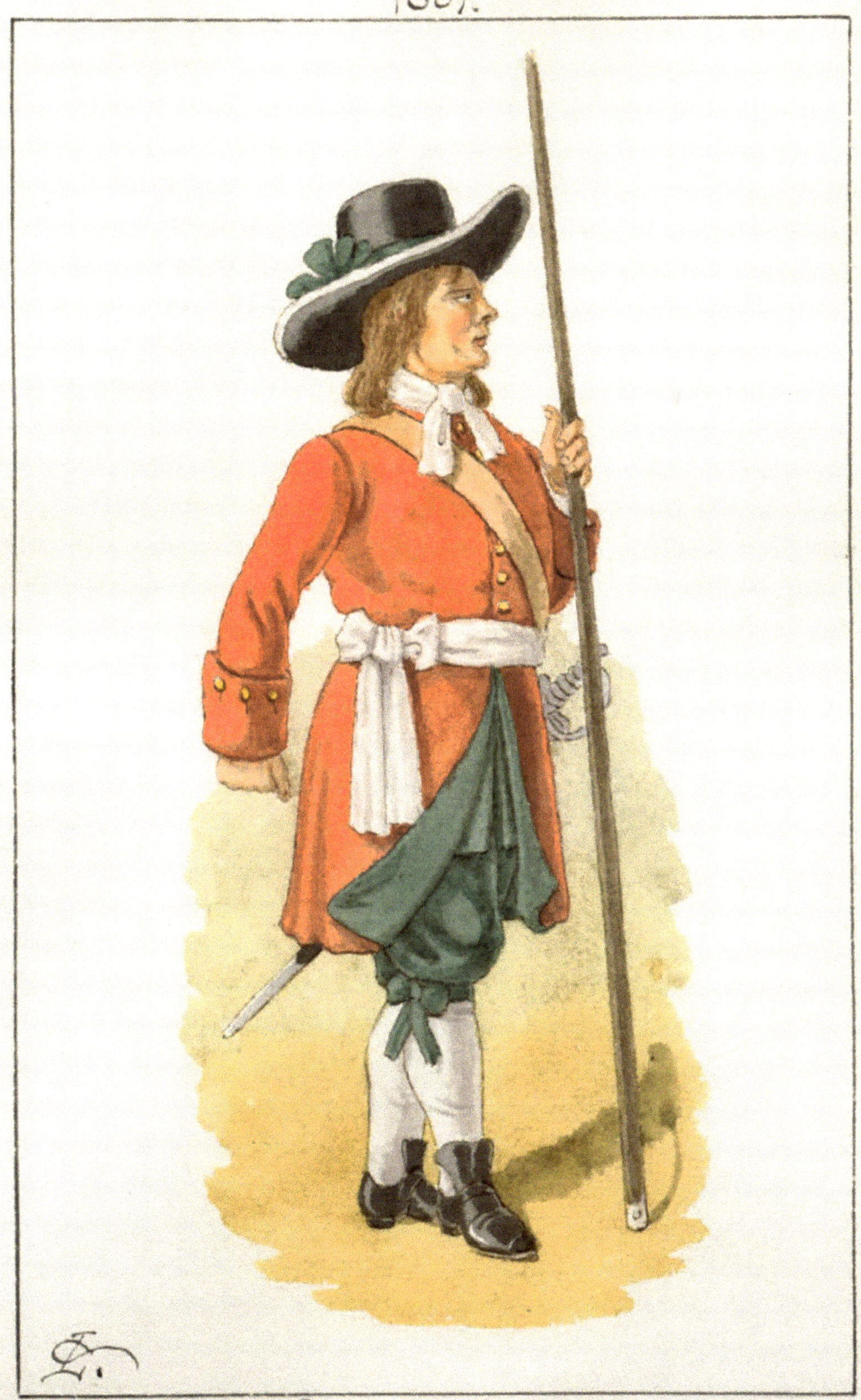

1st. Tangier Regt. Pikeman
now 2nd. Queens.

20 – 1st TANGIER REGIMENT GRENADIERS, NOW 2nd QUEEN'S, 1687

Grenadier companies had been added to infantry regiments by 1678, their distinctive, flat-fronted, fur caps more convenient when throwing grenades than the wide-brimmed hats worn at the time. A companion painting to Plate 19, Lyall's grenadier is shown with a brown leather pouch for storing grenades, an axe tucked into his belt, and a bandolier holding six cartridges. There would have been a further half dozen at the back.

1687.

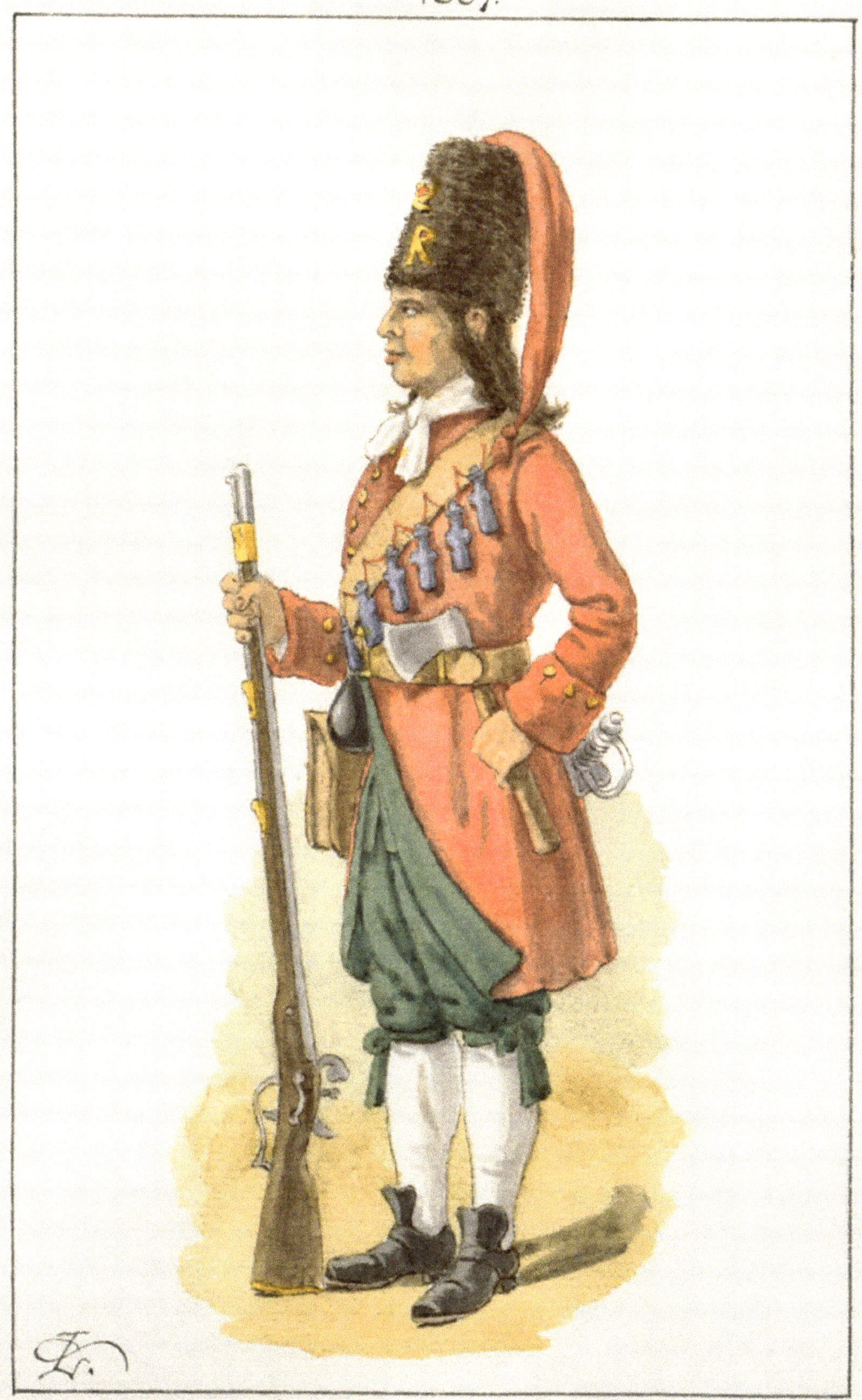

1st Tangier Regt. Grenadiers.
now 2nd Queens.

21 – TRAIN, PIONEERS, 1688

Once again, Charles Lyall has drawn his inspiration from one of the colour plates included with Captain RJ MacDonald's *The History of the Dress of the Royal Regiment of Artillery*. The author placing a date of '1660-1702' with his illustration. Uniform historian WY Carman notes that English gunners by the end of William's reign [1702] were wearing red or crimson coats faced blue. The year 1716 and the formation of the Royal Regiment of Artillery, however, saw the return of blue, this time with scarlet facings. But here we have in the long coat, with its wide gold lace, and the breeches and hose tied with orange ribbons, the early blue. Orange for the cuffs and waistcoat, which has a gold edging of lace. Captain MacDonald makes an interesting point regarding the hat. Of felt and replacing the helmet, it would have had a small steel cap sewn inside '...for protection from sabre cuts.'

1688.

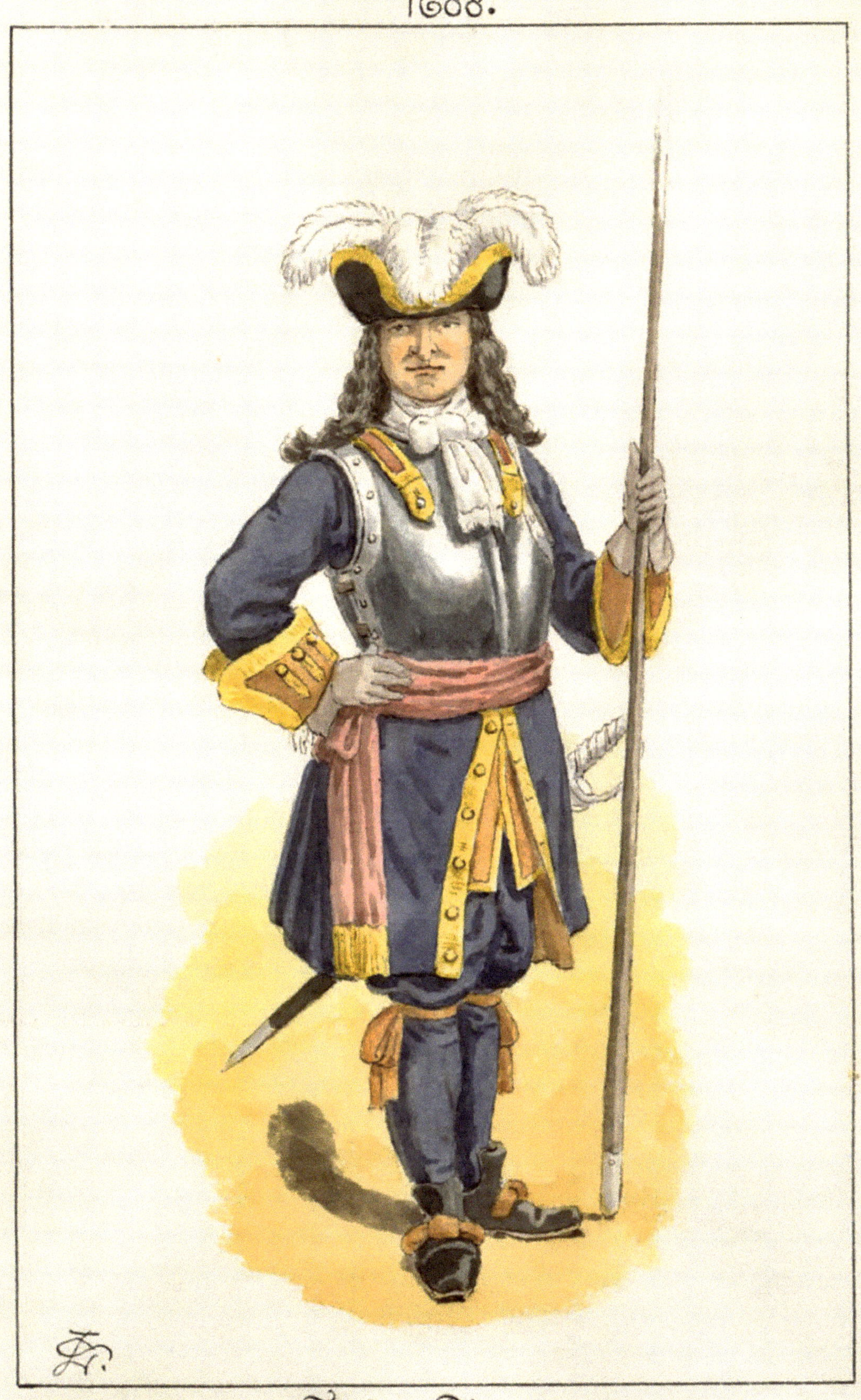

Train-Pioneers.

22 – 5th FOOT, 1688

Here we have the regiment raised in 1674 known as the Holland Regiment which, in 1751, took on the title of 5th Regiment of Foot, and in 1881, the Northumberland Fusiliers. Early service in Holland had been under the command of the Prince of Orange, the year 1688 seeing the colonelcy of the regiment, now in England, pass to Lieutenant-General Thomas Tollemache, formally of the Coldstream Guards. Although later well known for its gosling-green facing, the first colour in use was yellow, Lyall indicating this by the lining to the long red coat. Green, however, for the breeches. Of an officer, the artwork is clearly based on one on the colour plates included with the Cannon's Historical Records series, that after I Spence and produced by GE Madeley of No 3 Wellington Street just off the Strand in London.

1688.

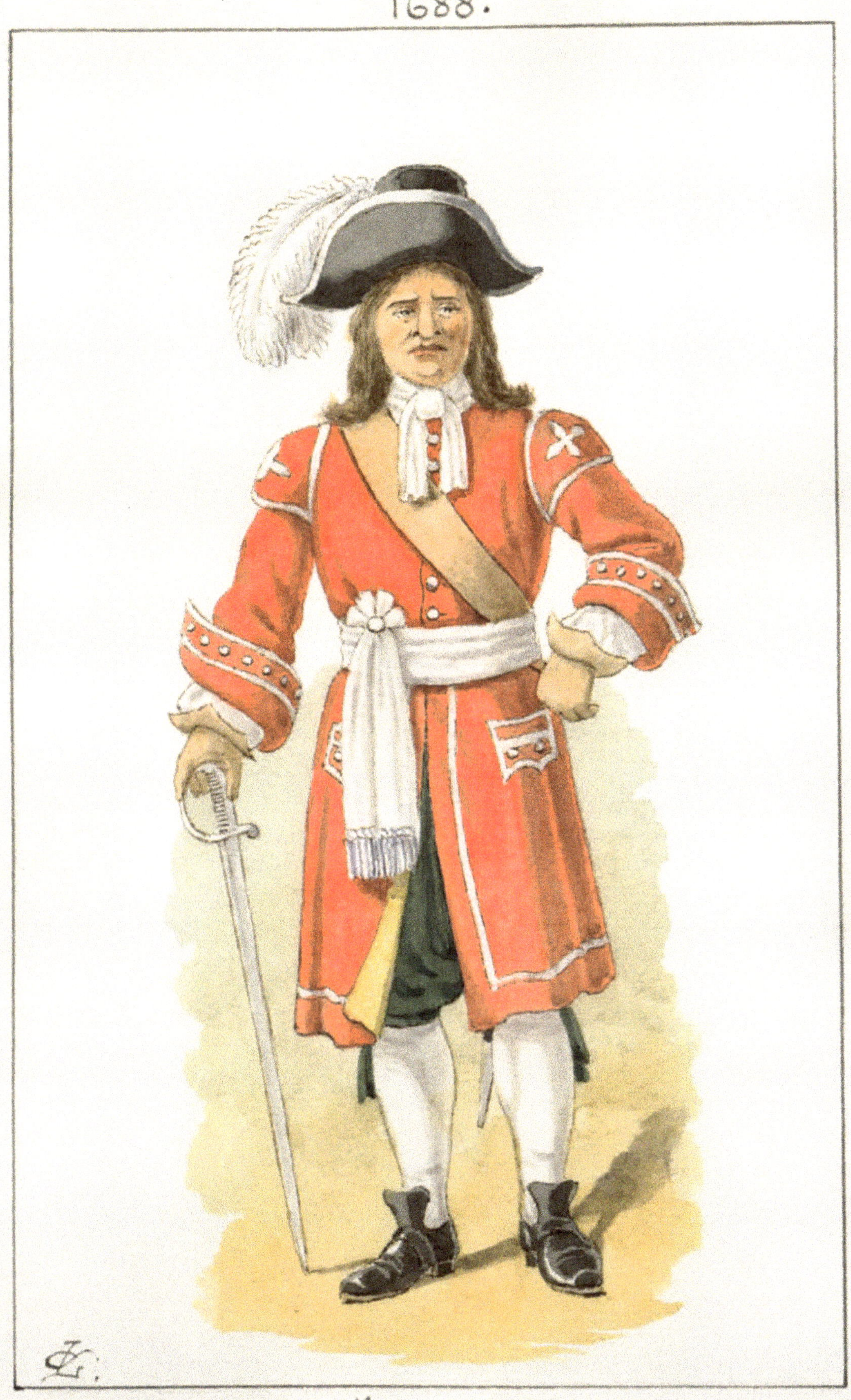

5th. Foot.

23 – TRAIN PIONEER, 1688-1702

Here we have an artillery pioneer of William and Mary's time. Having fled England in December 1688, King James II subsequently landed in Ireland with a French force of some 5,000 men in March of the following year. It then followed on 1 June that a warrant was issued directing that a train of artillery should immediately be prepared for shipment to Ireland. Part of the list of ordnance and other stores drawn up for the expedition included the following requirements for pioneers: 'Large blue coats lined with orange – 40, Orange waistcoats – 40, Blue breeches – 40 pairs, Blue stockings, 40 pairs and Caps embroidered with a shovel at the front – 40.' Charles Lyall seems to have followed this order to the letter, including all the uniform detail in his painting which also includes a drooping red bag with gold tassel to the headdress, a brown leather belt, orange garters and orange ribbons for the shoes.

1688–1702.

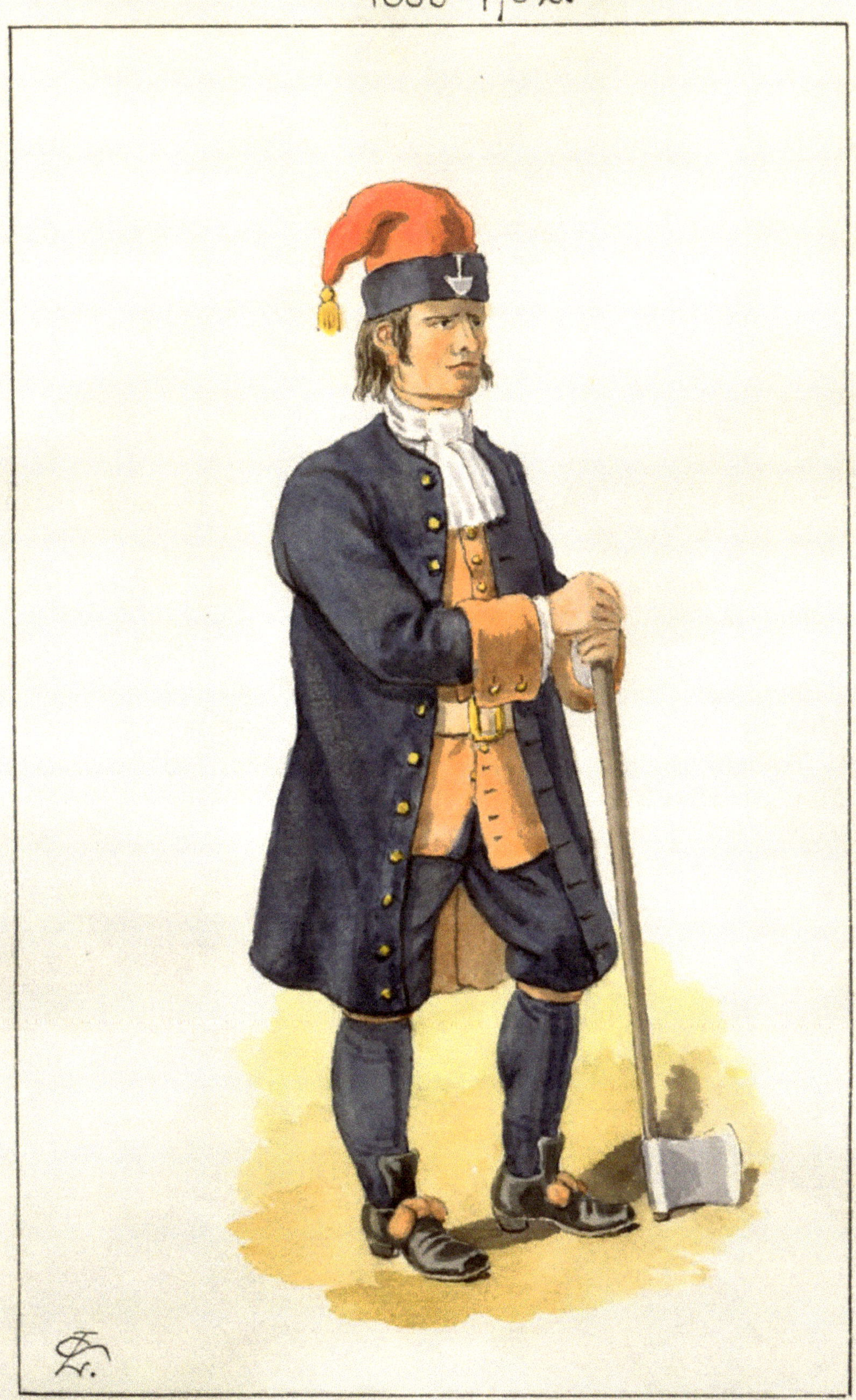

Train. Pioneer.

24 – COLONEL LANGSTON'S FIFTH HORSE, 1693

The subject holds a carbine at his right hip and wears a long scarlet coat with wide blue cuffs edged across the top with gold lace and showing three gilt buttons and buttonhole loops. The lining of the coat is of the same blue and has double gold lace buttonhole loops placed singularly down to the hem. A steel cuirass with gilt fittings is worn, and a white sash tipped with a blue fringe. The tall, wide-brimmed grey hat has a white band and flowing white feathers placed on the left side. The horse furniture is white, edged with scarlet, and carries the cypher of William III. The artist's date coincides with Lieutenant-General Francis Langston's appointment as colonel of the regiment in 1693. The Fifth Horse was re-designated as the 1st Irish Horse (or Blue Horse) in 1746, and as 4th Royal Irish Regiment of Dragoon Guards in 1788.

1693.

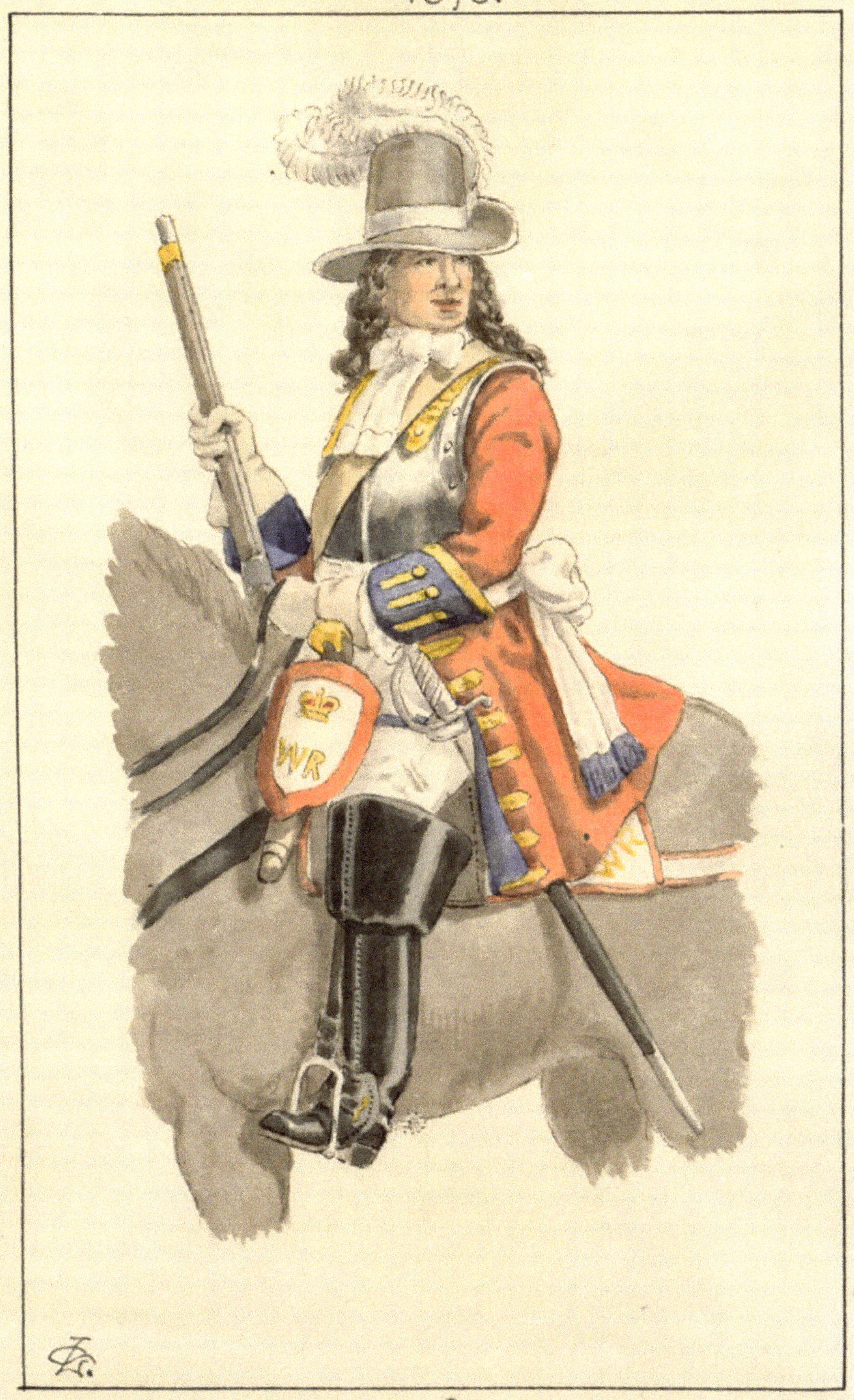

Colonel Langston's
Fifth Horse.

25 – TRAIN OF ARTILLERY, 1702-14

Save for the horse being a grey instead of black, Charles Lyall's painting is almost identical in detail to Plate II in Captain RJ MacDonald's book, *The History of the Dress of the Royal Regiment of Artillery*. Accompanying his image, Captain MacDonald writes, 'This plate represents an Officer of high rank in the Train of Artillery during Marlborough's wars on the continent. He wears a cuirass under his long coat, encircled by a crimson sash; the large cavalry boots called gambadoes, with silver spurs. A three-cornered laced cocked hat is worn; also a large peruke [wig].' Queen Anne reined from 1702 to 1714, Lyall however has shown the horse furniture with her predecessor's 'WR' cypher.

1702–14.

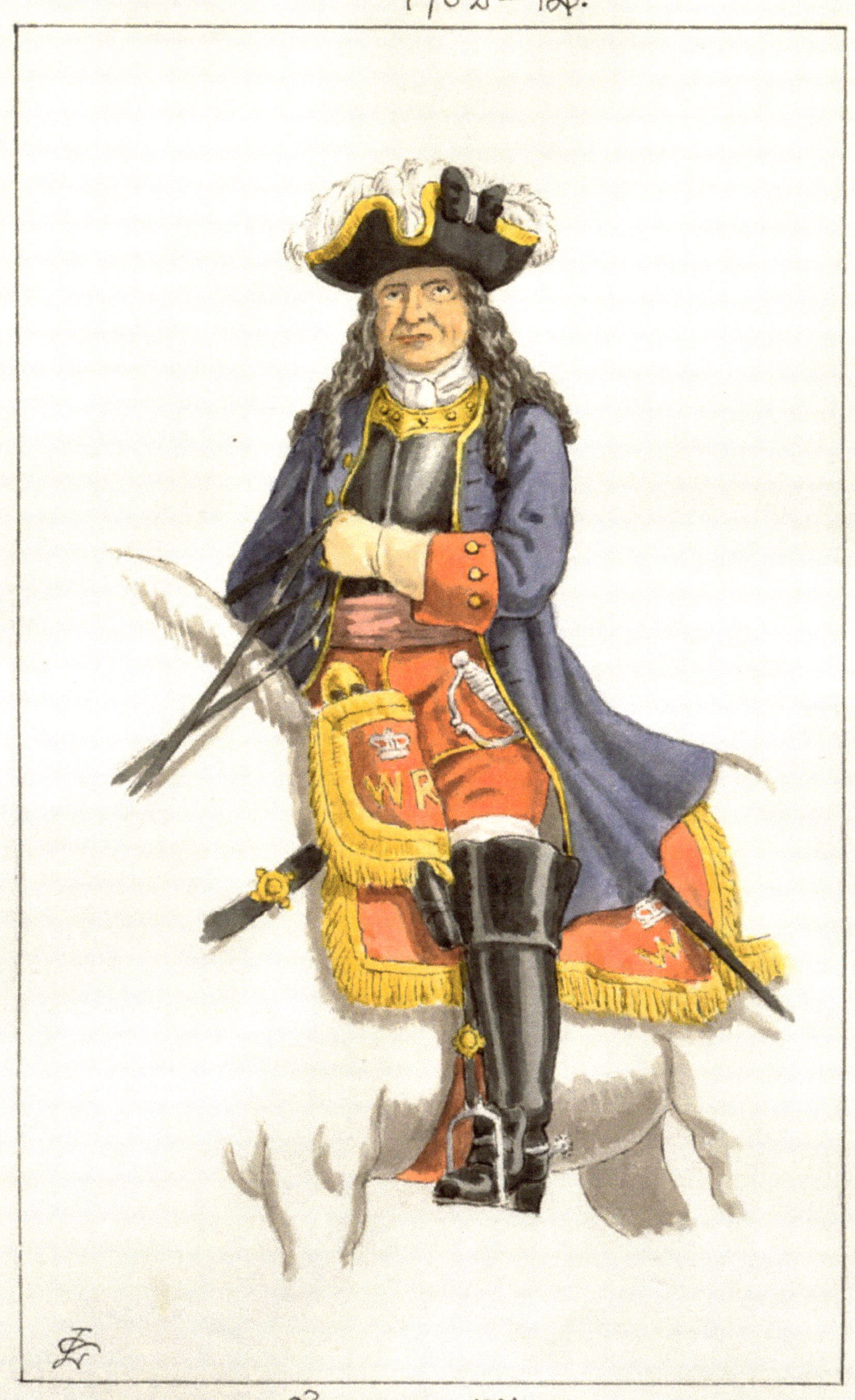

Train of Artillery

26 – 2ND N.B. DRAGOONS, SCOTS GREYS DISMOUNTED, 1704

Laden down with heavy wide buff belts, a cartridge box full of ammunition, a musket, bayonet and sword, the trooper slogs his way forward without his horse. The cumbersome black boots, with their wide knee protectors and silver spurs, also do much to increase the burden of a marching soldier during Queen Anne's time. The Royal Regiment of North British Dragoons was numbered as 2nd in 1751, 'Scots Greys' (hitherto a nickname) not appearing in the official title until more than one hundred years later in 1866. Having been raised in Scotland in May 1678, by 1687 the regiment's coats were being made of red cloth with blue serge linings, as shown in Lyall's painting. The tricorn hat of the time is trimmed with white lace.

1704.

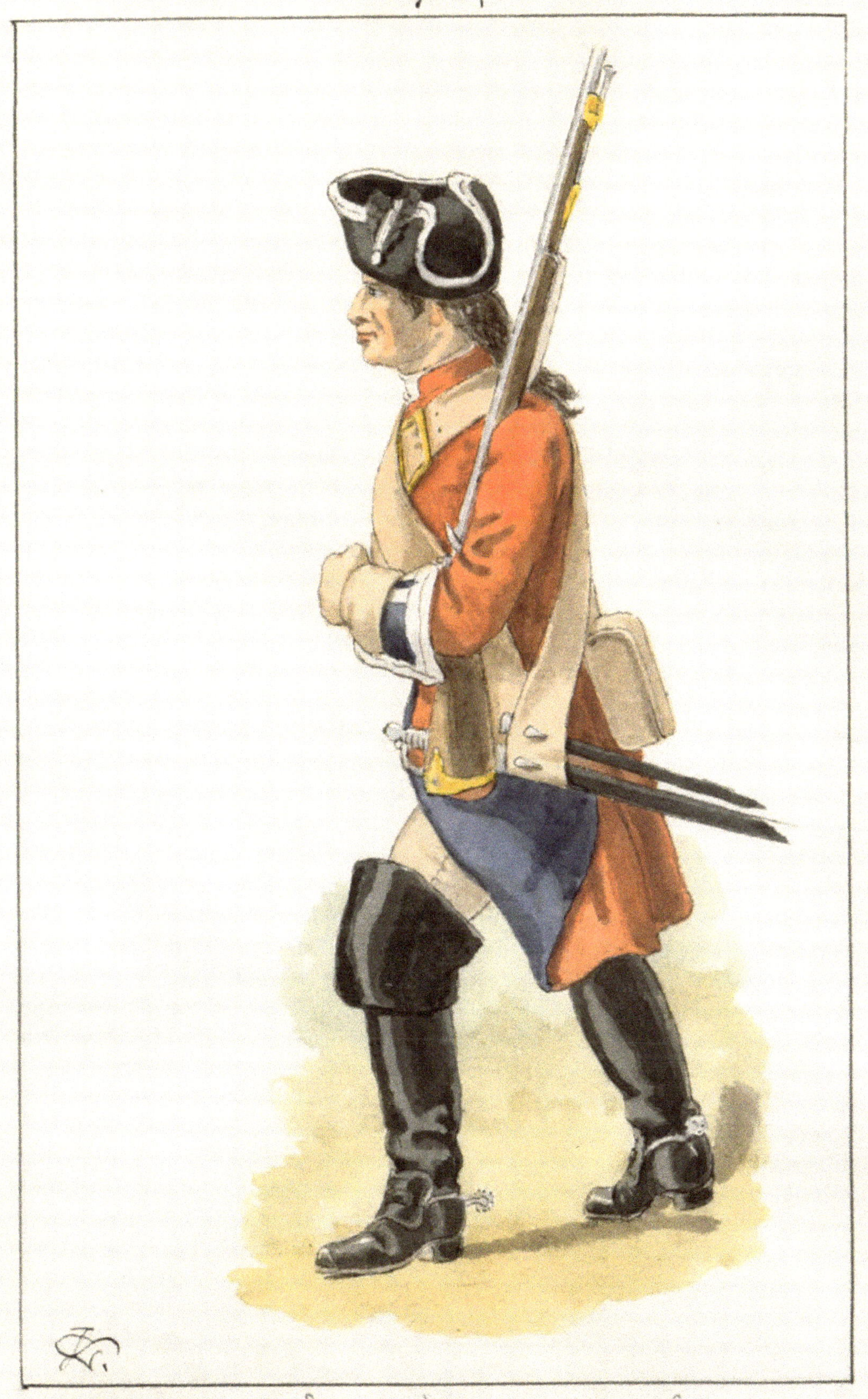

2nd N. B. Dragoons. Scots Greys.
Dismounted.

27 – 2ND N.B DRAGOONS SCOTS GREYS TRUMPET MAJOR, 1704

Save for his rich, thick gold lace, turned up cuffs reaching almost to the elbow, a black hat trimmed with gold, the epaulette and elegant wig, Charles Lyall's trumpet major of the 2nd North British Dragoons is dressed much the same as his dismounted colleague in Plate 26. Note how he is armed with a sword, which is drawn and held in the right hand. Two years before the date of Lyall's painting, the Scots Greys had embarked for war service, disembarking in Holland in the spring of 1702 under the command of John Churchill, Earl of Marlborough. Action at Blenheim followed on 13 August 1704, the regiment leaving Germany soon afterwards.

1704.

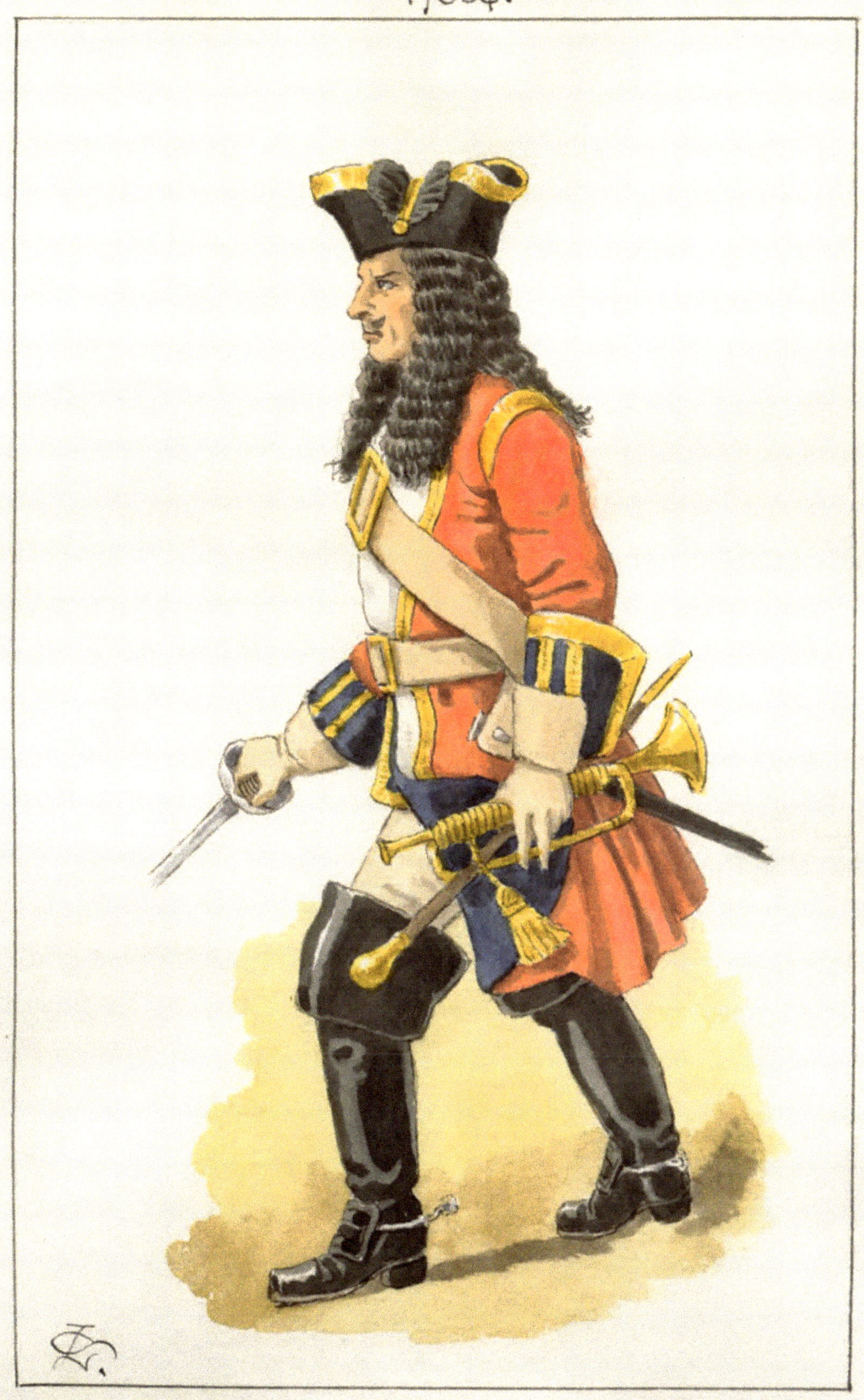

2nd N. B. Dragoons. Scots Greys.
Trumpet Major.

28 – BRITISH FOOT, 1710

The year is 1710, Queen Anne in the eighth year of her reign and the British infantry are still known by the names of their colonels. Charles Lyall's infantryman wears a long red coat with blue collar and cuffs decorated with white lace. His wide belts are of buff leather, one over the left shoulder attached to a large pouch, the other around the waist with a fitting attached to carry a sword and bayonet. The hat is of black felt with white lace all around, the breeches are white and fastened just below the knee with black garters. The gaiters are open at the front to reveal white hose.

1710.

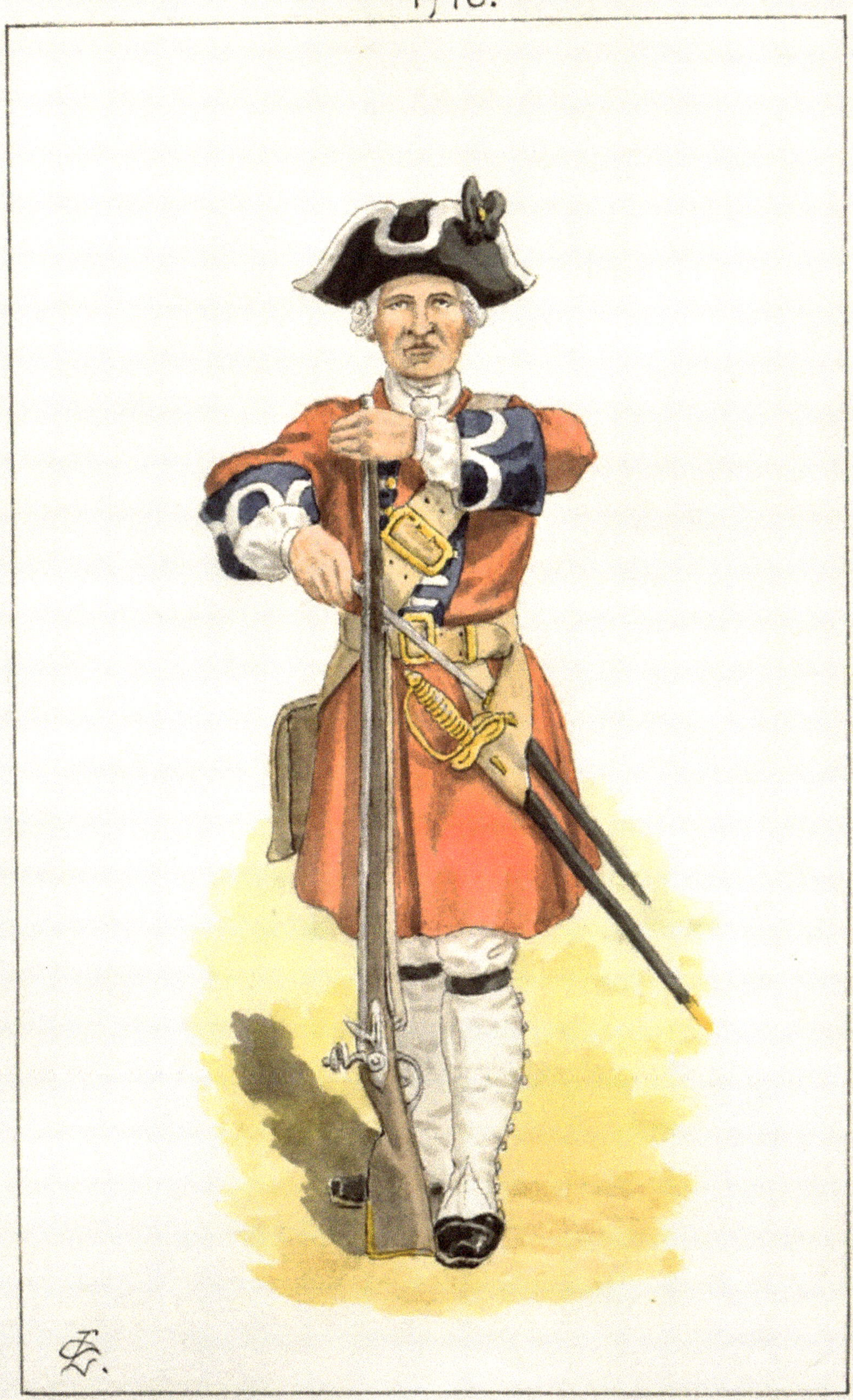

British Foot.

29 – THE CAMERONIAN REGIMENT OF FOOT, PIPER 1713

After service on the Continent, George Preston's Regiment (the 'Cameronians') in 1713 returned home for service in Ireland. Charles Lyall shows a piper of about this time who wears the regiment's pale yellow facings, seen here used for the cuffs, the waistcoat and coat linings. Tartan trews tied with green ribbons at the ankles have replaced breeches. For the headdress, a flat bonnet with diced border and a distinction for the pipers in the form of a single heron's feather at the front. Known by the names of its successive colonels until designated as 26th Regiment of Foot in 1751, the regiment would provide the 1st Battalion The Cameronians (Scottish Rifles) in 1881.

1713.

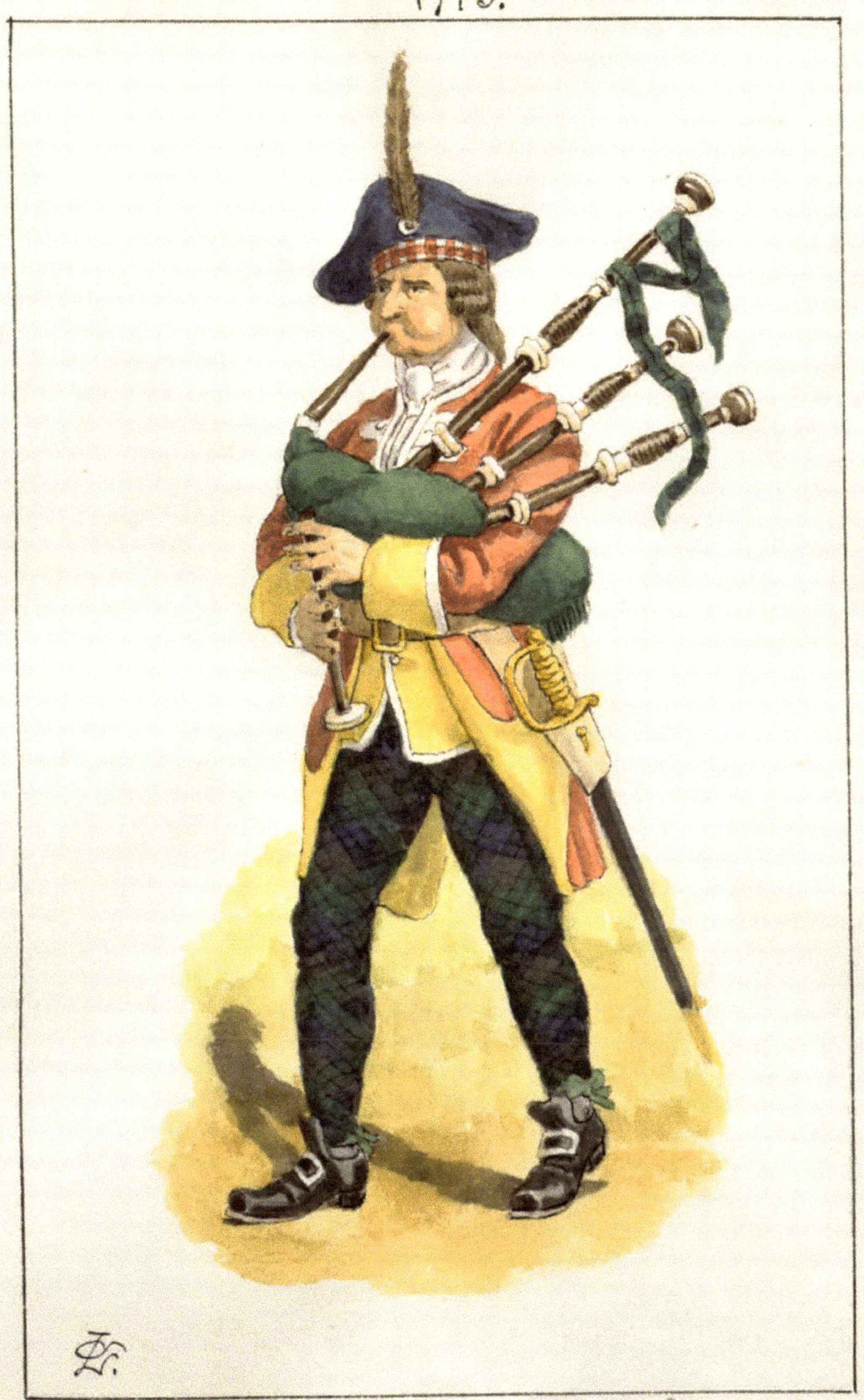

The Cameronian Regt. of Foot.
Piper.

30 – THE CAMERONIANS REGIMENT OF FOOT, GRENADIER 1713

With his red coat, yellow cuffs, lapels, waistcoat and linings, his cap and trews, the grenadier in Charles Lyall's painting looks much the same as his piper colleague in Plate 29. He does, however, have wide leather belts with heavy brass buckles, one of which carries a pouch which has an axe attached.

1713.

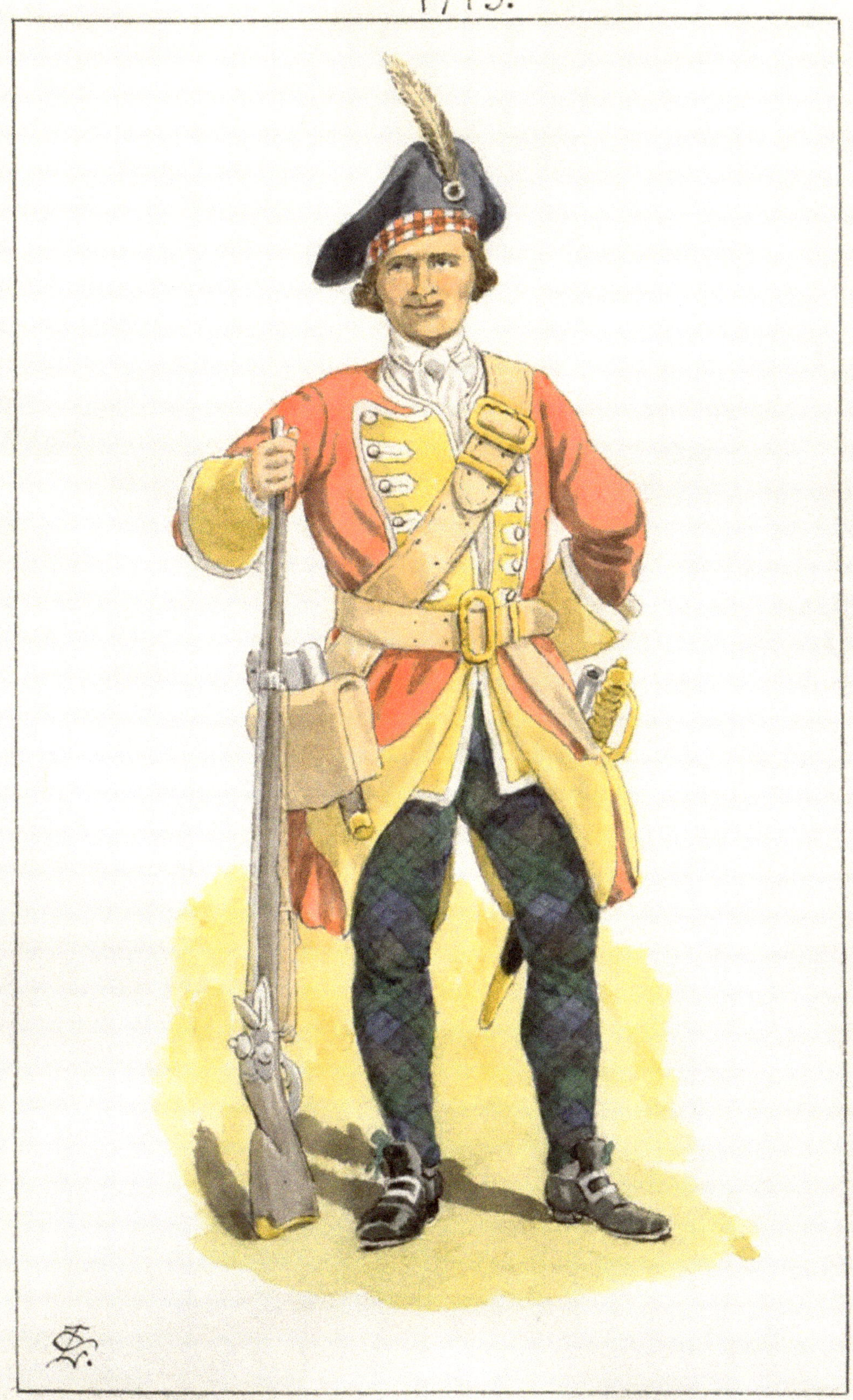

The Cameronian Regt. of Foot.
Grenadier.

31 – DRAGOONS, 4TH REGIMENT 1714-60

In 1714, and then known by the name of its colonel Sir Robert Rich, the regiment was stationed in Ireland. On page forty-three of his history of the 4th Dragoons, Richard Canon notes that in '...the autumn of 1715, when the Earl of Mar having erected the Pretender's standard in the Highlands, and summoned the disaffected clans to arms, it was ordered to proceed to Scotland, to take part in the suppression of this rebellion.' Various stations in England followed until in the summer of 1742 the regiment proceeded to Flanders, not quitting the Continent until the winter of 1745. In 1751 the regiment ceased to be known by the name of its colonel and instead took on the title of 4th Dragoons. It was in this year also that a royal warrant was issued regarding the clothing of regiments, the direction for the 4th being for the coat,—scarlet, double-breasted, without lapels, lined with green; slit sleeves turned up with green, the button-holes worked with narrow white lace, set on two and two; the buttons of white metal, set on two and two; a long slash pocket in each skirt; and a white worsted aiguillette on the right shoulder. The waistcoat and breeches were green. The hats were black with white lace and ornamented with a white loop and black cockade. For his painting, Lyall as we see has followed these instructions quite closely, except that he has placed the aiguillette on the left shoulder. Ending with Lyall's date of 1760, this year would find the 4th Dragoons stationed close to London where they were employed on public duties.

1714–60.

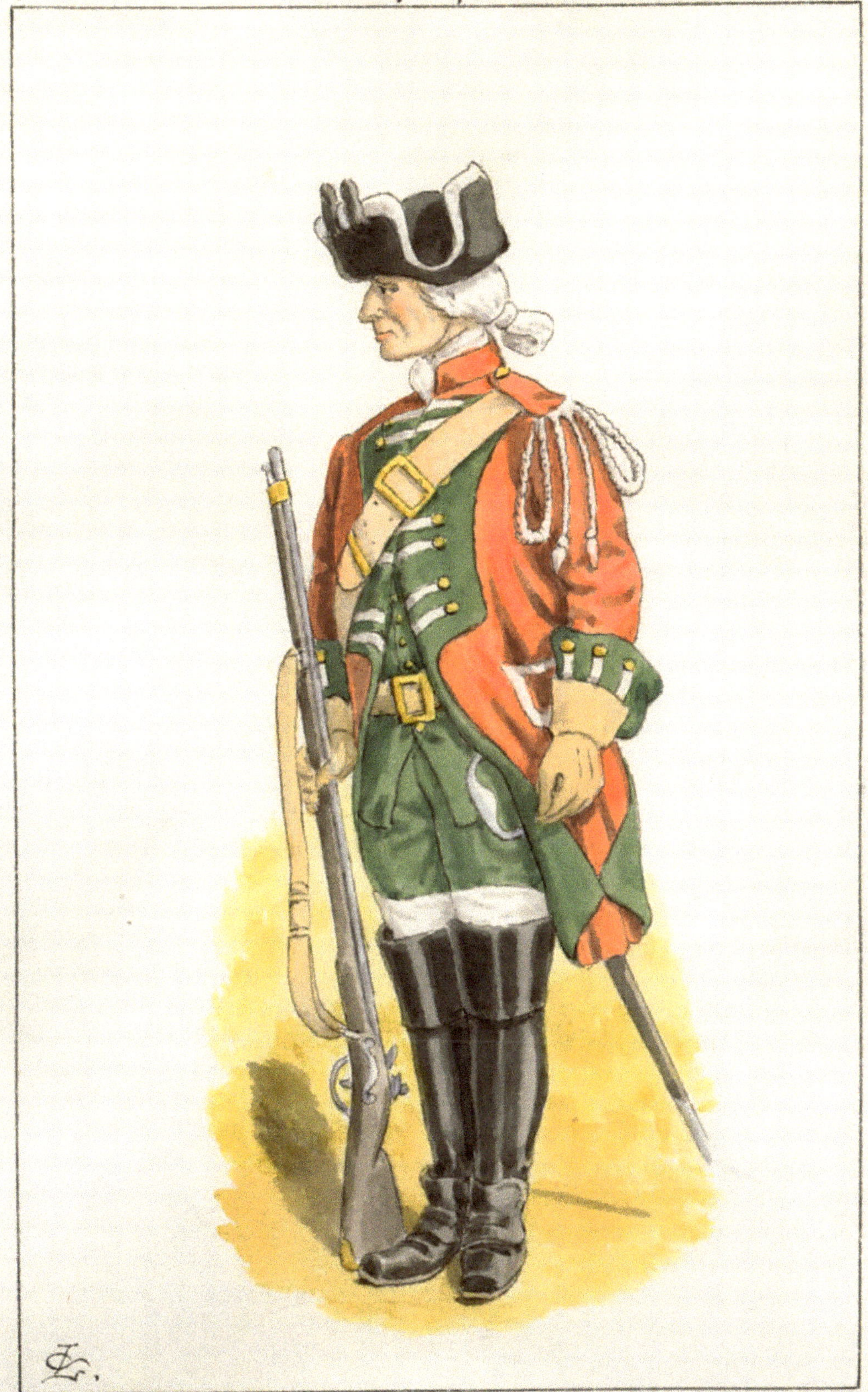

Dragoons.
4th Regt.

32 – REGIMENT OF INVALIDS, 1718

From the Royal Hospital in Chelsea, army pensioners (Invalids) were for many years drawn in time of war to man Invalid companies. Their role, to relieve regular soldiers in garrisons. It would be in 1719, the year after Charles Lyall's caption date, that an entire regiment of invalids from Chelsea were raised, this to become the 41st Regiment in 1751, then 1st Battalion Welsh Regiment in 1881.

1718.

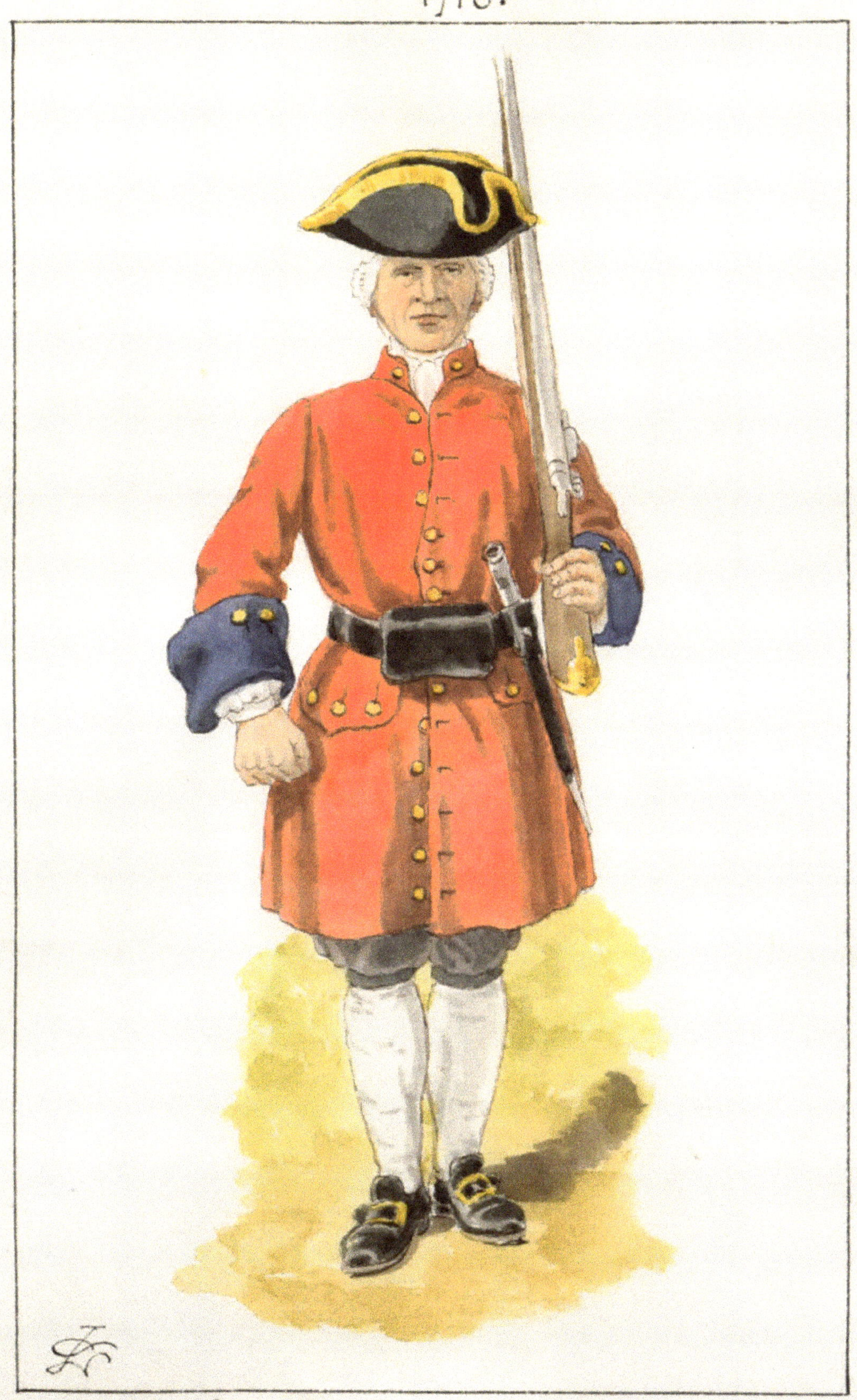

Regiment of Invalids.

33 – FIRST REGIMENT OF FOOT GUARDS, GRENADIER 1726

It was necessary to safeguard the musket when throwing a grenade, so straps were fitted to the weapon that allowed it to be slung over the shoulder in the manner seen in Charles Lyall's painting. But the wide-brimmed infantryman's hats of the day made this a difficult operation and subsequently a flat-fronted cap was developed for grenadiers. Small at first, they later grew taller and with a front made from cloth of the facing colour—blue in the case of the First Regiment of Foot Guards—and with an embroidered crown over an eight-pointed star charged with the red cross of St George within the Garter. The red flap below carries the device of the White Horse of Hanover with the motto *Nec aspera Terrent* (By difficulties undaunted) across the top edge. The large black pouch with its 'GR' cypher holds the grenades.

1726.

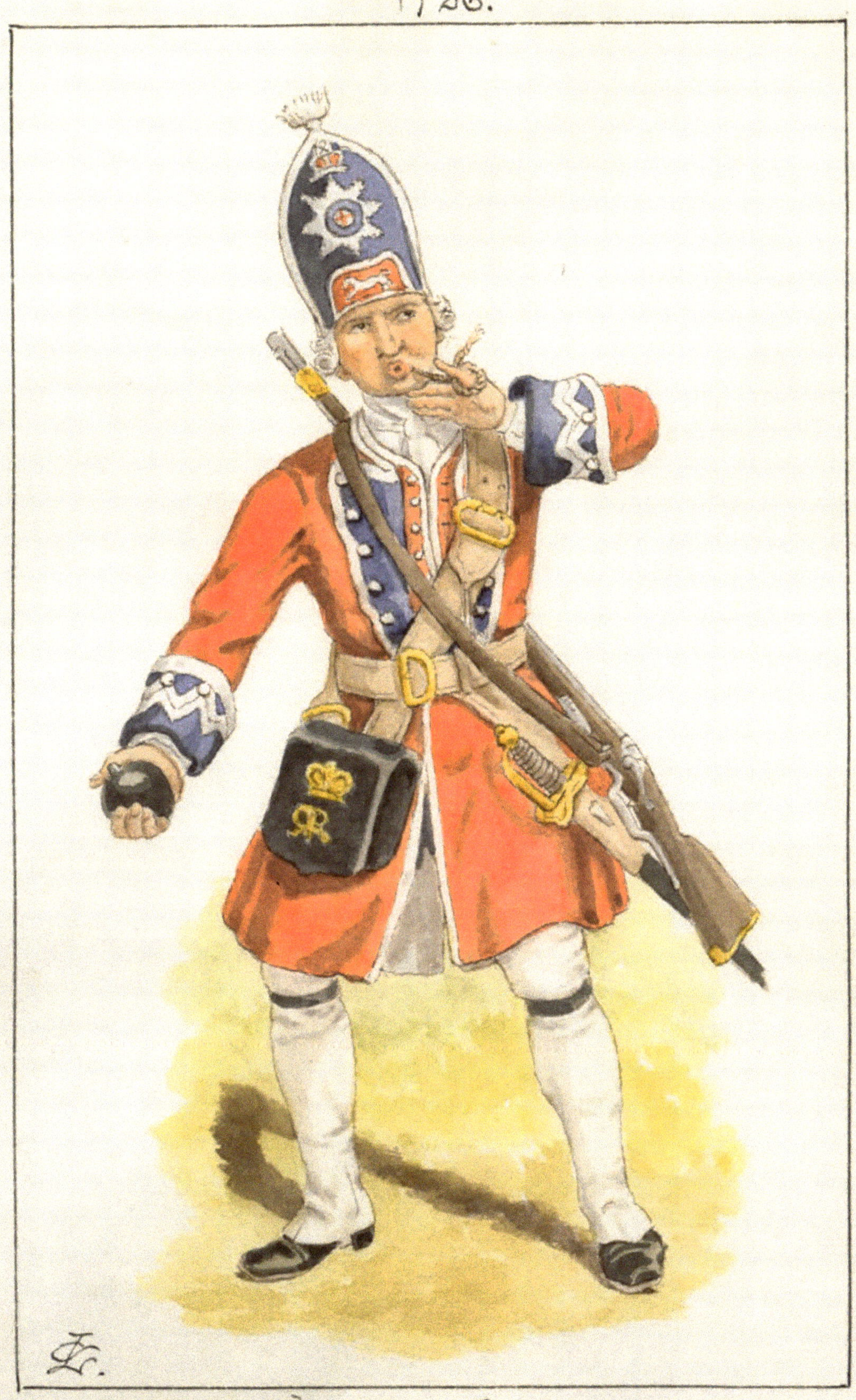

First Regt. of Foot Guards
Grenadier.

34 – ROYAL ARTILLERY DRIVER, 1785

Charles Lyall's image has clearly been taken from a sketch by Captain RJ MacDonald (see page 29 of *The History of the Dress of the Royal Regiment of Artillery 1625-1897*). The long coat is blue, red for the tall collar, wide cuffs and coat lining. Its buttons each bear the Ordnance Arms of three cannon balls and three cannons on a shield. The driver's long brown untidy hair flows from beneath a black leather cap with a wide peak. Untidy also are the drooping white cloth gaiters which are held in place by straps passing underneath the footwear at the instep.

1785.

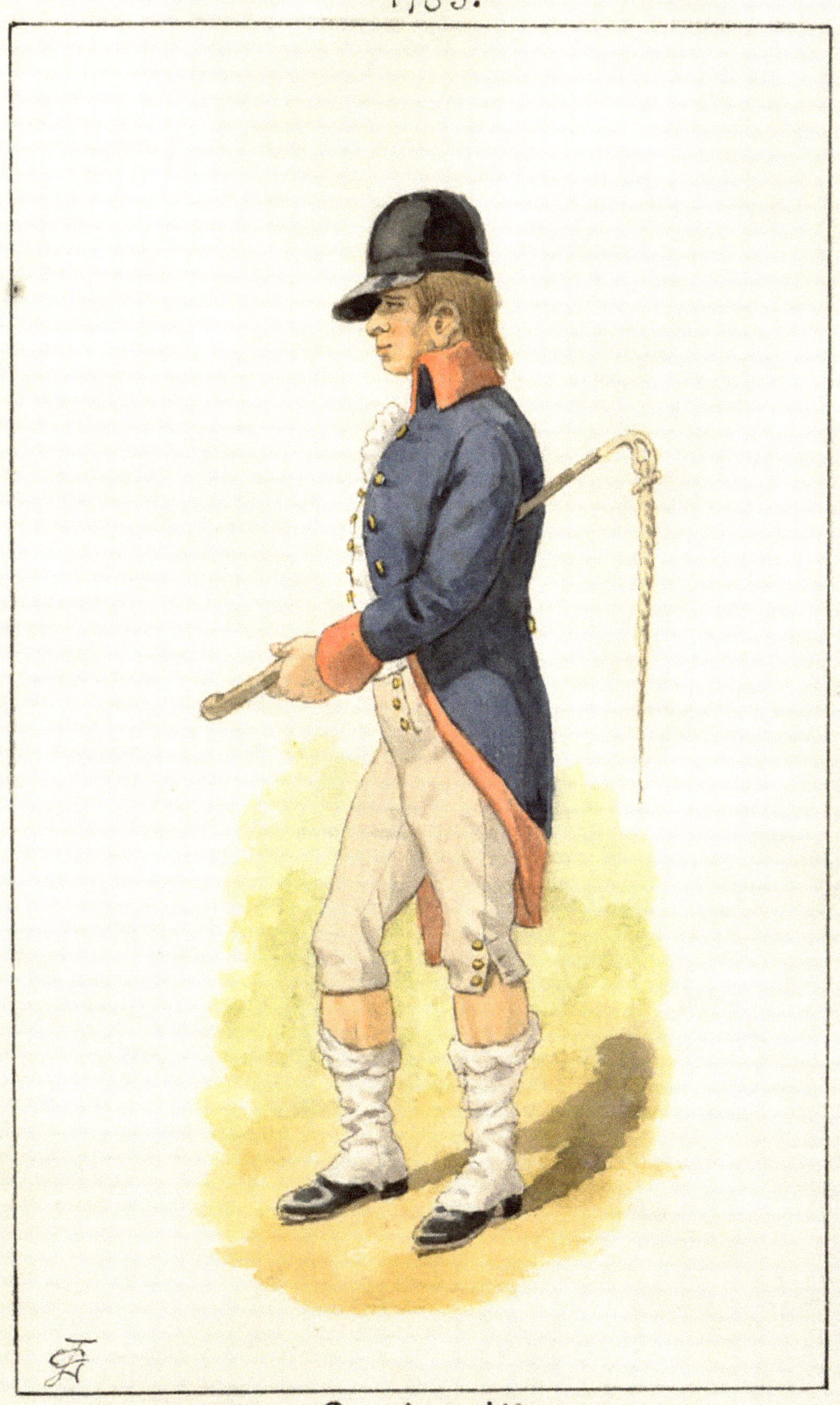

Royal Artillery.
Driver.

35 – 9TH FOOT, OFFICER 1785

Charles Lyall shows this officer wearing a long scarlet coat with yellow collar, lapels and cuffs, silver lace and buttons. The white lining of the coat is clearly seen, and a crimson sash is worn around the waist. A white waistcoat and breeches are also worn with black gaiters buttoned up at the sides. The headdress is a black felt hat with wide silver lace forming an edge to the brim, a black cockade fixed with a line of silver lace and buttons, and a short white plume. A silver gorget hangs down from the officer's neck and his sword-belt carries an oval plate. For the period under consideration, the plate seems to be that described by Major Parkyn—'an oval silver plate with a high beaded rim and in the centre the figure of Britannia with a scroll below inscribed 9 Regt.'—on page 98 of his book *(Military) Shoulder-Belt Plates and Buttons*. The artist's date is exactly one hundred years after the formation of the regiment in 1685, the 9th in 1881 becoming the Norfolk Regiment.

1785.

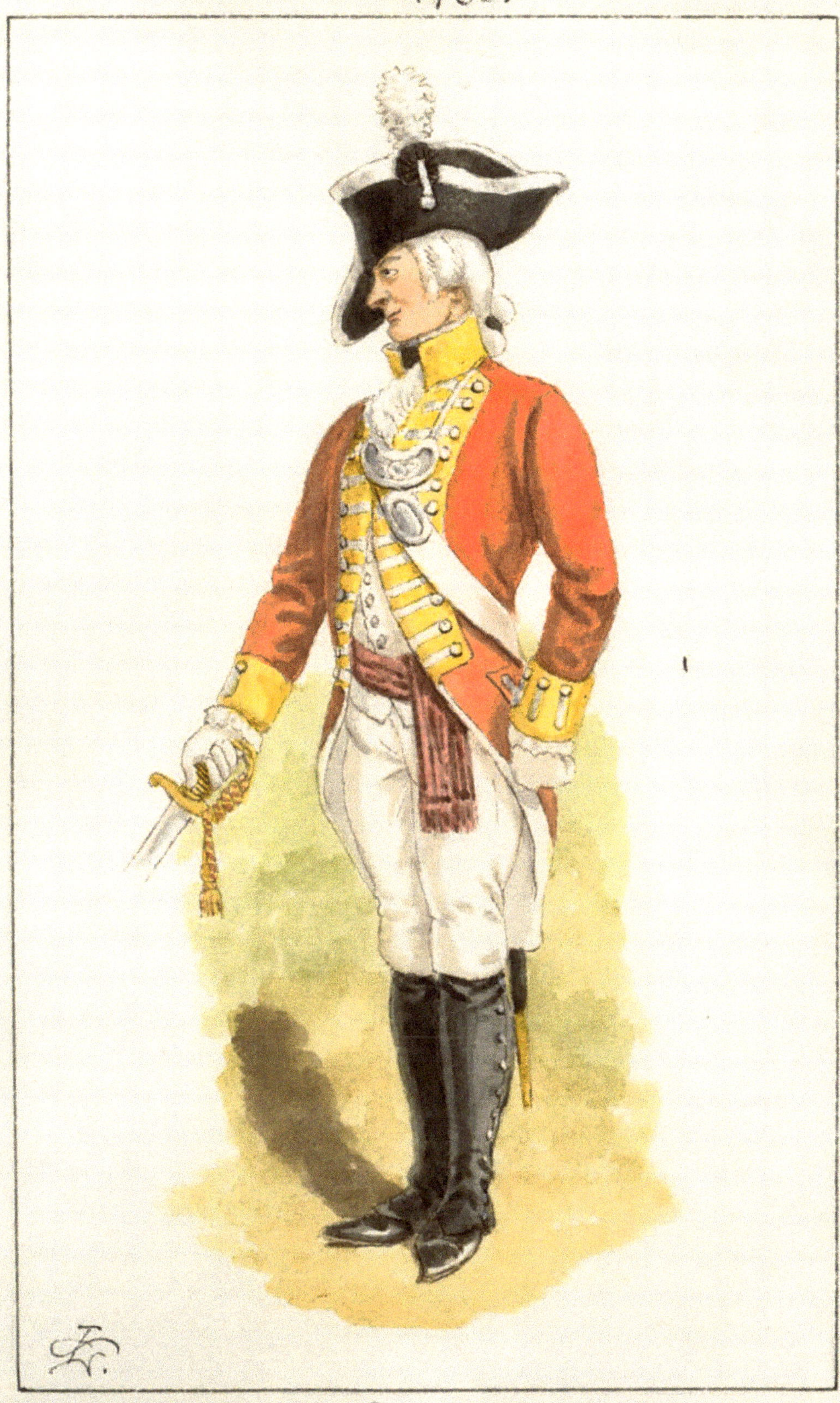

9th Foot. Officier.

36 – 9TH FOOT, PRIVATE 1785

The first facings of the 9th Regiment are on record as having been orange, changing later to green. In 1733, however, authorisation was given to revert back to the original orange, this colour by 1747 being described as yellow. A similar shoulder-belt plate (attached to the bayonet frog-belt) to that of the officers (see Plate 35), but brass for other ranks and with a crown above the figure of Britannia. Three buttons on each side for the breeches, ten for the long, black, cloth gaiters.

4

1785.

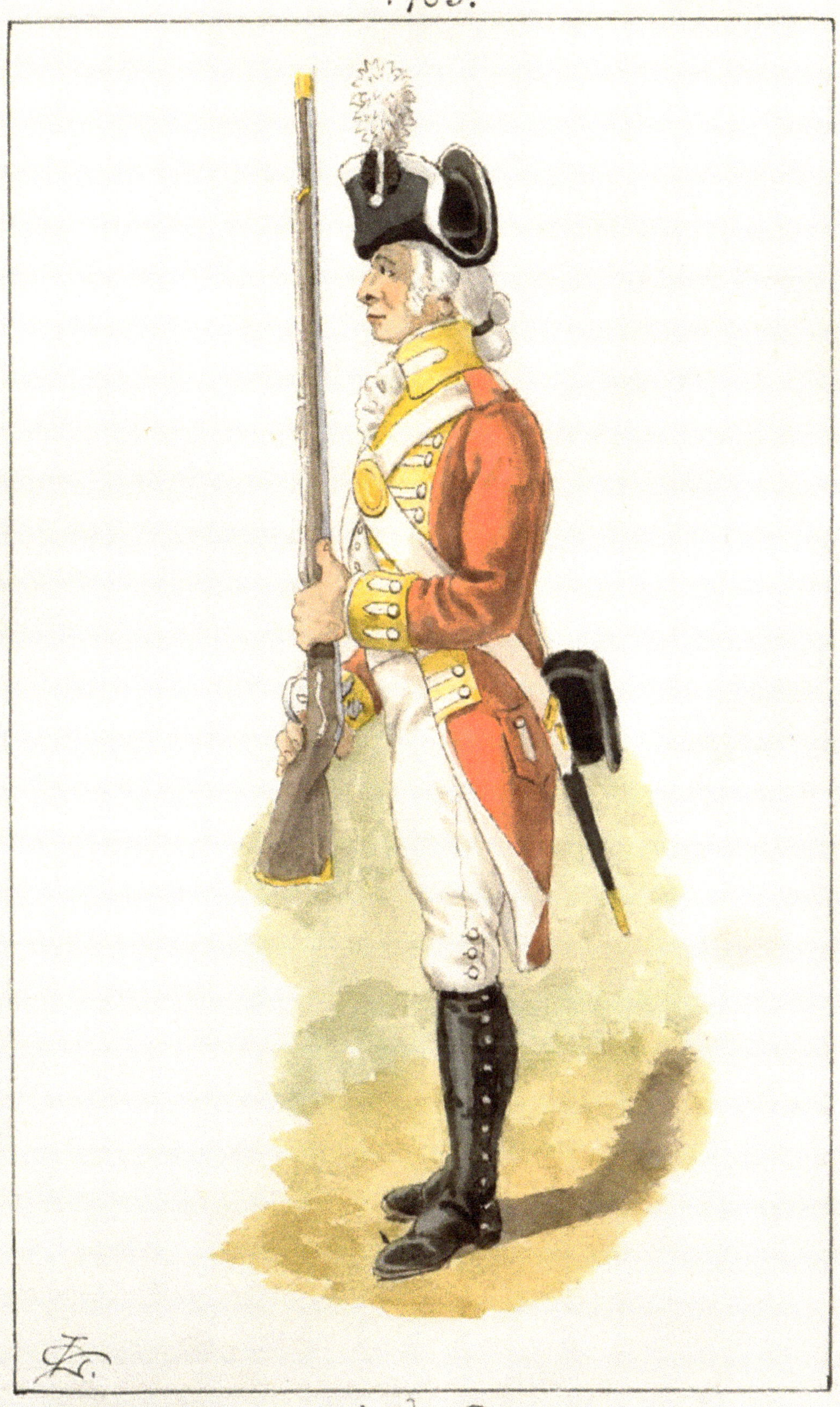

9th Foot, Private.

37 – 12th SUFFOLK REGIMENT, 1785

Raised in 1685 by Henry Howard, 7th Duke of Norfolk, and known by the names of its successive colonels until designated as the 12th Regiment of Foot in 1751. 'East Suffolk' was added to the title in 1782. The year 1785 saw the regiment stationed at home, Webb's regimental history recording an order of 5 April, '...to march in two divisions...to Sunderland and Tynemouth.' The author goes on, 'While on the march, an order was received to proceed, with all haste to Newcastle, Gateshead, and Westgate, in aid of the civil power.' This Charles Lyall painting suggests white facings—Cannon mentions white ribbons and coat linings being worn in June 1686—but yellow was later adopted and in use certainly by 1742. An interesting and unusual rear view by the artist showing the pouch-belt and pouch, and over the right shoulder the belt holding the bayonet frog. It had only been the year before Lyall's caption date of 1785 that infantry soldiers had been directed to cease supporting the bayonet via a waist belt. Note also how the queue—the hair gathered at the back—was bound with ribbon to form a long tail.

1785.

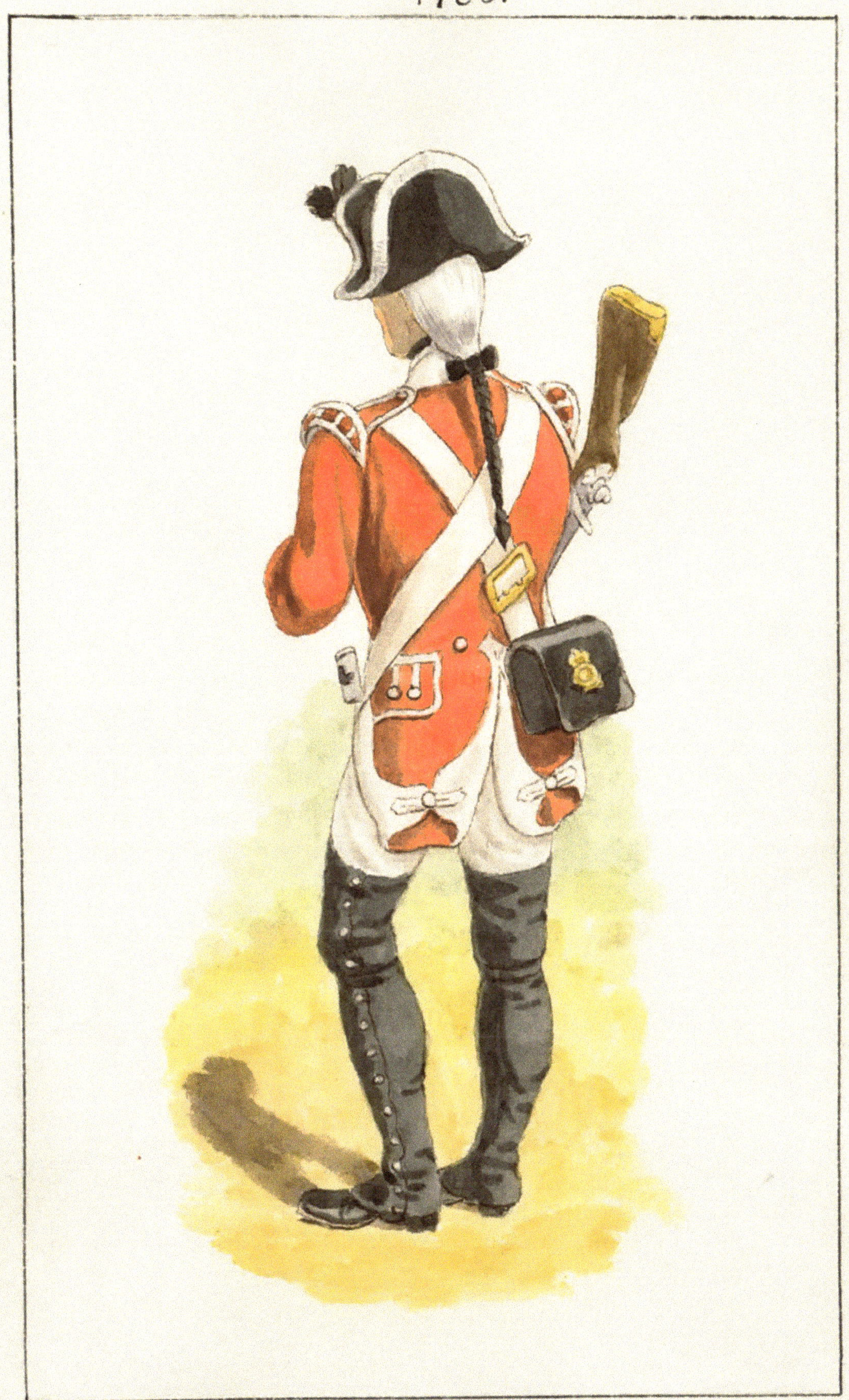

12th. "Suffolk" Regiment.

38 – SAPPERS AND MINERS, WORKING DRESS 1786

We will see in Plates 39 and 40 how in 1787 the coats for working dress were white. In the previous year, however, red was the colour, and we turn to TWJ Connolly for details: 'The working dress was a plain long red jacket in winter, and a linen one in summer, with a single row of large brass buttons, wide apart, down the front. It descended to the hips, opened from the chest upwards to show the shirt, and from that point downwards to show the waistcoat. The collar and cuffs were of yellow cloth. Under the jacket a waistcoat was worn—in summer linen, in winter flannel.' As we can see, the hat was white.

1786.

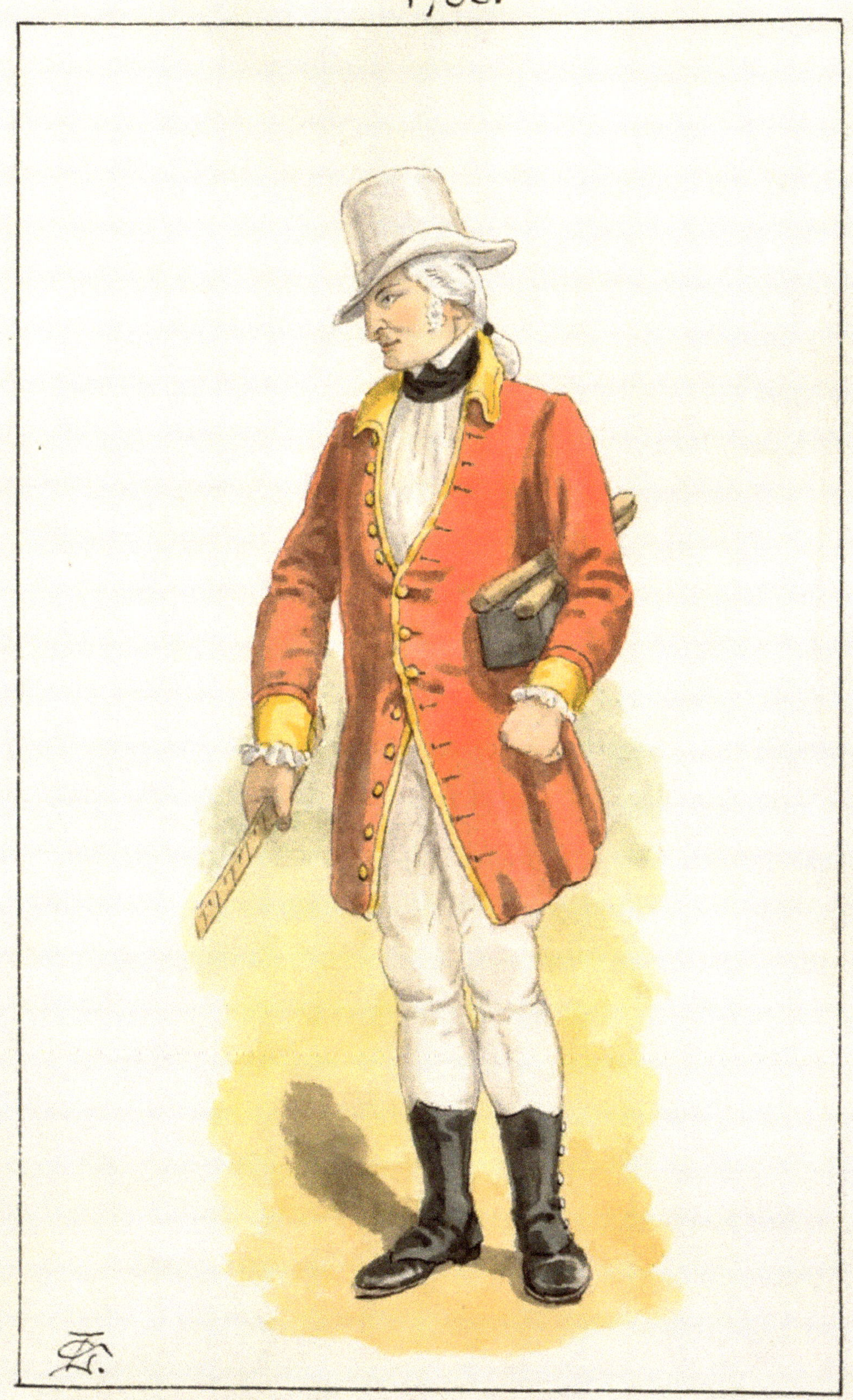

Sappers & Miners.
Working Dress.

39 – SAPPERS AND MINERS OFFICER, WORKING DRESS 1787

Charles Lyall's inspiration for this study of a Sappers and Miners officer in working dress has come from Volume 1 of TWJ Connolly's *History of the Royal Sappers and Miners*, (Longman, Brown, Green, Longmans & Roberts, 1857). Although the full dress of the corps consisted of a blue coat with long skirts and black facings, a working dress existed which is described by TWJ Connolly as follows: 'The working dress was a plain white raven duck, or canvas frock, reaching nearly to the ankles, with a rolling collar, and brass buttons down the front; white duck waistcoat and pantaloons, tongued and buttoned at the bottom, and plain black felt hats. Leather stocks and frilled shirts were also worn. The hair was queued but not powered.' The Connelly print (M&N Hanhart after GB Campion) also shows a sapper who wears a plain hat as described (see Plate 40). His officer's headgear, however, has the gold lace band as depicted by Lyall.

1787.

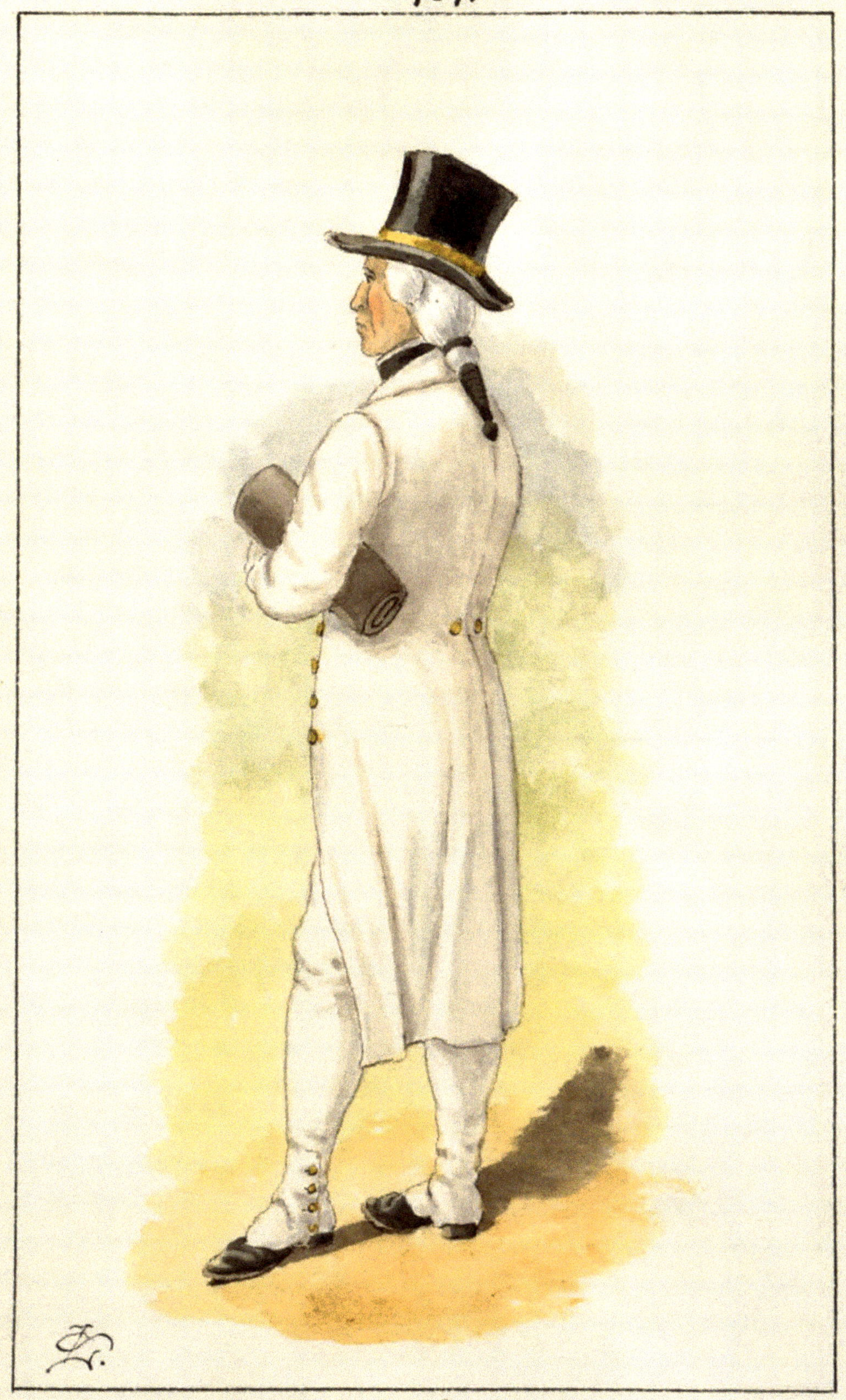

Sappers & Miners.
Officer. Working dress.

40 – SAPPERS AND MINERS, WORKING DRESS 1787

From the same source as Plate 39, we can now see a frontal view of the white raven duck, or canvas frock coat with its rolling collar and brass buttons. The waistcoat and pantaloons too, with their button arrangements, the plain black felt hat without gold band, the leather stock and frilled shirt. The dress seemingly more civilian in appearance than military, the figure looks quite like a carpenter calling at some Georgian home to fix new sashes to the upstairs windows.

1787.

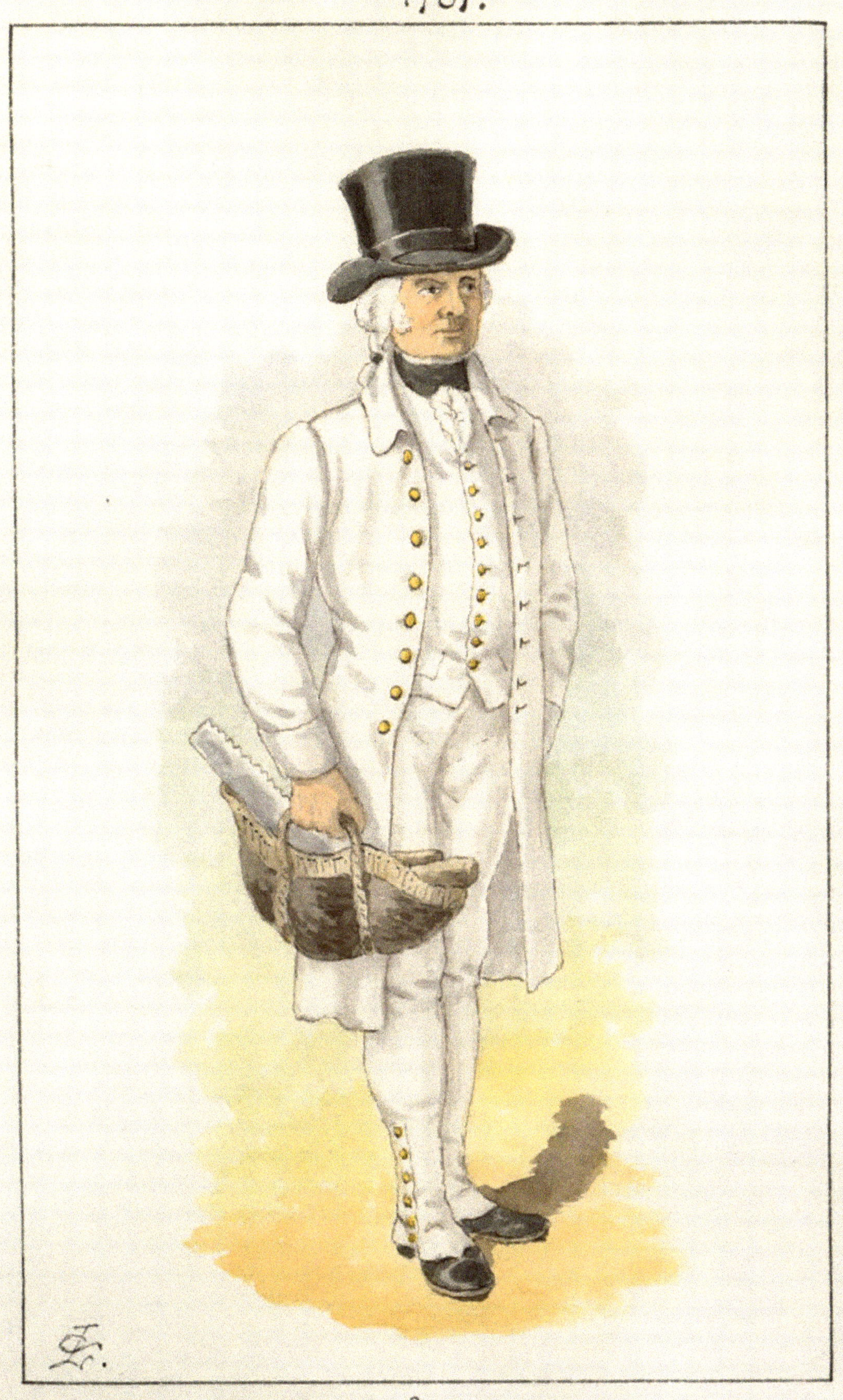

Sappers & Miners
Working Dress.

41 – SAPPERS AND MINERS, DRUMMER 1787

Charles Lyall's inspiration for this study of a Sappers and Miners drummer has come from the third colour plate in Volume 1 of TWJ Connolly's *History of the Royal Sappers and Miners* (Longman, Brown, Green, Longmans & Roberts, 1857). Connolly explains the drummer's lace as being '…broad livery lace of a quality like tape, bearing the Ordnance arms of three guns and three balls, extending from the collar downwards in parallel stripes.' As we can see, the tape also forms a border around the shoulder strap and appears in several lines down the arms. 'The drummers' (Connolly again) 'were armed with brass-handled swords, short in the blade, but broader than the sergeants, and black scabbards with brass mountings.' Interestingly, Charles Lyall shows a rope-tension drum with blue hoops painted with red wavy lines, the gold shell being emblazoned. Connolly's plate, however, has the drummer carrying a plain gold drum with red hoops.

1787.

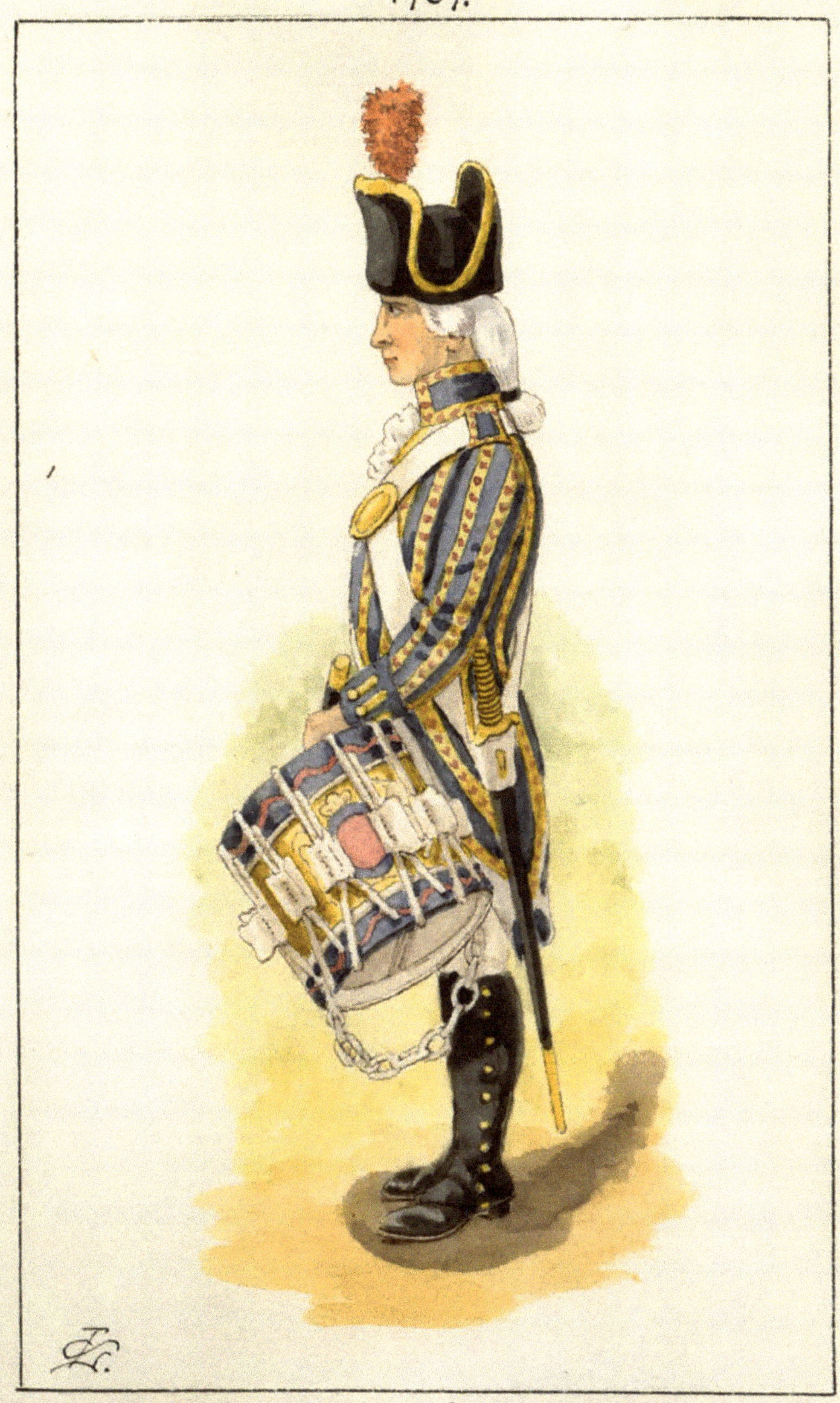

Sappers & Miners.
Drummer.

42 – SAPPERS AND MINERS, SERGEANT 1787

Also inspired by the third plate in TWJ Connolly's book (see Plate 41) is this watercolour by Charles Lyall of a sergeant in 1787. Of the arms of the corps, Connolly records that they '… were those common to the period—firelocks, pouches and cross belts of buff leather pipe-clayed. The sergeants had pikes, and long narrow thrust-swords—the latter purchased at their own expense….' Note the yellow grenades on the white turnbacks.

1787.

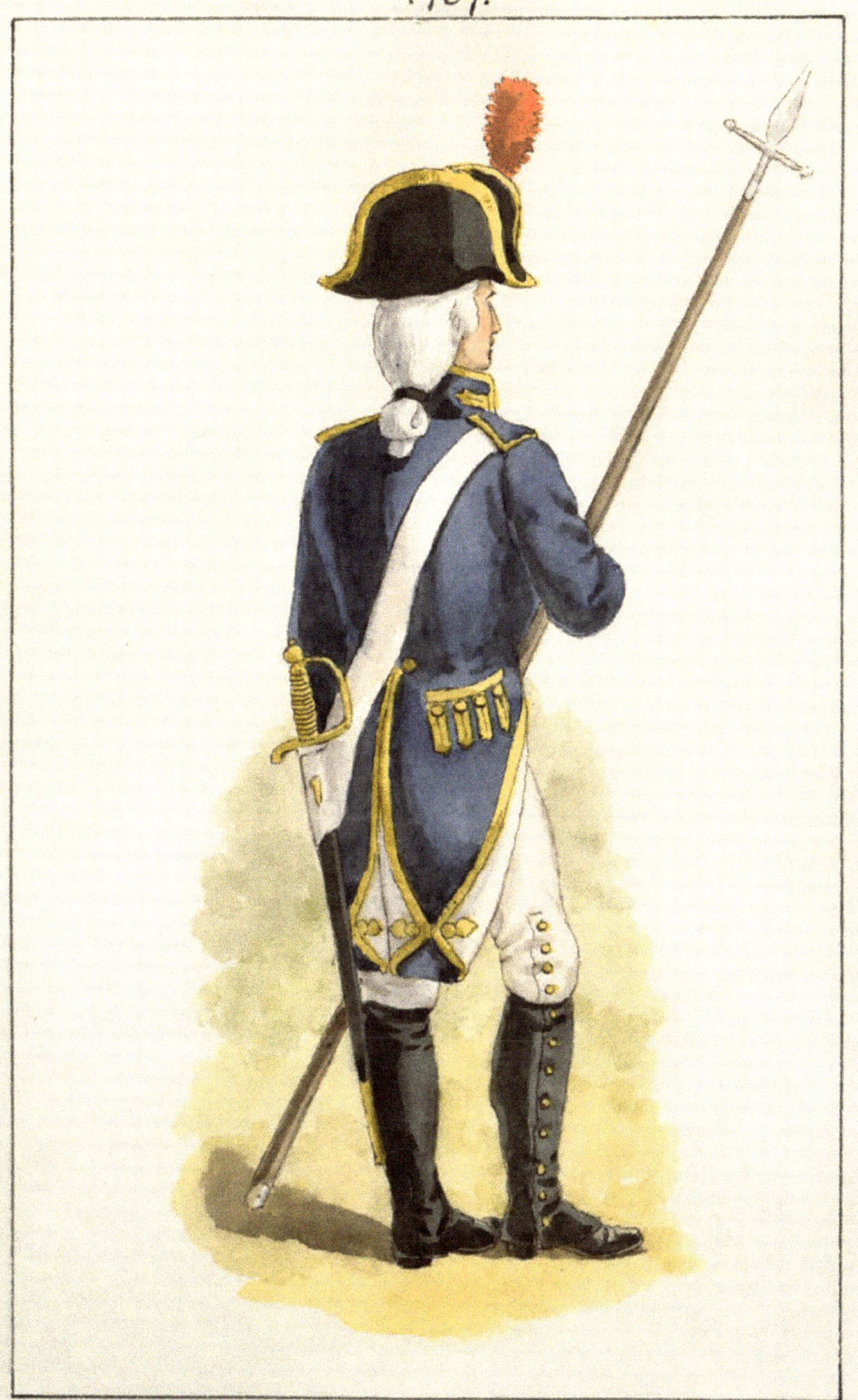

Sappers & Miners.
Sergeant.

43 – SAPPERS AND MINERS, OFFICER 1787

In this study of a Sappers and Miners officer for 1787, we see wide gold lace, a gold cockade and red feather plume on the bi-corn hat. For the coat, gold epaulettes, pointed buttonhole loops and a gold edging that runs from the collar all the way down to the skirts. Similar lace also for the white waistcoat which has two pockets. A crimson sash is worn tied at the left side, and black buttoned gaiters.

1787.

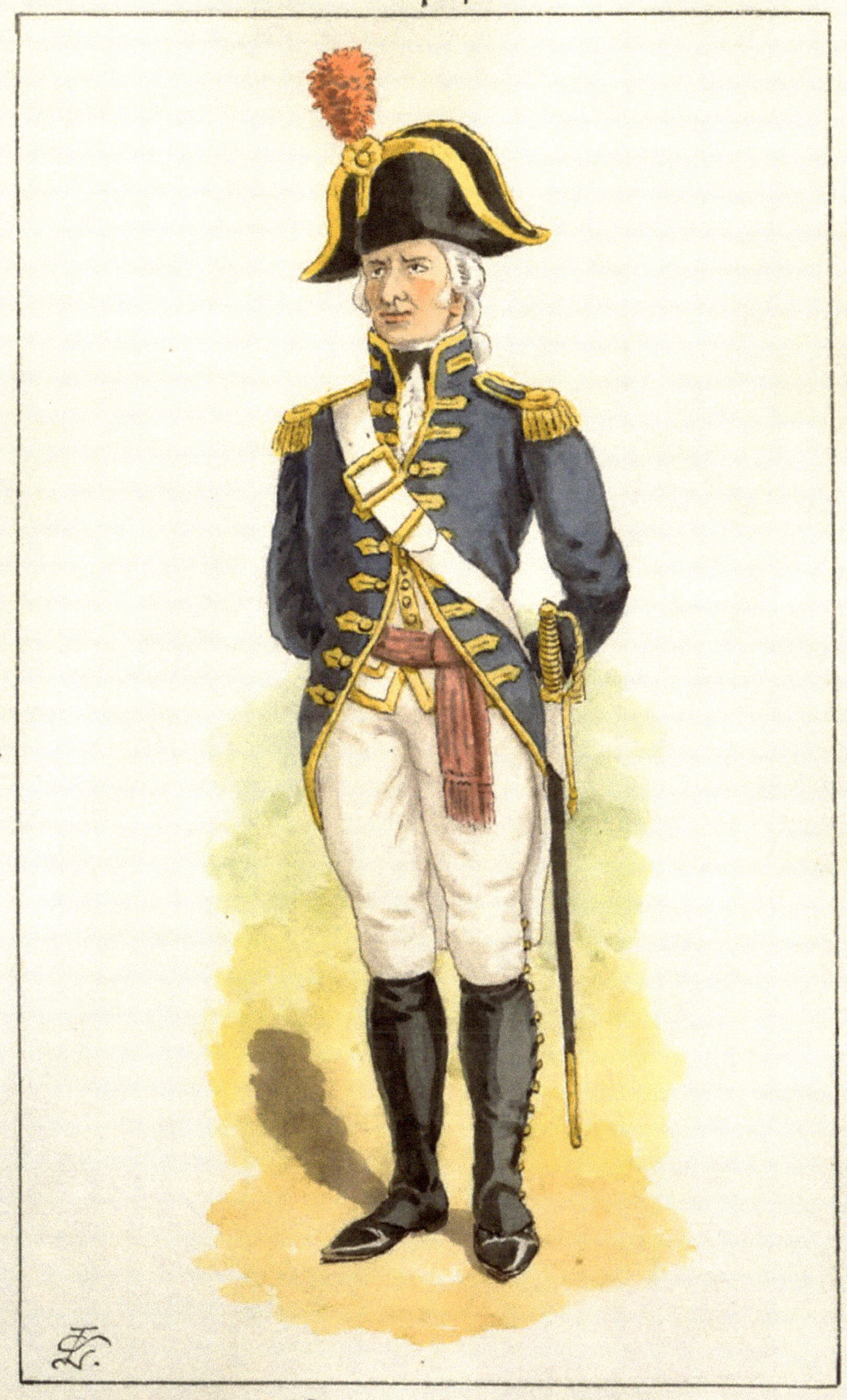

Sappers & Miners.
Officer.

44 – 74TH HIGHLANDERS, 1787

Three regiments, all disbanded, would be known as 74th before that featured here was raised in Glasgow in 1787 by General Sir Archibald Campbell. The painting is very much based on that facing page one of *Historical Records of the 74th Regiment* by Richard Cannon who describes the uniform worn at formation as being 'the full Highland garb of kilt and feathered bonnet, the tartan being similar to that of the forty-second regiment, and the facings white.' In the following year, and to answer the call for reinforcements, a detachment of the 74th embarked for India where, notes Cannon, kilts were found to be unsuitable for the climate.

1787.

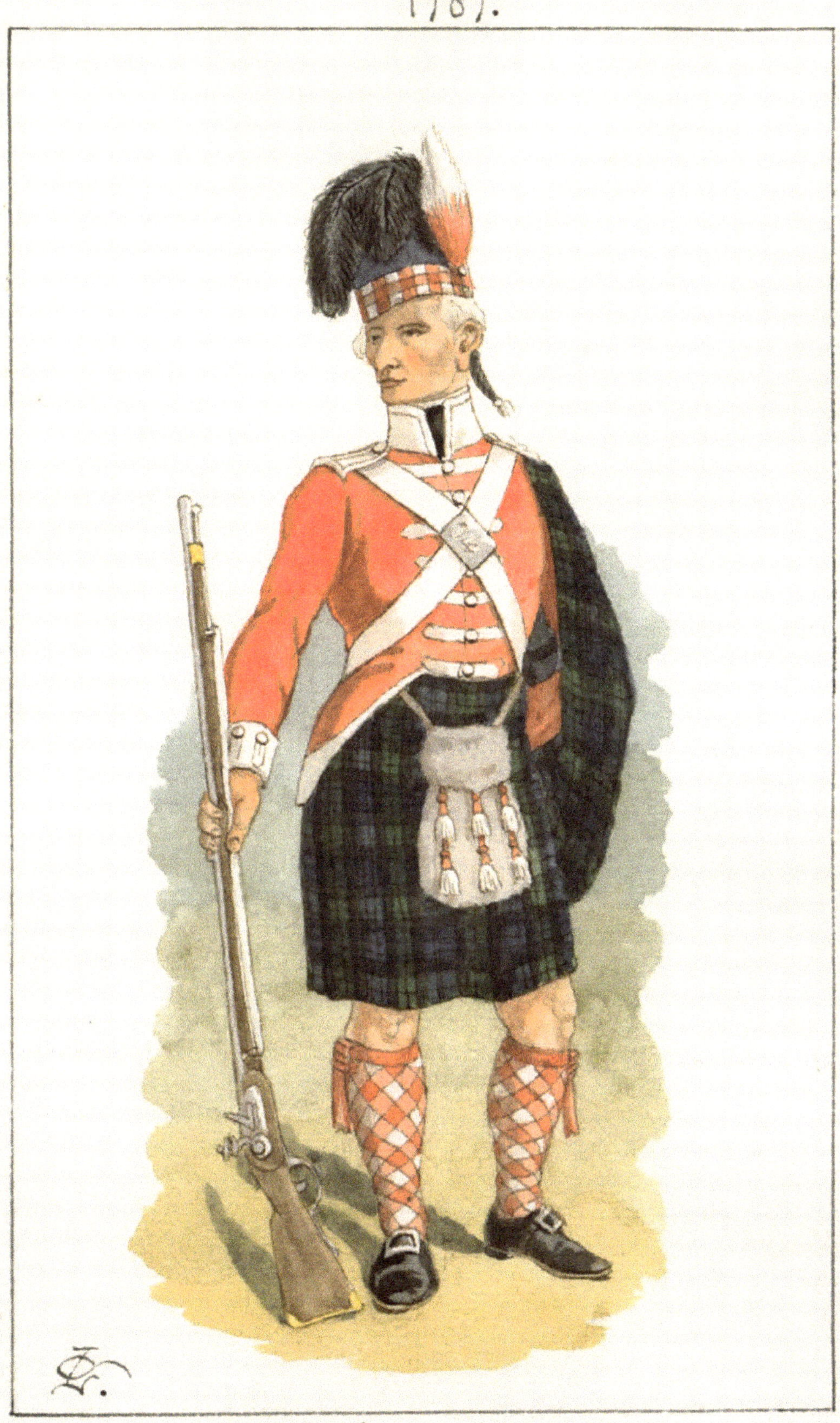

74th. Highlanders.

45 – LIFE GUARDS, 1788

The following order was issued on 26 March 1788: 'The two Troops of Life Guards and Horse Grenadier Guards to cease on 24 June next and instead of said Troops there shall be two Regiments of Life Guards.' It is from this date that the Army List would now show two regiments, the 1st and 2nd Life Guards, an arrangement that would last until 1922 and the amalgamation as the Life Guards. Charles Lyall gives no indication as to troop or regiment. There were, however, slight differences in appearance, such as in the colour of the horse furniture, viz red for the 1st Troop and blue for the 2nd. And on the uniforms, all blue collars for the 1st, red with a blue front for the 2nd.

1788.

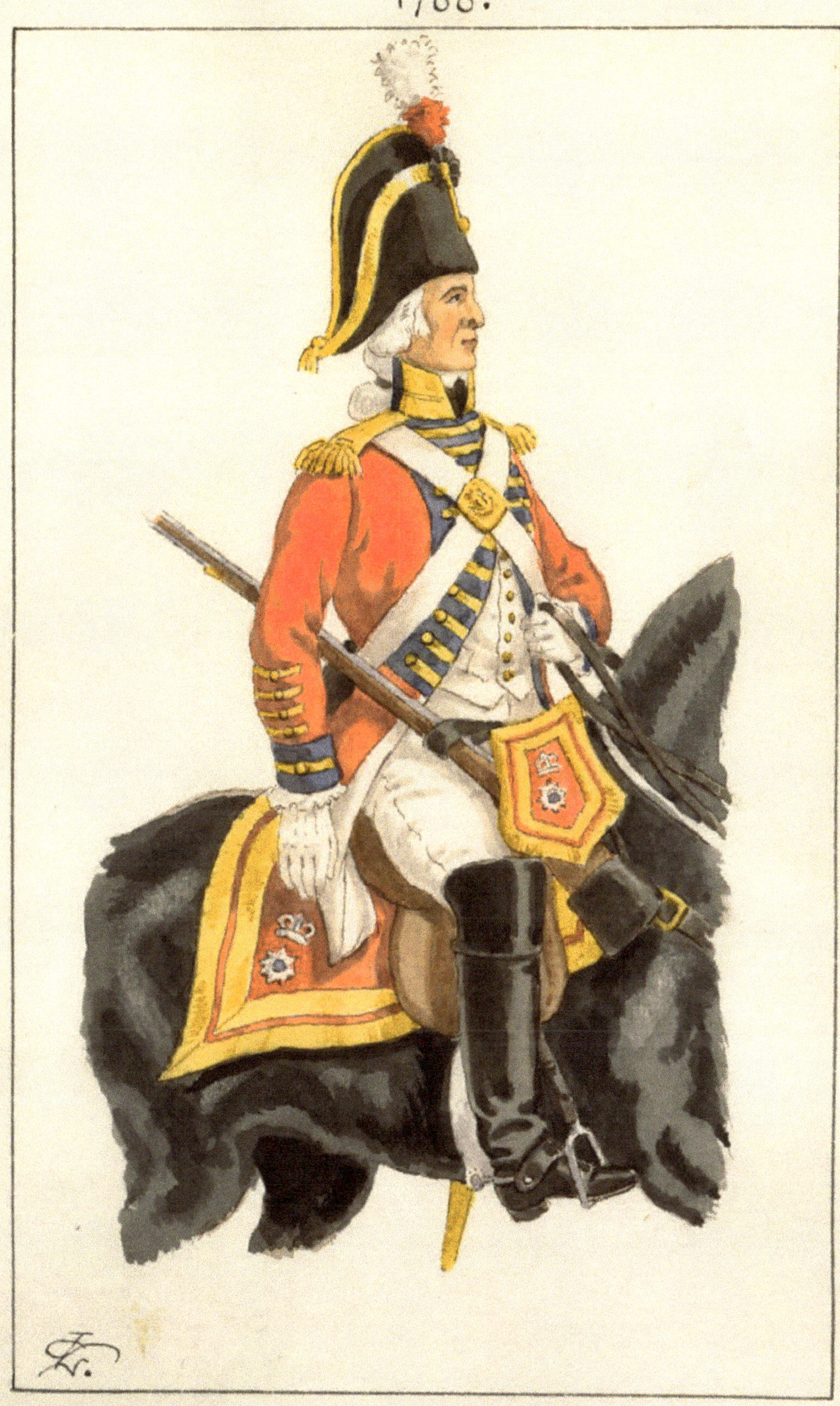

Life Guards.

46 – FOOT DRUMMER, 1788

It was the custom that the colours of drummers' coats were the reverse of those worn by the rest of the regiment—red with blue facings would become blue with red facings, or in the case of Charles Lyall's painting, buff with red facings. To this were added the blue fleur-de-lys decorated lines of lace down the sleeves and other parts of the coat that distinguished the musician. Although many proficient drummers do hold their left-hand stick in a fist-like grip (correct for the right hand) it would be considered by most percussion teachers that what Lyall has shown (the stick in the middle of the four fingers) is correct—certainly in the military.

1788.

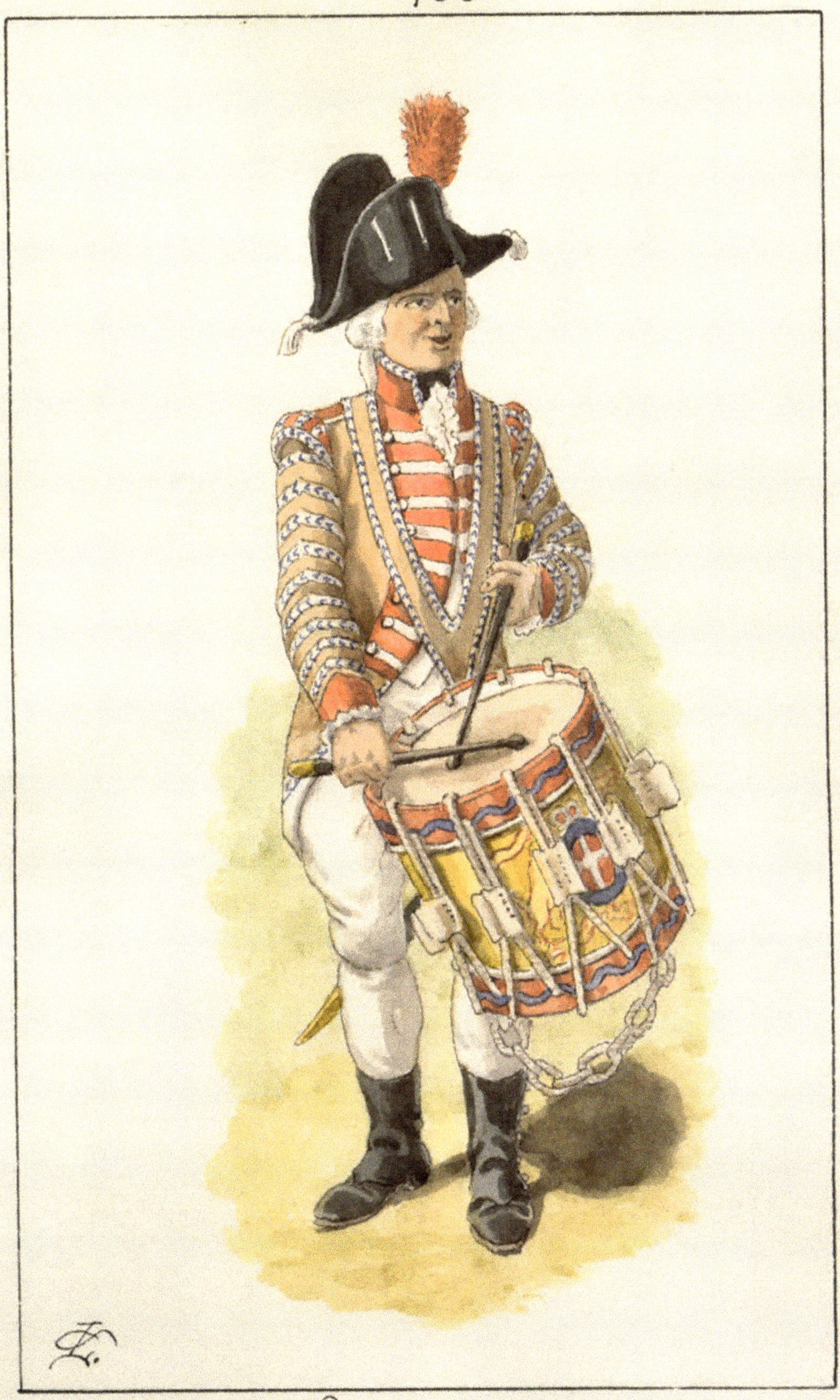

Foot. Drummer.

47 – LIFE GUARDS, 1790

Charles Lyall shows a dismounted officer, his scarlet coat has long tails that reveal a white lining, a blue collar with heavy gold lace at the front, gold lace across the chest, on the blue cuffs and up the lower arms. The headdress is a bicorn black hat which has a wide band of gold lace and a short white-over-red plume.

1790.

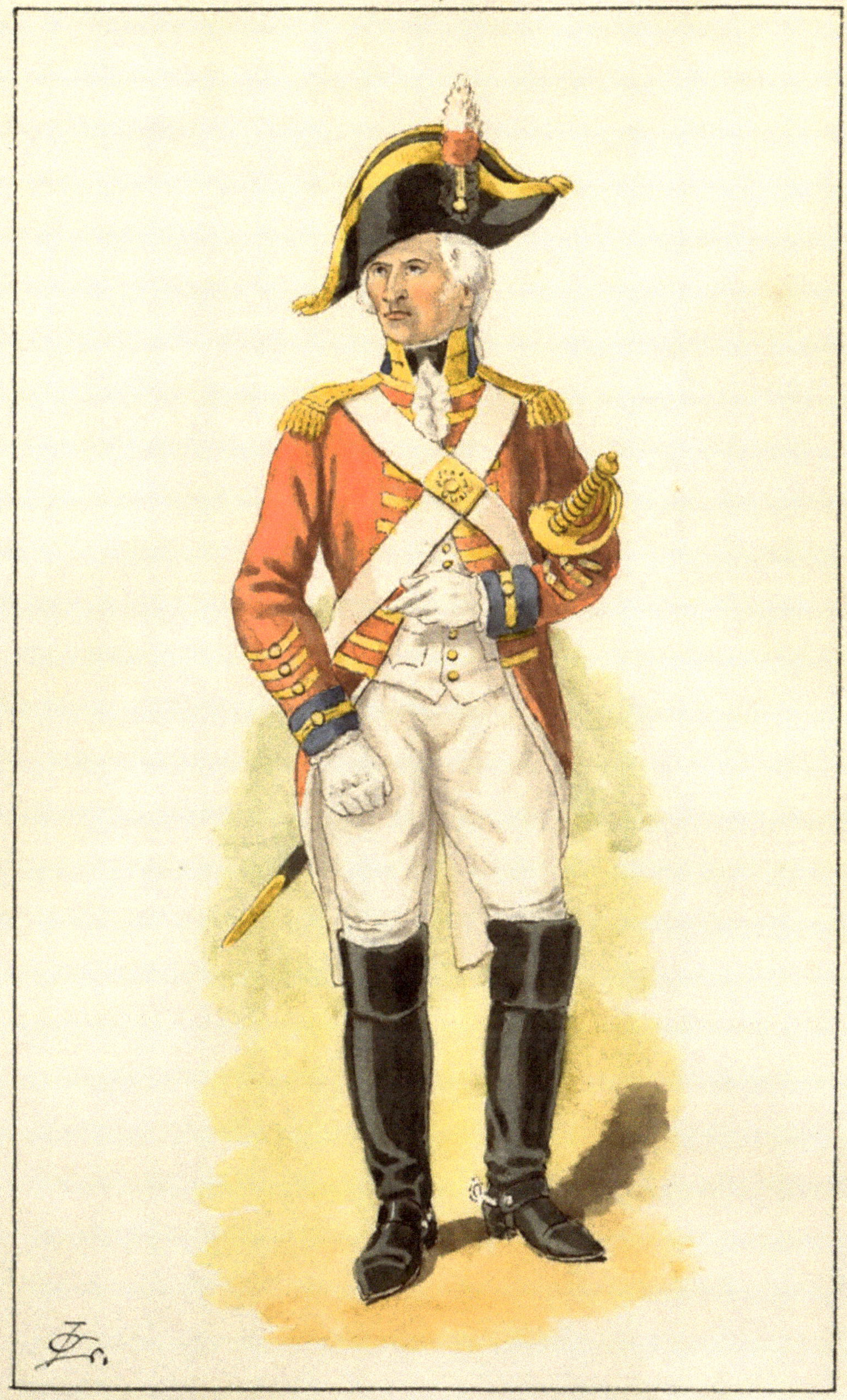

Life Guards.

48 – GENERAL OF LIGHT DRAGOONS, 1790

The image here is clearly based upon that of Lieutenant-Colonel Banastre Tarleton painted by Joshua Reynolds in 1782 and now on show at the National Gallery in London. With both arms resting on a supported raised left leg, and the subject looking away to his right, the pose is the same in both works. At the age of twenty-one, Tarleton had volunteered for service in the American Revolutionary War, climbing rapidly through the ranks to become commander of the British Legion and, later, a general. But as a hard and ruthless fighter, he would gain the reputation of a 'butcher' and was to be involved in a number of questionable atrocities, notably that of 29 May 1780 in which some 260 Americans surrendering under a white flag were either killed or severely wounded. To the American forces the term 'no quarter offered' soon became 'Tarleton's quarter'. Tarleton, the inventor of the Tarleton cavalry helmet, wore a short green jacket with gold lace, black collar and cuffs. But here Charles Lyall has given his 'General of Light Dragoons' a blue jacket with red facings and a helmet with gilt fittings, red turban and white feather.

1790.

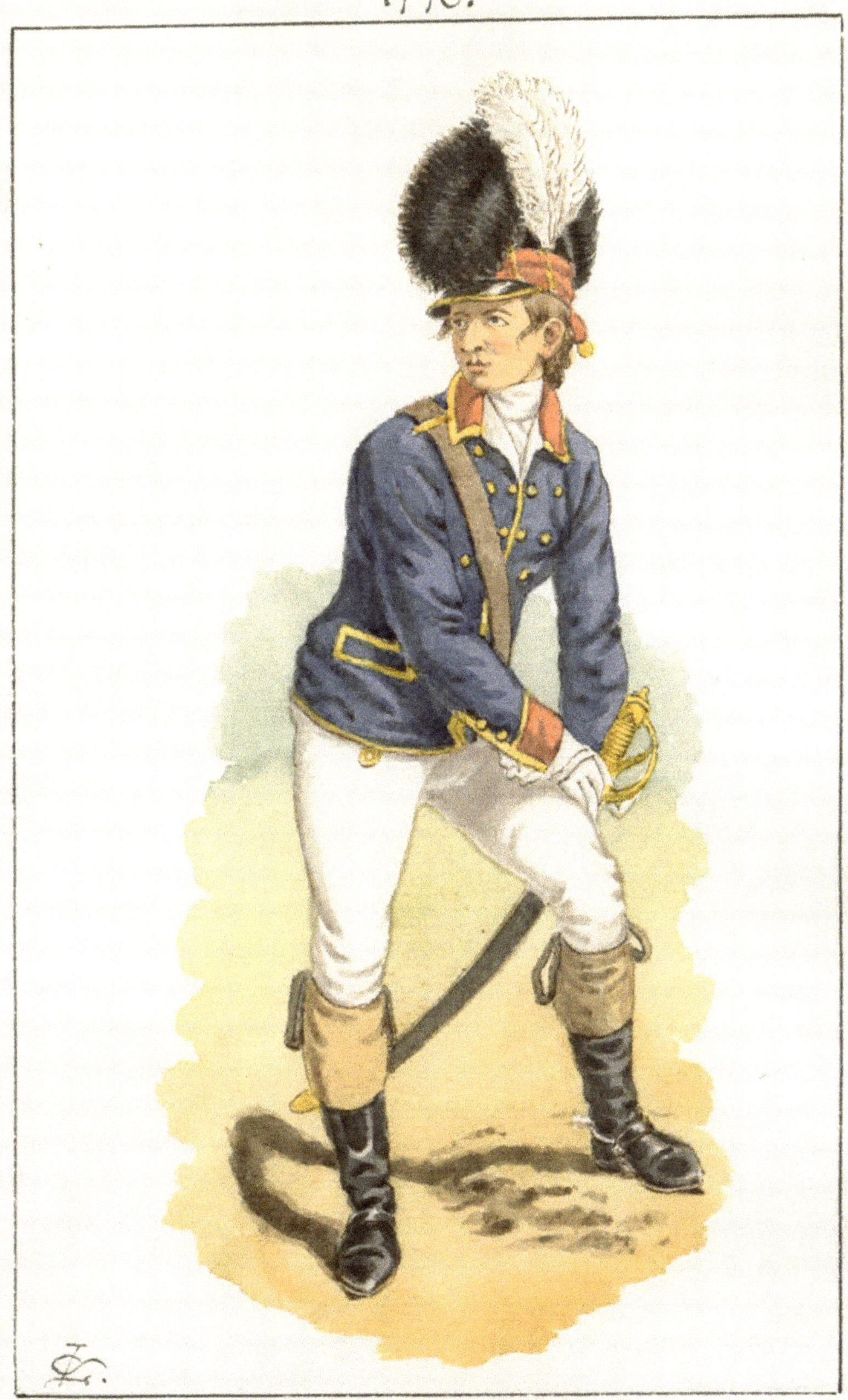

General of Light Dragoons.

49 – 13TH LIGHT DRAGOONS, 1790

A mounted figure with sword drawn wearing a light blue jacket with light green collar, shoulder straps and cuffs, all three edged with white lace. White lace also across the chest, down the front of the jacket and around the bottom edge. The helmet has silver fittings, a light green turban and a long flowing black hair plume. White breeches are worn with black boots rising to just below the knee. The horse furniture is the same colour as the facings, edged with white lace and carrying a star-shaped ornament. The regiment had been raised as dragoons in 1715 by Brigadier General Richard Munden, receiving the numerical designation of 13th in 1751. It became a light dragoon regiment in 1783, then hussars in 1861.

1790.

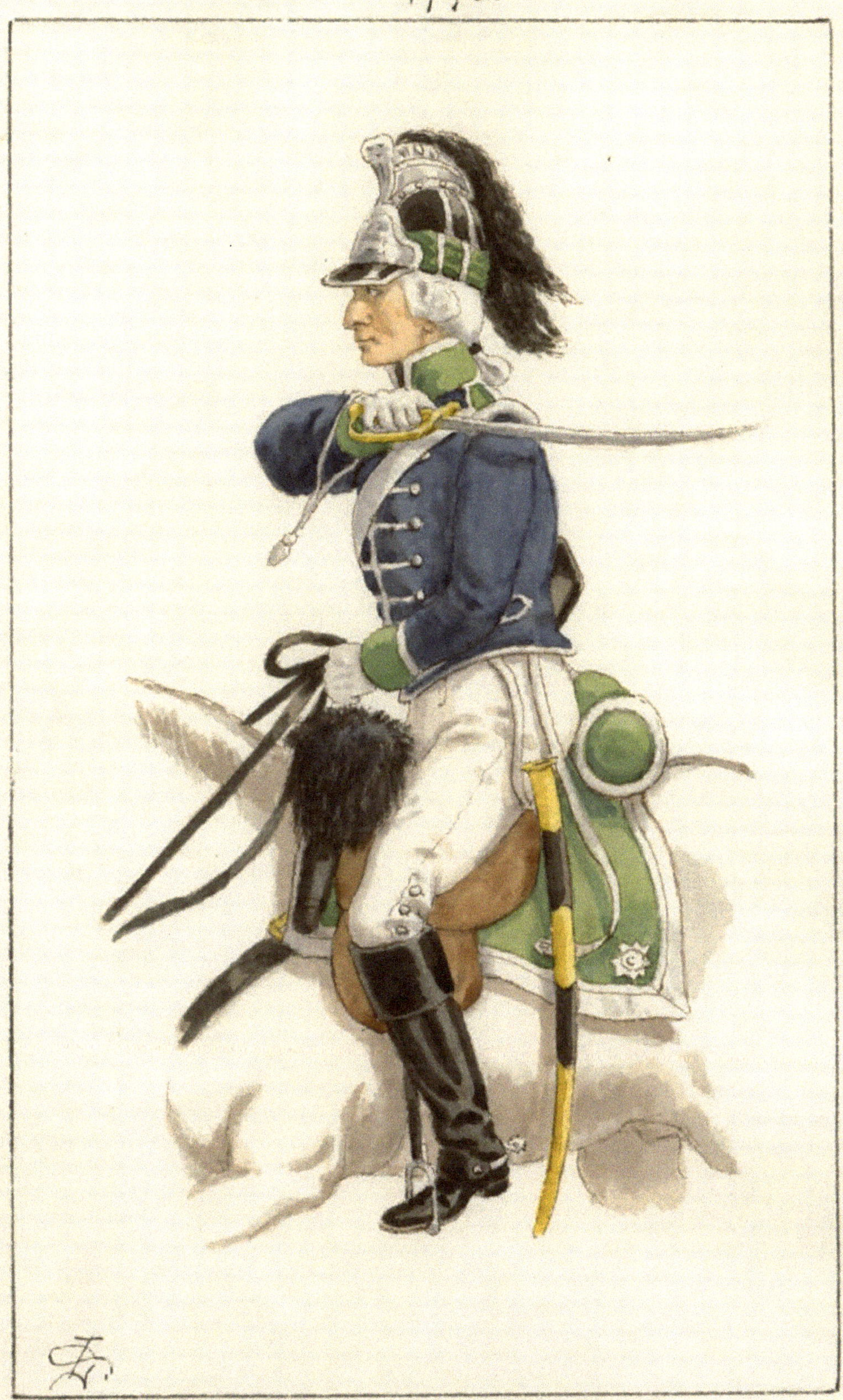

13th. Light Dragoons.

50 – 22nd LIGHT DRAGOONS, 1790

Chichester and Burge-Short, in their list of disbanded cavalry regiments, mention a 22nd Light Dragoons raised for home service in 1779. Regarding the uniform worn by this corps, the writers make reference to a costume print held by the British Museum from which they give the following description: '...a rifle-green Hussars dress, with green hanging jacket, black helmet, rifle-green horse-furniture, and apparently, as a badge, the White Rose and Crown.' This seems to point, in part anyway, towards Charles Lyall's '1790' 22nd Light Dragoons. There is, however, a discrepancy in dates as the Earl of Sheffield's regiment was disbanded seven years earlier in 1783. Two other regiments with the same number must be considered, one raised in 1794 and disbanded in 1802, the other dating from 1802 to 1819 and wearing grey.

1790.

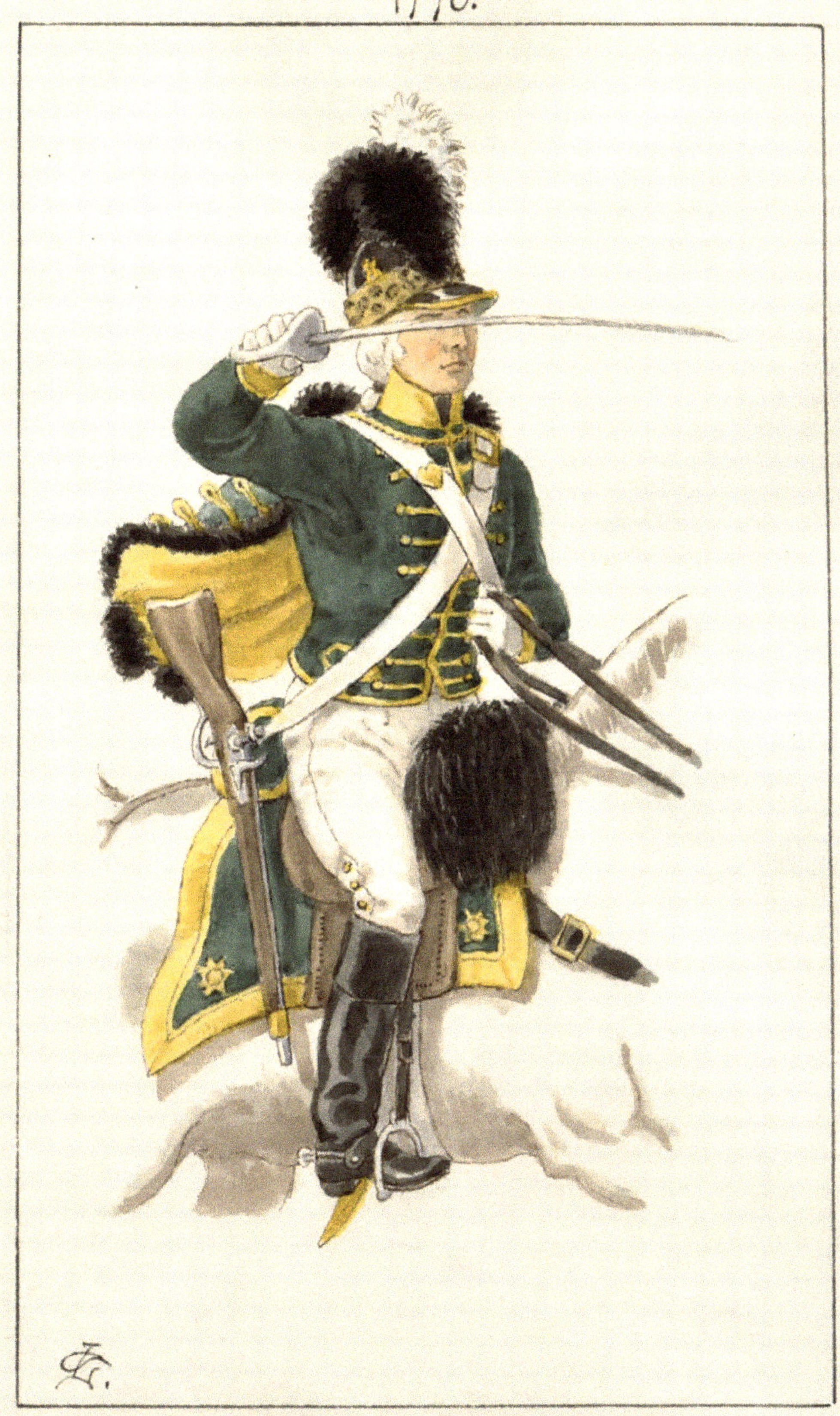

22nd Light Dragoons.

51 – FIRST REGIMENT OF FOOT GUARDS, GRENADIER DRUMMER 1790

Charles Lyall shows the regiment's red coat and blue facings together with the drummer's lace and fringed shoulder wings distinctions. As a grenadier a fur cap is worn, the front of which is charged with the Royal Arms. The drum is of the rope tension type with a blue, emblazoned shell. The wooden rims, top and bottom, are painted red, white and blue outside, the insides having a blue wavy line (a worm).

1790.

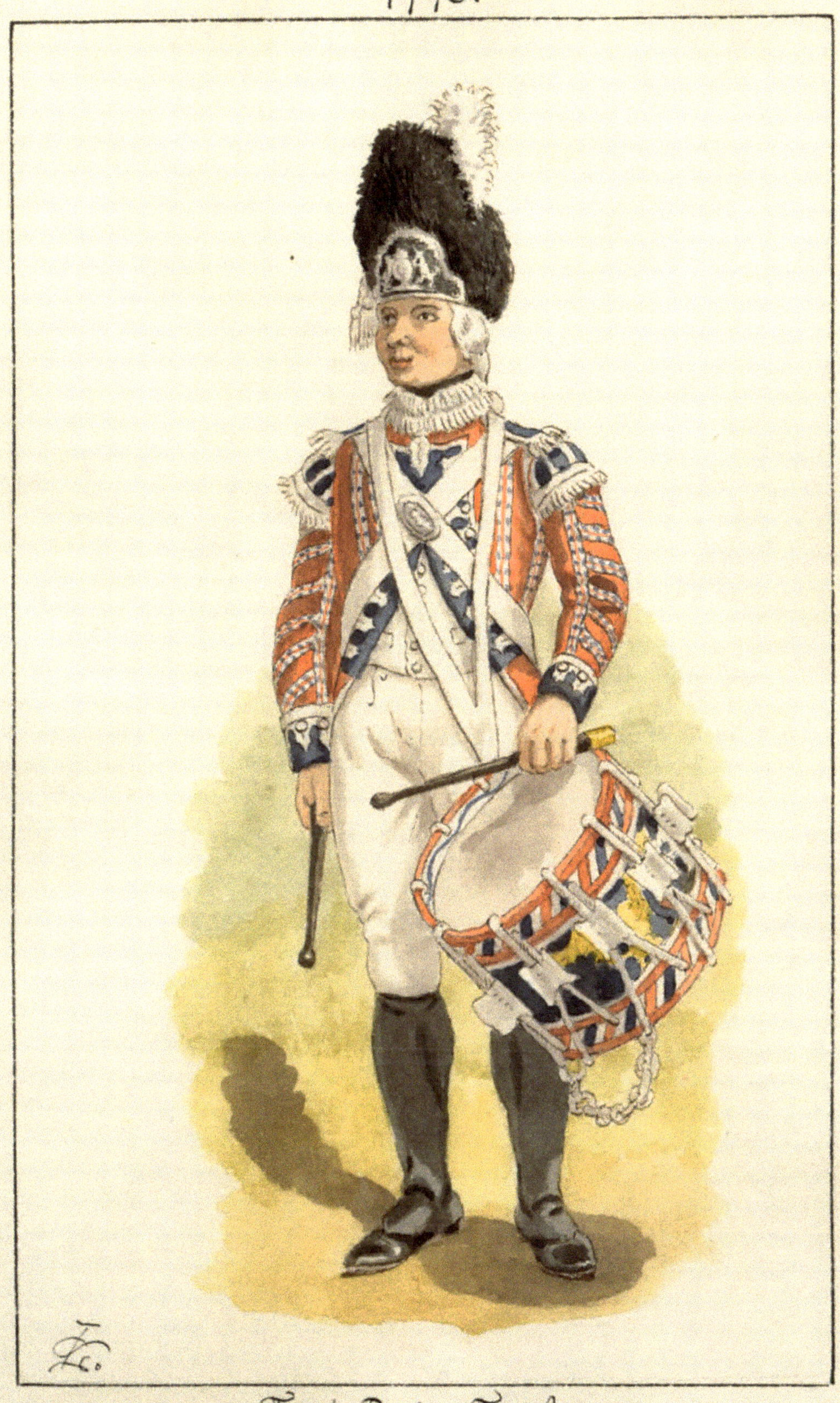

First Regt. of Foot Guards.
Grenadier, Drummer.

52 – FIRST REGIMENT OF FOOT GUARDS, SERGEANT 1790

A distinction of his rank, the sergeant has gold lace all around his blue collar and shoulder straps which end with gold fringes. Gold is used also for the lapels, cuffs and pocket buttonhole loops. These is a white and crimson sash and the traditional halberd held in the right hand. The oval gilt sword-belt plate was engraved with the design of a crowned garter.

1790.

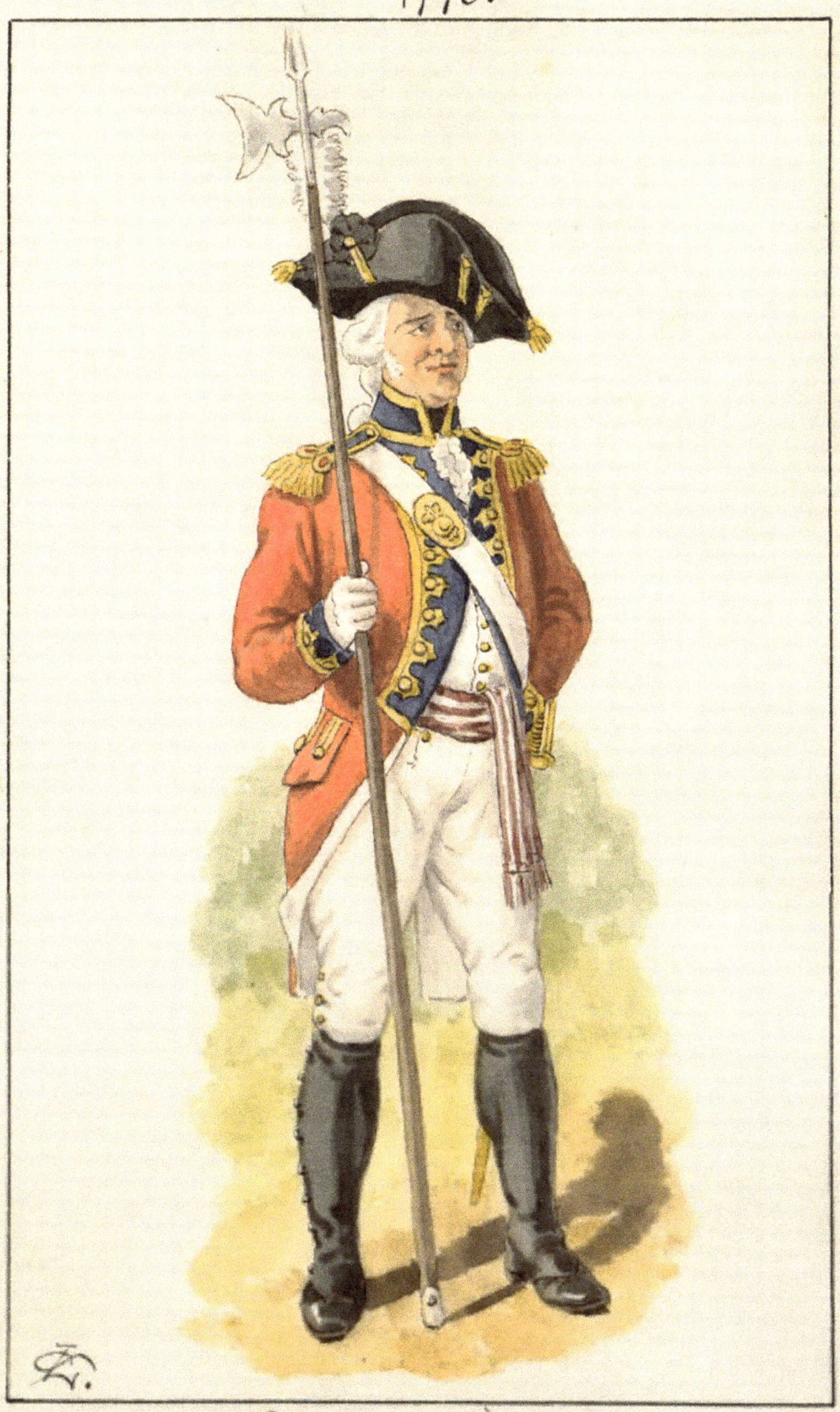

First Regt. of Foot Guards.
Sergeant.

53 – FIRST REGIMENT OF FOOT GUARDS, GRENADIER 1790

Of the same date as the Sergeant in Plate 52, the red coat and blue facings are this time adorned by white lace. The tall fur cap has a red-over-white plume, a Royal Arms device at the front and white tassels on the right side. The breeches are secured by three buttons at the knee, the black gaiters fastened on the outside by eleven small buttons. Charles Lyall provides a side view this time which clearly shows the coat's white lining, a black leather pouch held by a wide white shoulder belt and a folded brown blanket held on the back by white straps.

1790.

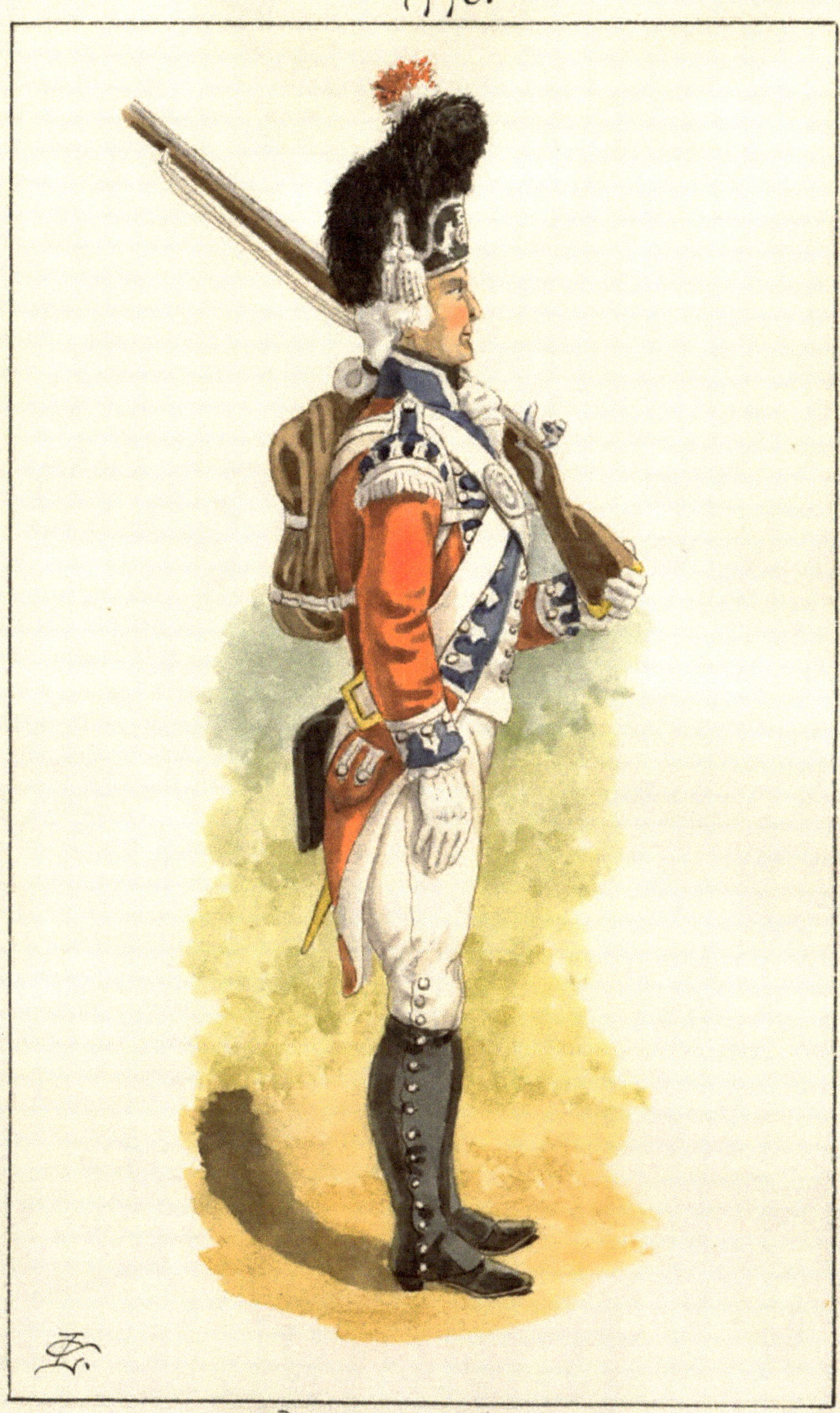

First Regt. of Foot Guards.
Grenadier.

54 – LIGHT HORSEMAN, 1790-95

The artist shows a light dragoon wearing a short blue jacket with thick black fur on the collar which runs all the way down the front to the tails and around each cuff. Yellow lace for the shoulder straps, wings and buttonhole loops, also as a decoration for a blue waistcoat. For the headdress, the Tarleton helmet invented by Lieutenant-Colonel Banastre Tarleton.

1790–95.

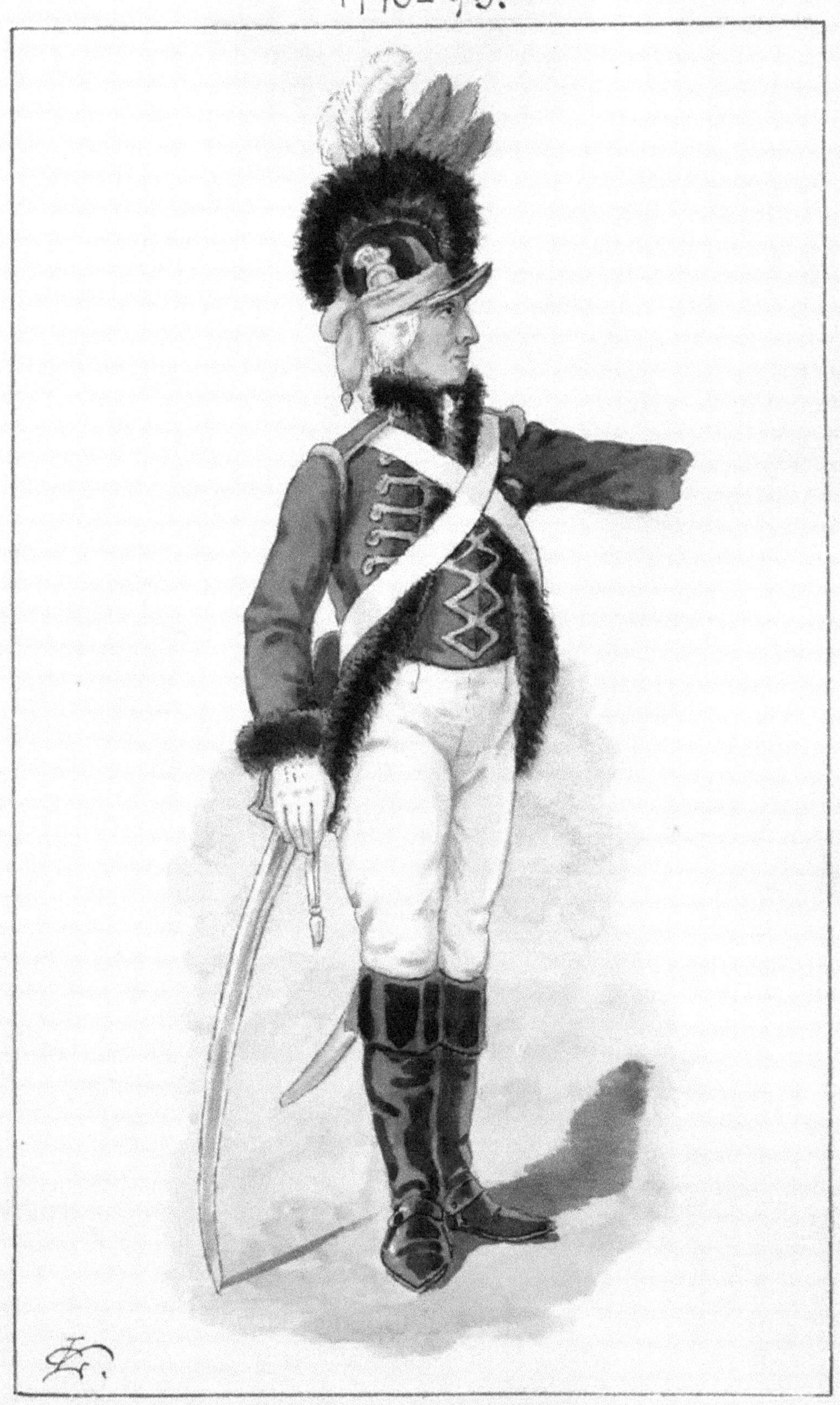

Light Horsemen.

55 – LIGHT INFANTRY, 1791

With no specific regiment mentioned, the caption for this painting is simply 'Light Infantry 1791'. WY Carman explains that light companies were sometimes removed from their regiments to form brigades, but this was only a temporary arrangement. And certainly several light infantry regiments were formed in time of war, but these again were temporary and would be disbanded when peace arrived. Permanent light infantry regiments, notes Mr Carman, did not appear until the nineteenth century. Charles Lyall gives green facings to the red coat which has shoulder wings and a high collar edged with white. The lining is white, as are the breeches which have three buttons at each knee. There are short black gaiters fastened by six buttons on the outside, and the waistcoat is red with white braid across the front. A black felt high-fronted cap is worn with a silver device at the front and feathers, one green, one white, on the right side.

1791.

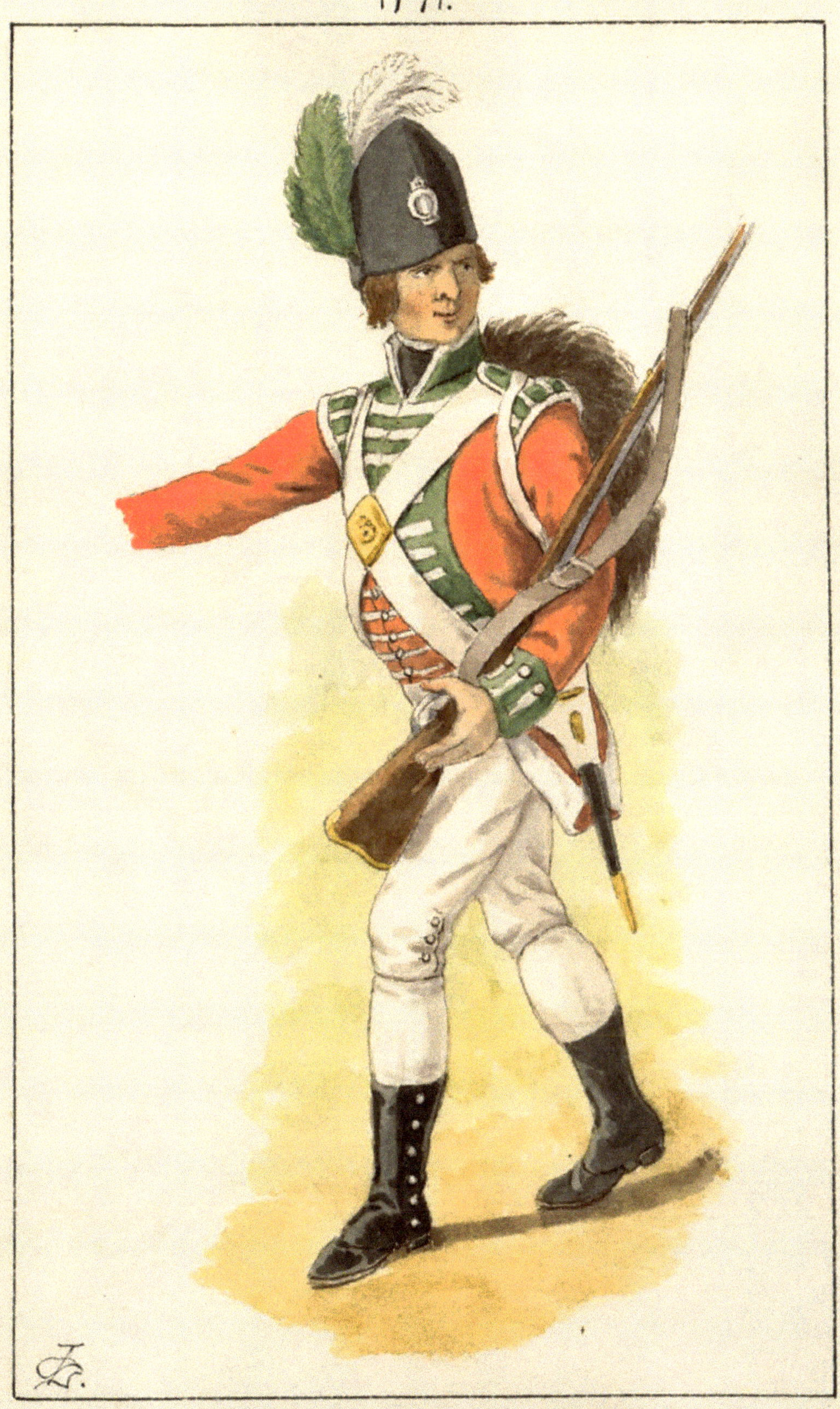

Light Infantry.

56 – 19th LIGHT DRAGOONS, 1792

This was the regiment raised in the Home Counties as the 23rd Light Dragoons for service in India in 1781. It was re-numbered as 19th in 1786, became lancers in 1817 and was disbanded in 1821. Reaching Madras in 1782, the regiment would spend the next twenty-five years in India where it would experience much action against Tippoo Sahib and during the campaign against the Mahrattas in 1803-4. For its distinguished conduct at the battle of Assaye the badge of an elephant was awarded, a distinction and battle honour which was later inherited by the 19th Hussars. Charles Lyall shows a blue jacket with primrose yellow facings and silver braid.

1792.

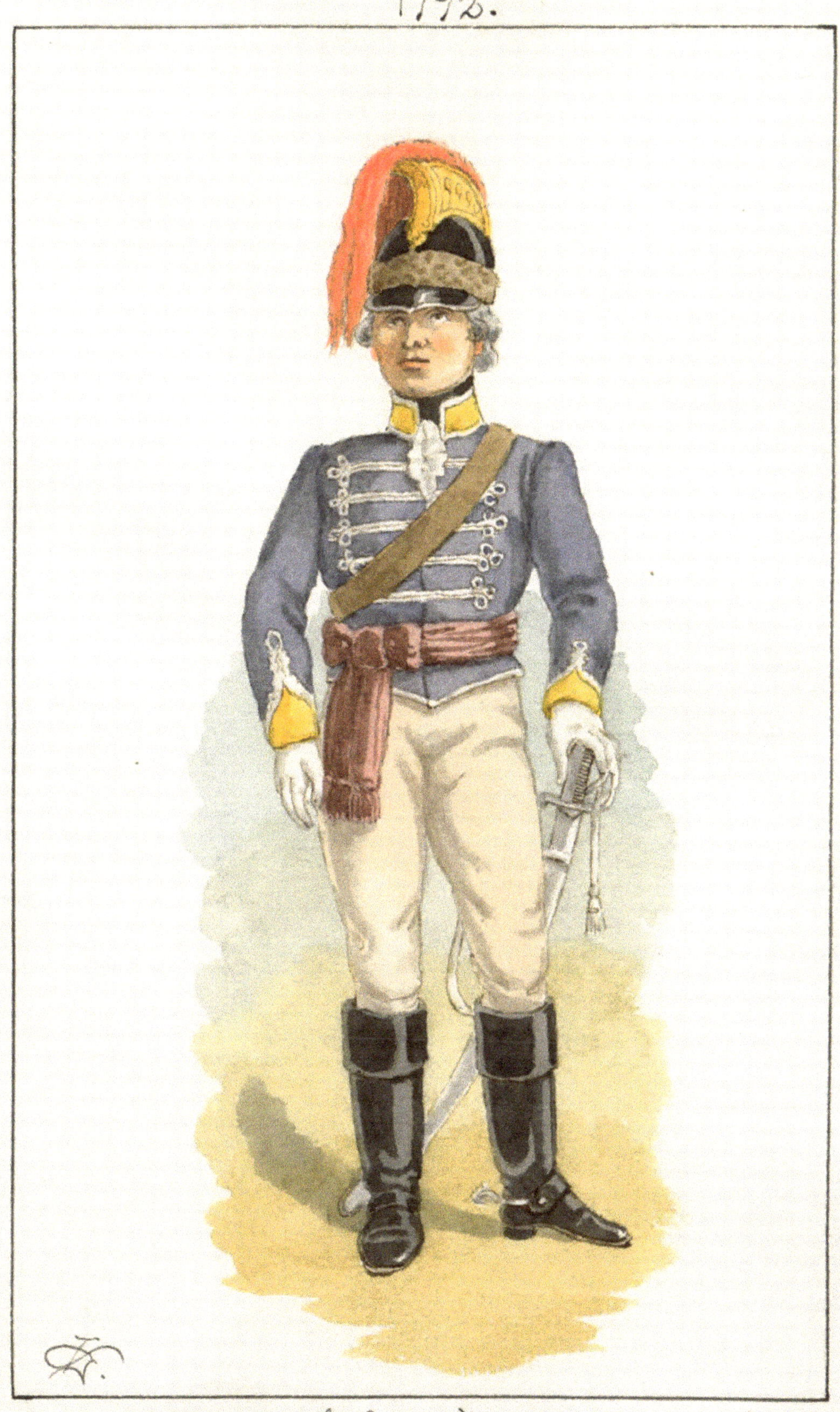

19th Light Dragoons.

57 – ROYAL ARTILLERY, DRIVER 1792

Charles Lyall's painting follows closely a sketch that appeared on page thirty of Captain RJ MacDonald's book, *The History of the Dress of the Royal Regiment of Artillery*. A smart black leather hat decorated with yellow lace and white plume; the long grey smock, however, looks very un-soldierlike.

1792.

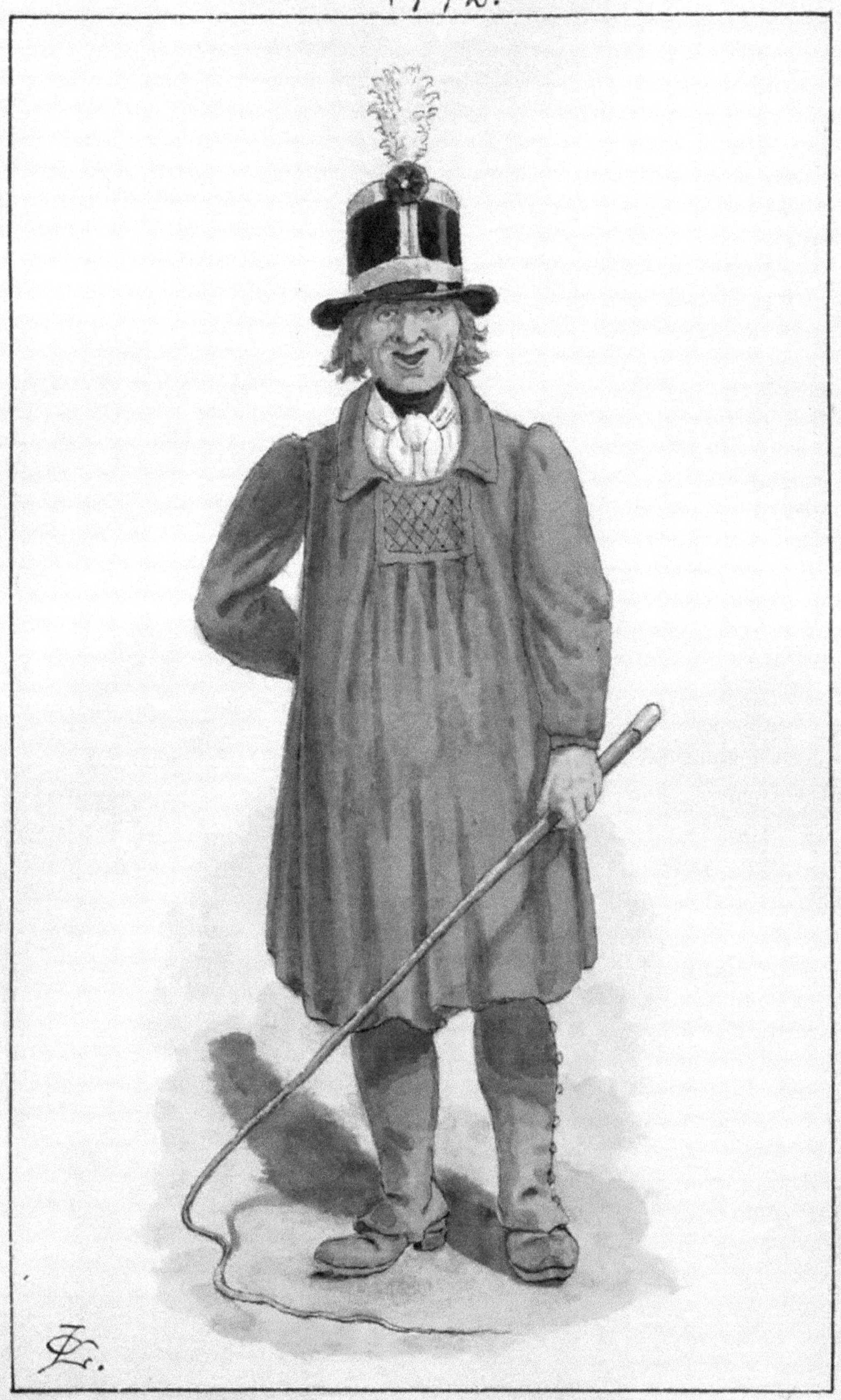

Royal Artillery.
Driver.

58 – SAPPERS AND MINERS, PRIVATE 1792

Uniforms, according to TWJ Connolly's *History of the Royal Sappers and Miners*, were issued every alternate year and consisted 'of a blue coat with long skirts, rolling collar, black cloth facings, white shalloon lining to the skirts, and lapels at the breast; which, with the slashes on the cuffs and pocket-hole, were laced with rectangular loops. Having a button at one end of the loop.' The writer goes on to say how the stock was of black leather and the gaiters 'of black cloth, which reached as high as the knee, and were secured round the leg by a row of small buttons, eighteen in number, on the outer seam. To prevent them twisting they were steadied by a button at the bend of the knee.' The black felt round hat, with its yellow lace and red plume, seen in Lyall's painting, was introduced in 1792.

1792.

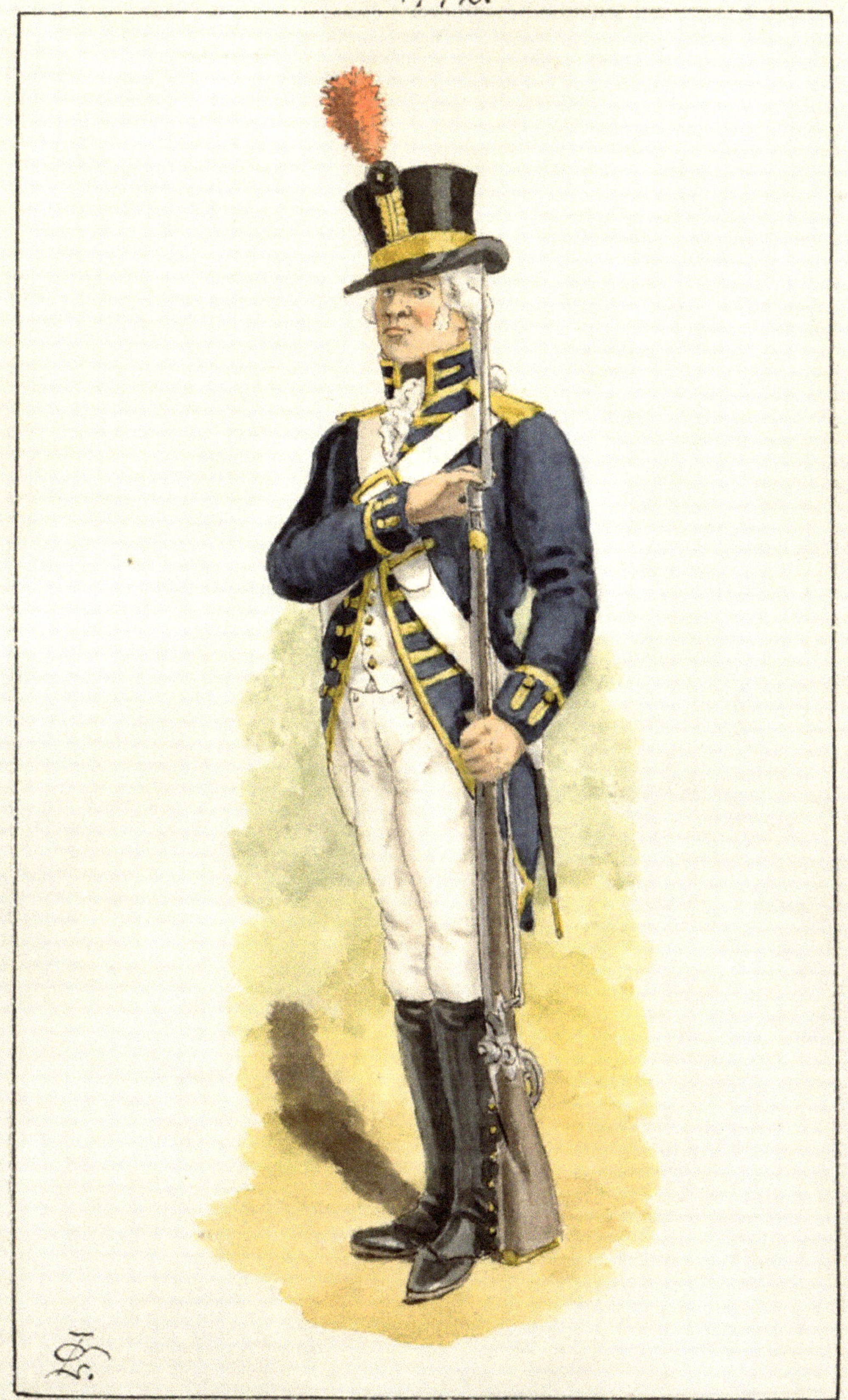

Sappers & Miners
Private.

59 – ROYAL HORSE ARTILLERY, 1793

Captain RJ MacDonald records that horse artillery had been introduced into the British Army in 1793 and shows in his book an officer of the 'Chestnut Troop' wearing very much the same uniform as that depicted in Charles Lyall's painting. The helmet is of a light dragoon type with a crimson turban and, unseen in the image, a white plume on the left side. 'The first Horse Artillery jacket,' notes Captain MacDonald, 'was after the style of the Chasseur jacket of the French Army…hooked at the collar, and sloped away towards a short skirt….' The breeches, 'well pipeclayed doe or buck skins,' are fastened at the knee with buttons.

1793.

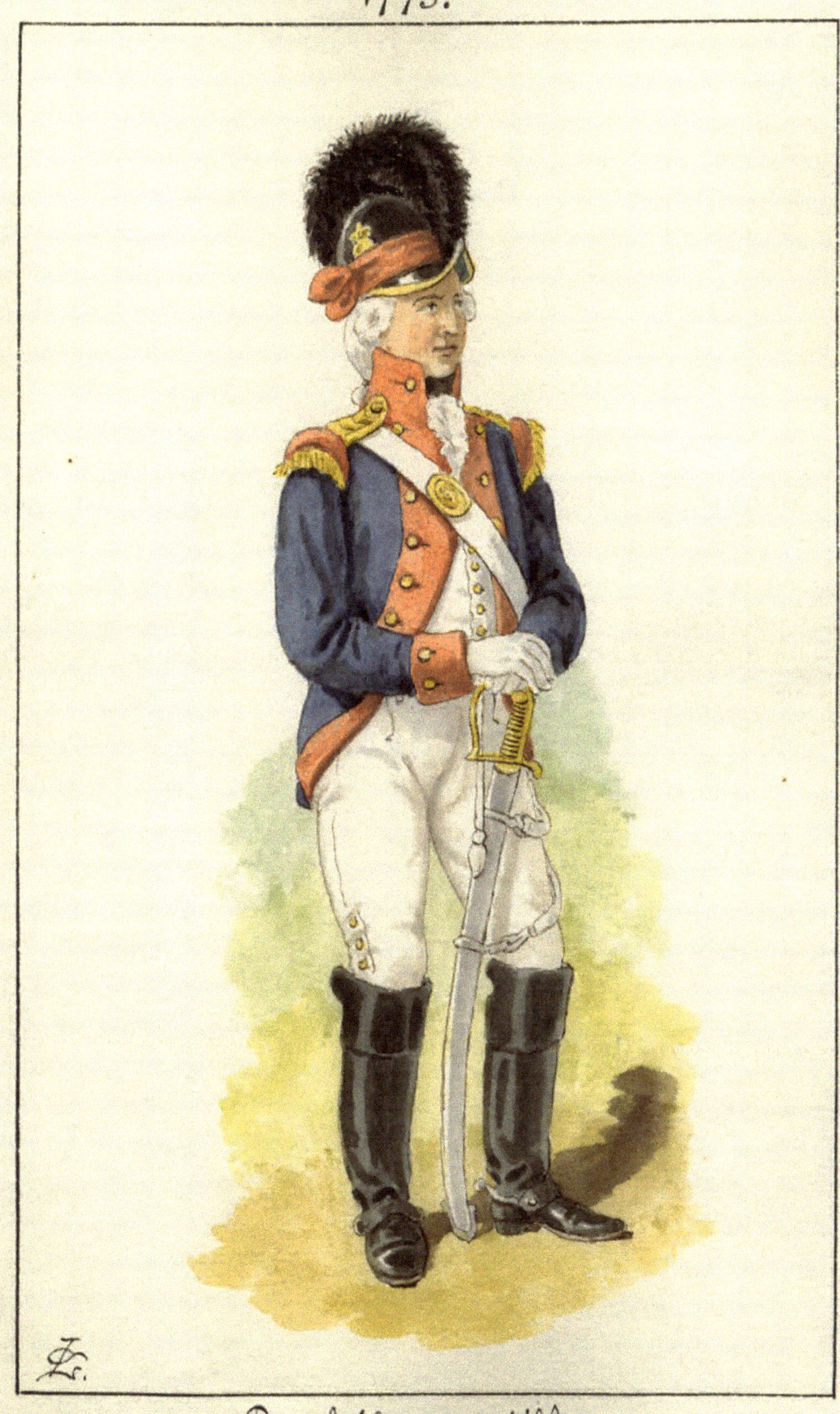

Royal Horse Artillery.

60 – 87TH ROYAL IRISH FUSILIERS, 1793

Charles Lyall's year of 1793 is that in which the 87th (The Prince of Wales's Irish) Regiment of Foot was raised by Major John Doyle, an officer who at the time was on half pay. The letter of service authorising formation was dated 18 September. Charles Lyall shows the original uniform worn by the regiment's light company which comprised one captain, two lieutenants, three sergeants, three corporals, two drummers, two fifers and fifty-seven privates. Black belts are worn, the oval brass plate being engraved with the Prince of Wales's plumes, coronet and motto above an Irish harp. The title of the regiment, 'The Prince of Wales's Irish', appears around the edge. An illustration of this item can be seen on page 306 of *(Military) Shoulder-Belt Plates and Buttons* by Major HG Parkyn. The 87th would provide the 1st Battalion Princess Victoria's (Royal Irish Fusiliers) in 1881.

1793.

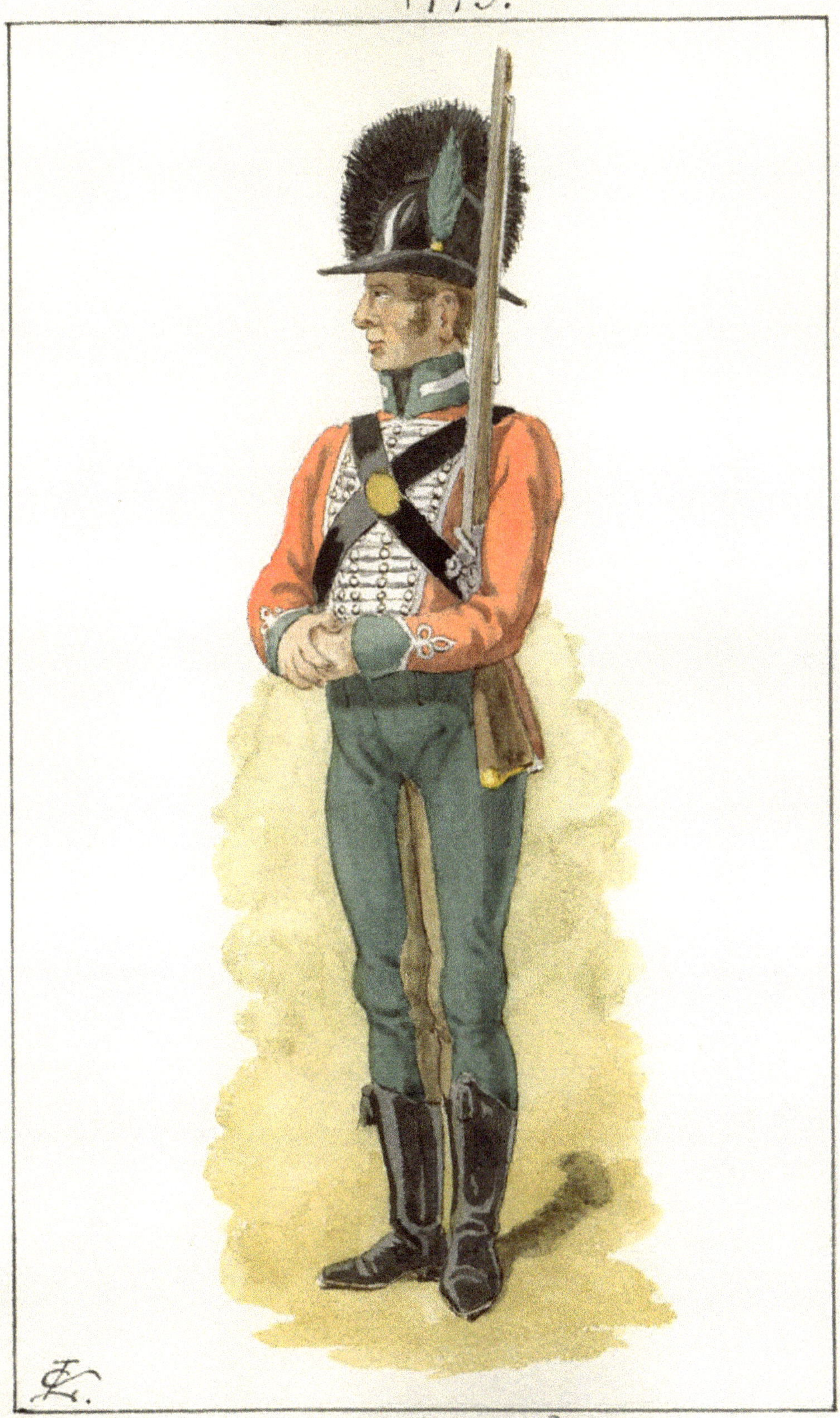

87th Royal Irish Fusileers.

61 – 2ND DRAGOON GUARDS, 1794

The regiment dates from the time of the Monmouth Rebellion when it was raised as the Earl of Peterborough's Regiment of Horse. There would be several changes in title, 2nd The Queen's Dragoon Guards appearing in the Army List after 1746. Having joined the British forces in Flanders in 1793, the following year saw the regiment present at the Siege of Landrécies in April and the action at Tournay on 10 May. Arrival back in England was in November 1795.

1794.

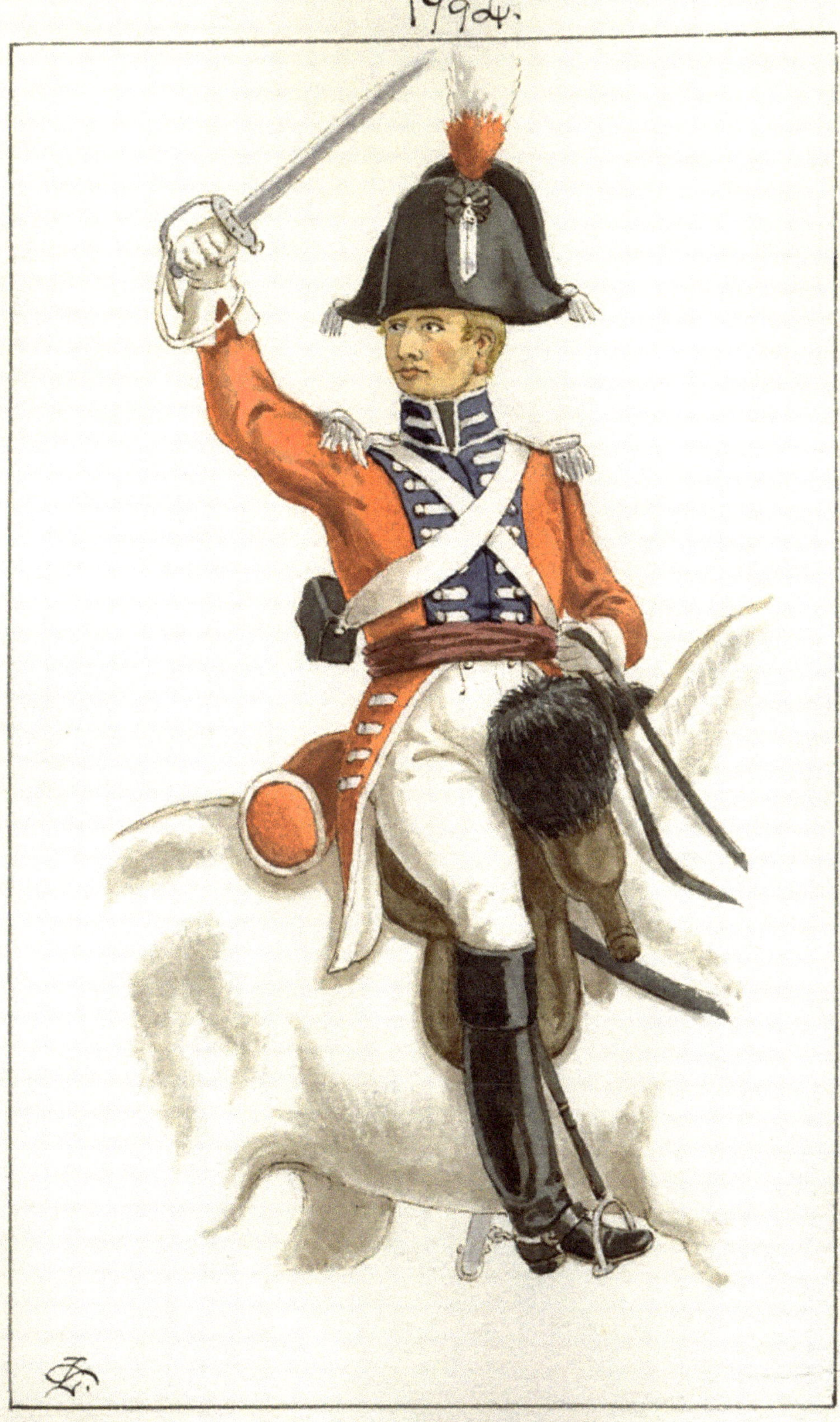

2nd. Dragoon Guards.

62 – ROYAL ARTILLERY, OFFICER 1794

This painting shows a field officer of 1794, Charles Lyall basing his painting on one of Captain RJ MacDonald's plates from *The History of the Dress of the Royal Regiment of Artillery 1625-1897*). With the right leg just slightly forward, the cane casually held out at an angle and the left hand grasping a crimson sash, Lyall's image follows the original pose almost down to the last detail. MacDonald, however, giving his subject the single gold epaulette of a company officer.

1794.

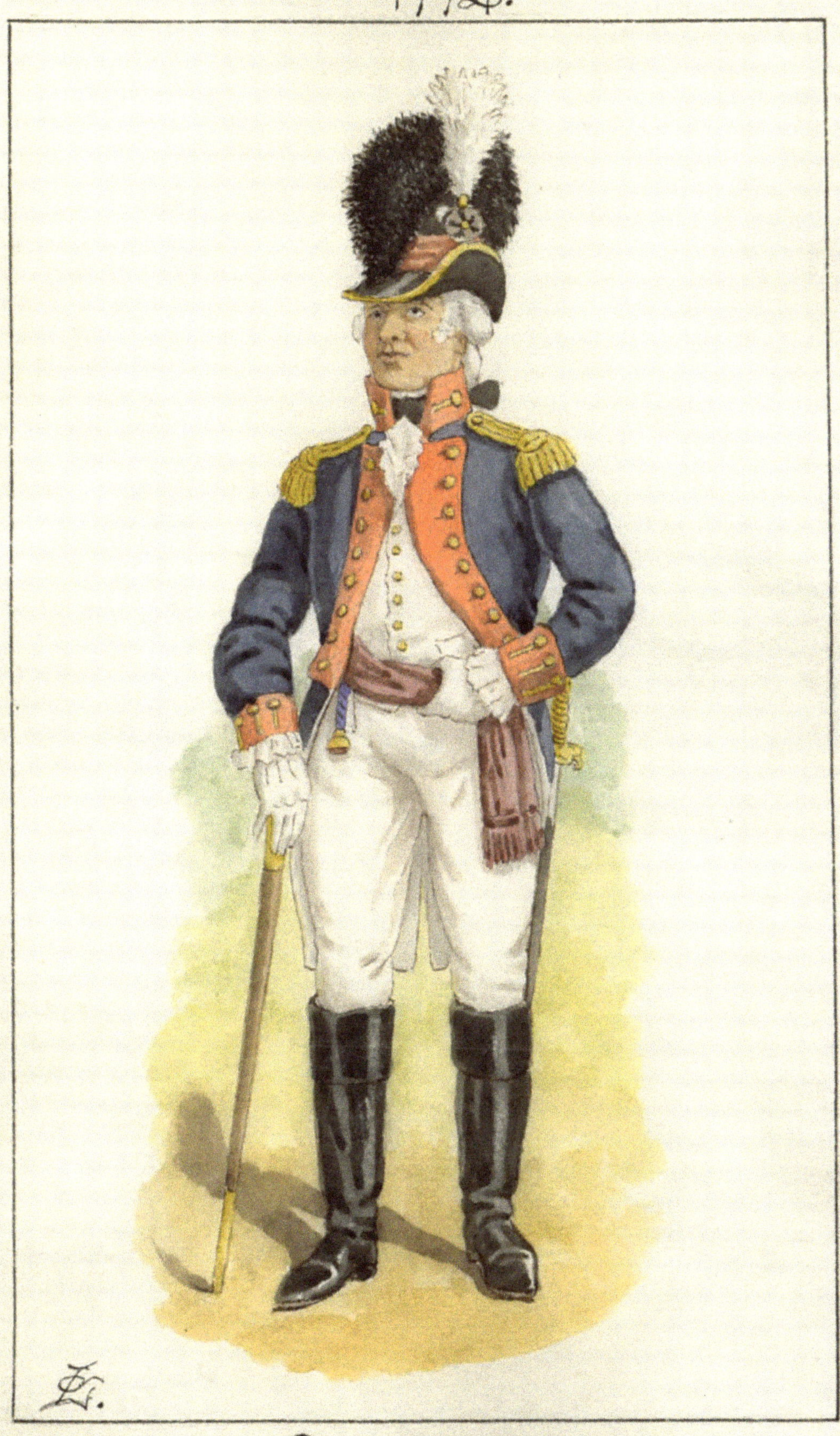

Royal Artillery
Officer.

63 – ROYAL ARTILLERY GUNNER, INDIA 1794

Captain MacDonald's book has the same image, save that the gunner is shown looking outwards while leaning on a sea wall. Charles Lyall paints the same uniform, MacDonald's accompanying text to his picture noting that 'The gunner is wearing his full-dress head-dress, from which was afterwards evolved the cap of the early part of the eighteenth century, and the chako of a latter period.'

1794.

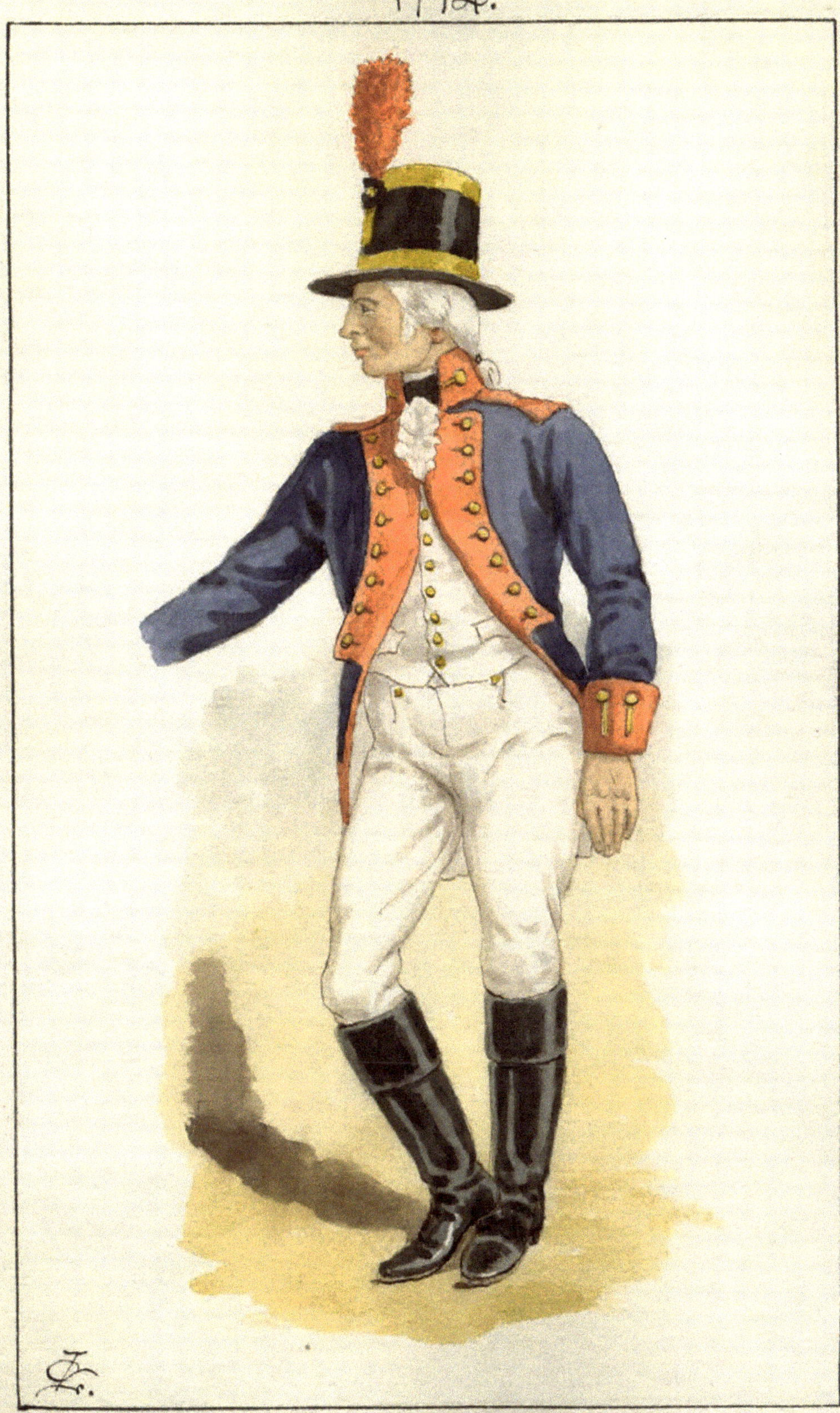

Royal Artillery.
Gunner.
India.

64 – 42nd ROYAL HIGHLANDERS, WEST INDIES UNIFORM 1794

Charles Lyall's caption date of 1794 is misleading as in that year the 42nd were in fact taking part in operations in Flanders. The regiment returned to England in April 1795 and it was not until 9 February 1796 that the Highlanders (and then only with five companies) reached the West Indies. The records of many Scottish regiments note how the kilt and Highland bonnet had proven impractical in hot climates.

1794.

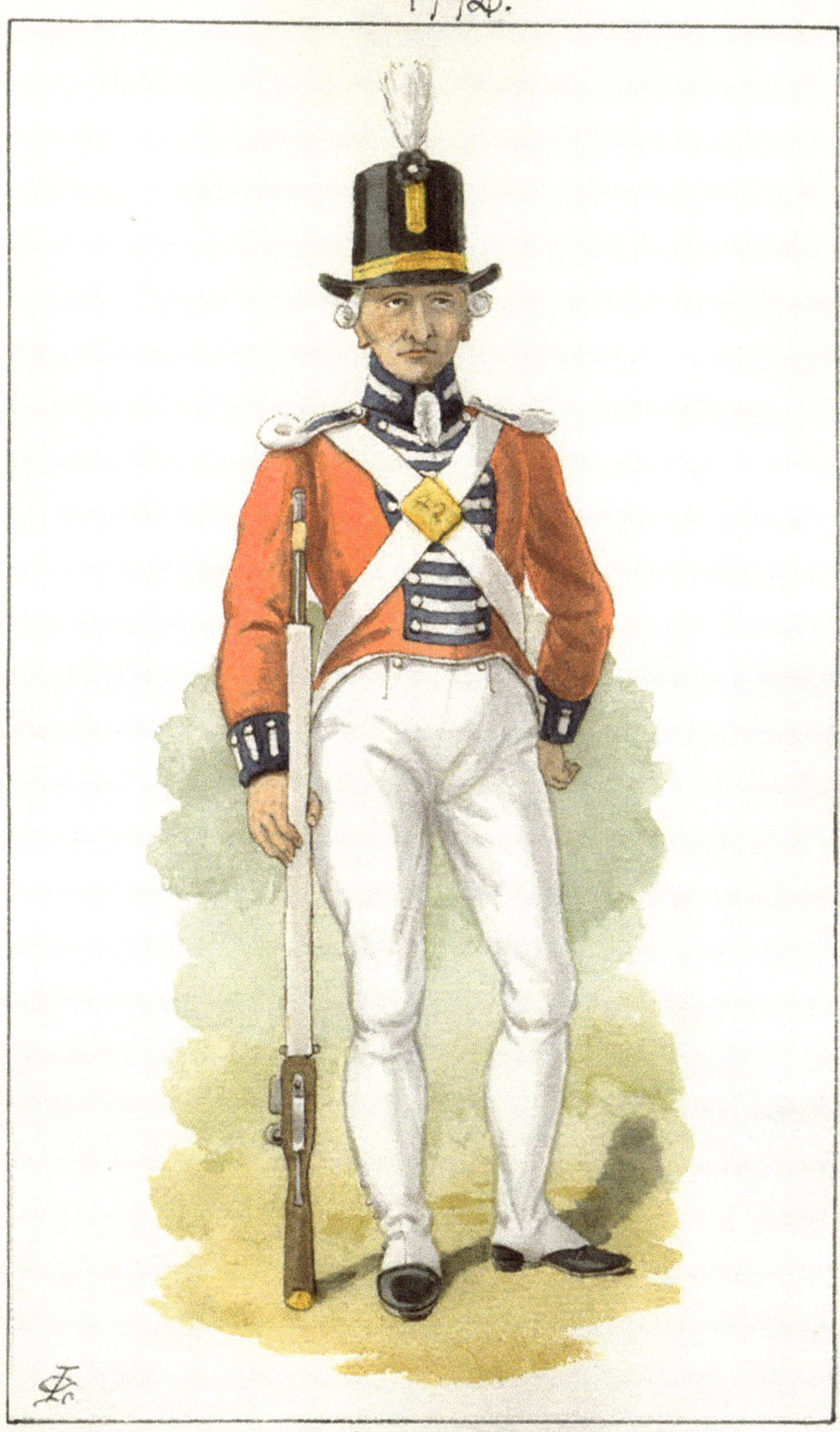

42nd. Royal Highlanders.
West Indies uniform.

65 – THE 90TH REGIMENT PERTHSHIRE VOLUNTEERS, 1794

The 90th (Perthshire Volunteers) are represented here by a private wearing a red coat with buff facings. When raised in 1794 the colour of the netherwear seen here led to the regiment's nickname of 'Perthshire Greybreeks'—breeks being a Scottish term for breeches. The regiment having been ordered to be trained and equipped as light infantry, the uniform would include shoulder wings and a light cavalry-style helmet. The 90th became the 2nd Battalion Cameronians (Scottish Rifles) in 1881.

1794.

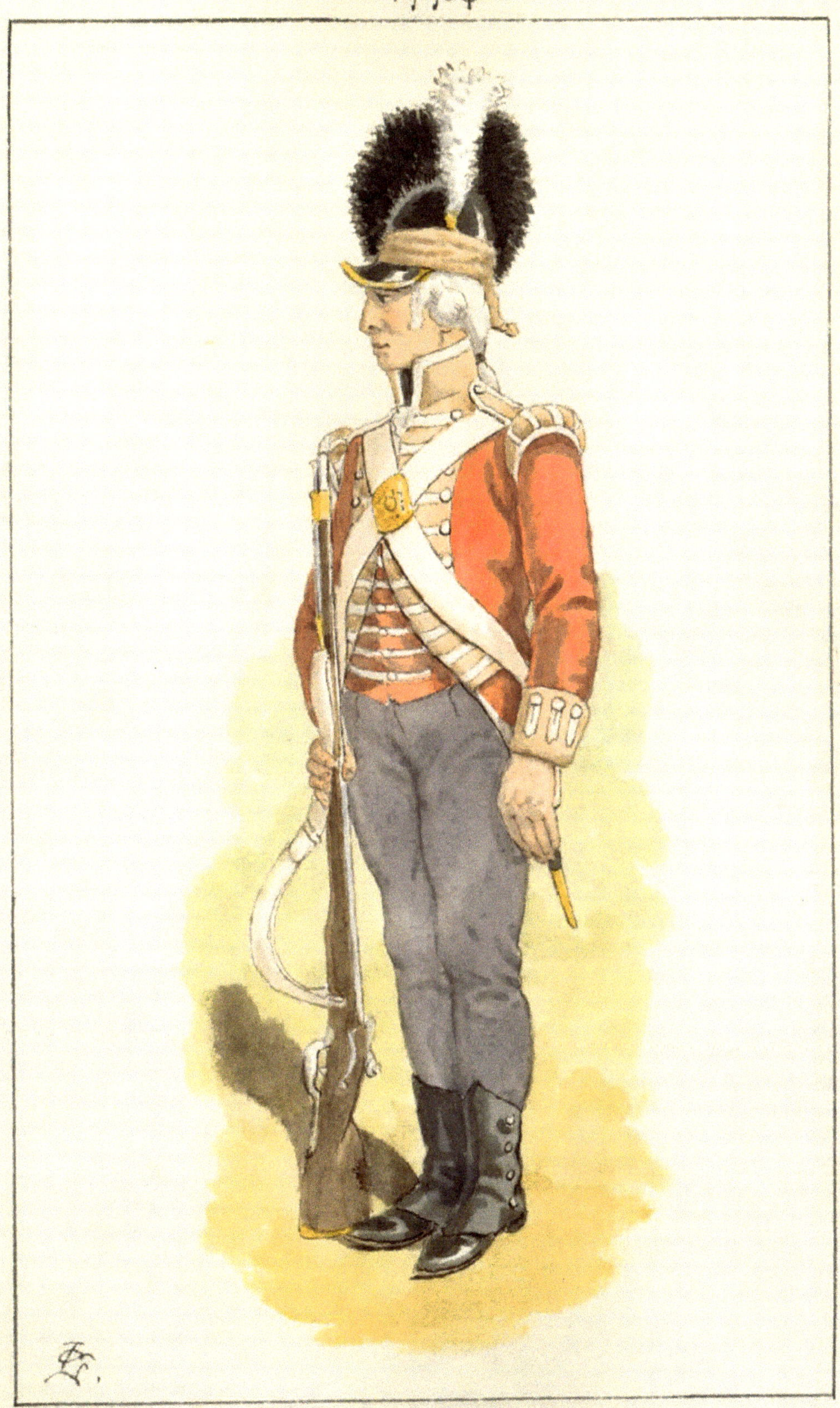

The 90th Regt.. Perthshire Volunteers.

66 – THE 90TH REGIMENT PERTHSHIRE VOLUNTEERS, OFFICER 1794

Charles Lyall's officer figure is much the same as his private soldier in Plate 65, save for the addition of fringes on the shoulder wings, black boots, white breeches instead of grey and the crimson sash worn around the waist. The sword-belt plate is oval.

1794.

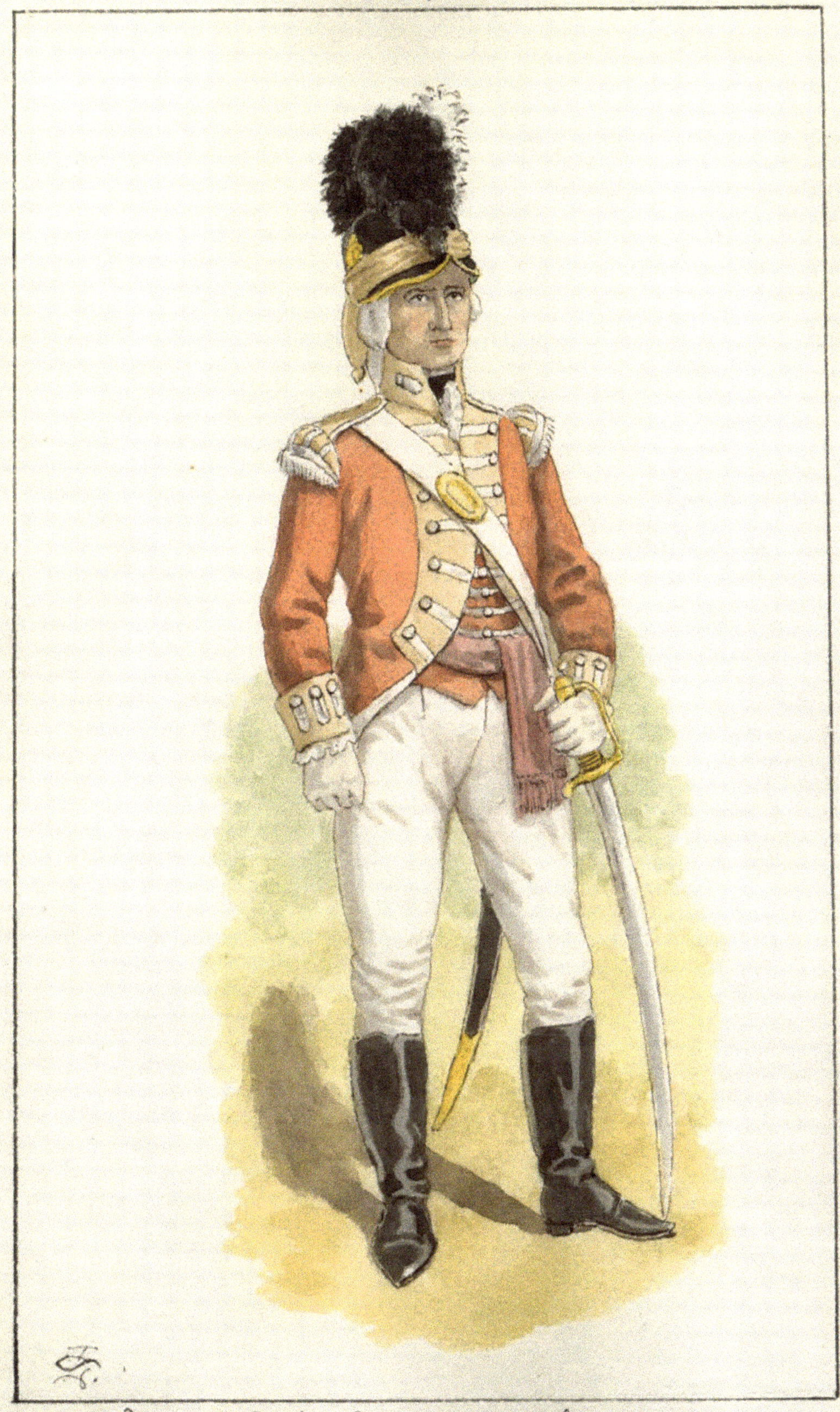

The 90th Regt. Perthshire Volunteers.
Officer.

67 – BETHNAL GREEN BATTALION VOLUNTEERS, 1794

Here demonstrating the second motion of the 'Support Arms' position is a member of the Bethnal Green Battalion Volunteers. The man's headdress is a cocked hat with a red-over-green feather and leopard-skin turban. His coat is red with blue facings. Charles Lyall has based his painting of this East End of London corps on one of the colour plates after Thomas Rowlandson, included in *Loyal London Volunteers*, published around 1797-8 by Rudolph Ackermann.

153

1794.

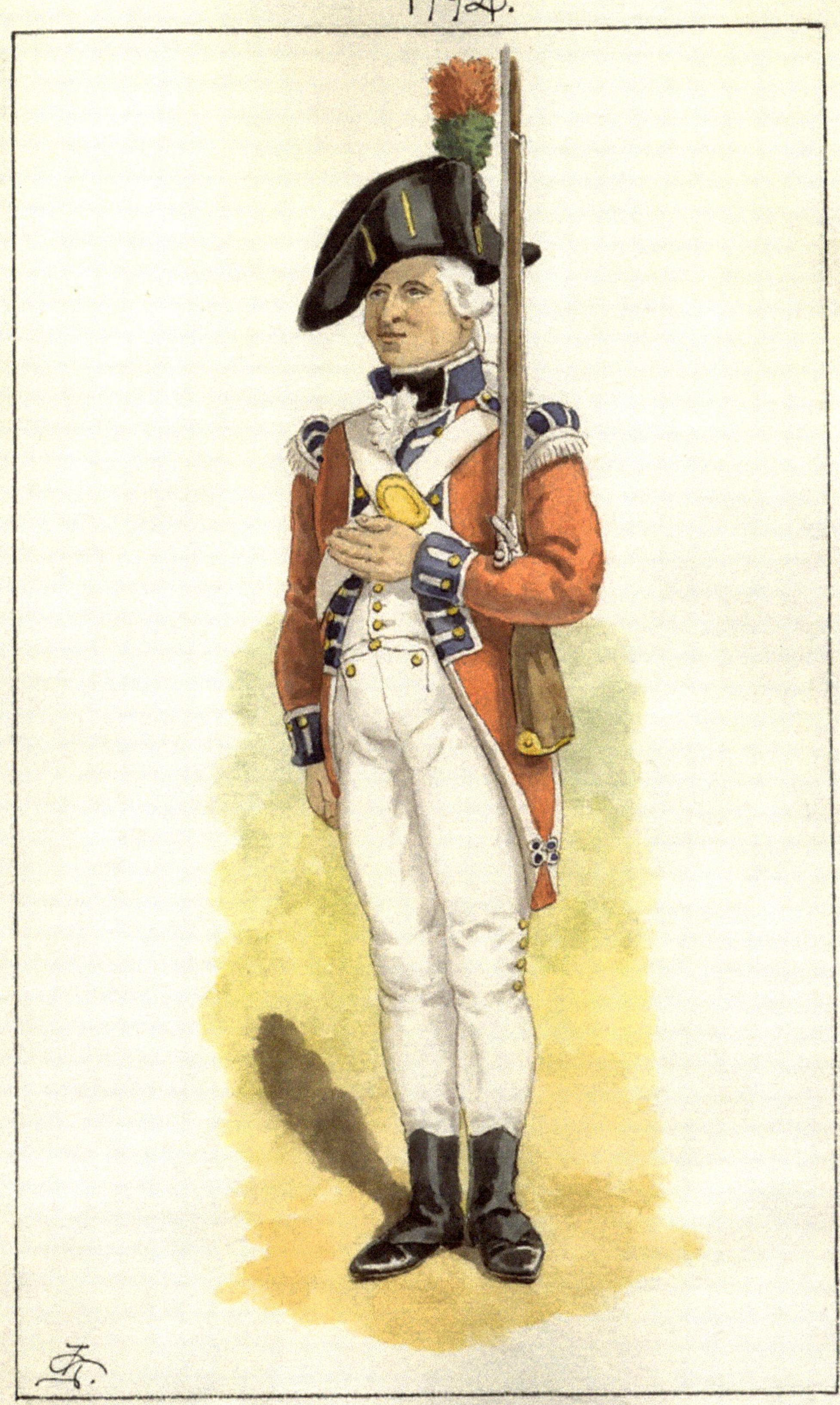

Bethnel Green Battalion
Volunteers.

68 – St MARTIN'S IN THE FIELDS VOLUNTEERS, 1794

There at the north-east corner of Trafalgar Square since its completion in 1726 stands James Gibbs's church of St Martin's in the Fields. The volunteer corps formed there comprised three battalion companies and Charles Lyall shows one of its number wearing a blue coat with red collar, shoulder straps, cuffs and piping. Trafalgar Square was not so named until 1832, the area at one time being known as Charing Cross from where all distances to London were measured. The parish, with an estimated 5,000 houses by 1786, was noted as one of the most densely populated in Georgian London.

1794.

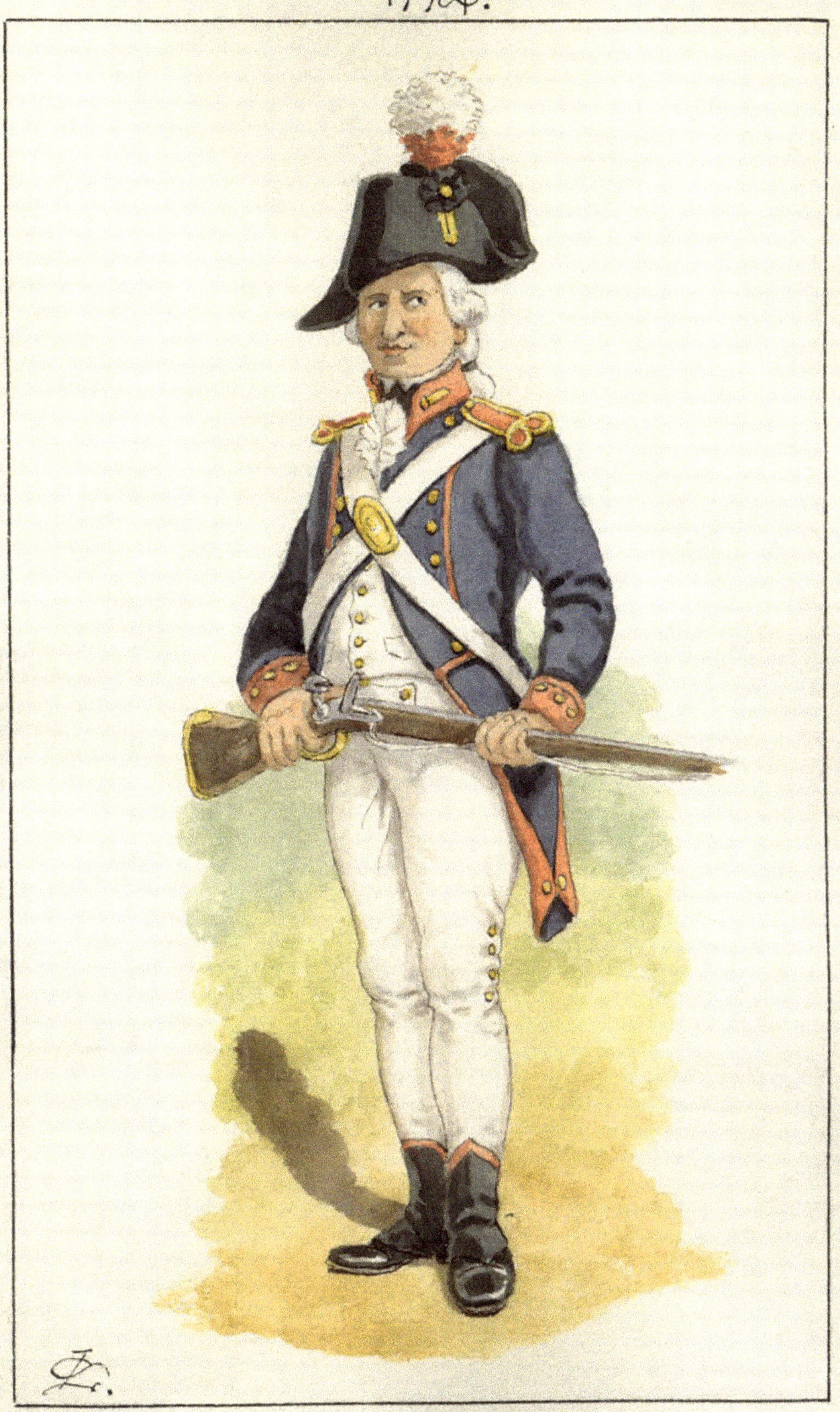

St. Martin's-in-the-Fields.
Volunteers.

69 – WANDSWORTH VOLUNTEERS, 1794

The officers' commissions in the Wandsworth Association Volunteers were not signed by the king until 19 July 1798. Charles Lyall shows a private of this South West London corps wearing a fur-crested headdress and a blue coat with red collar, lapels and cuffs.

1794.

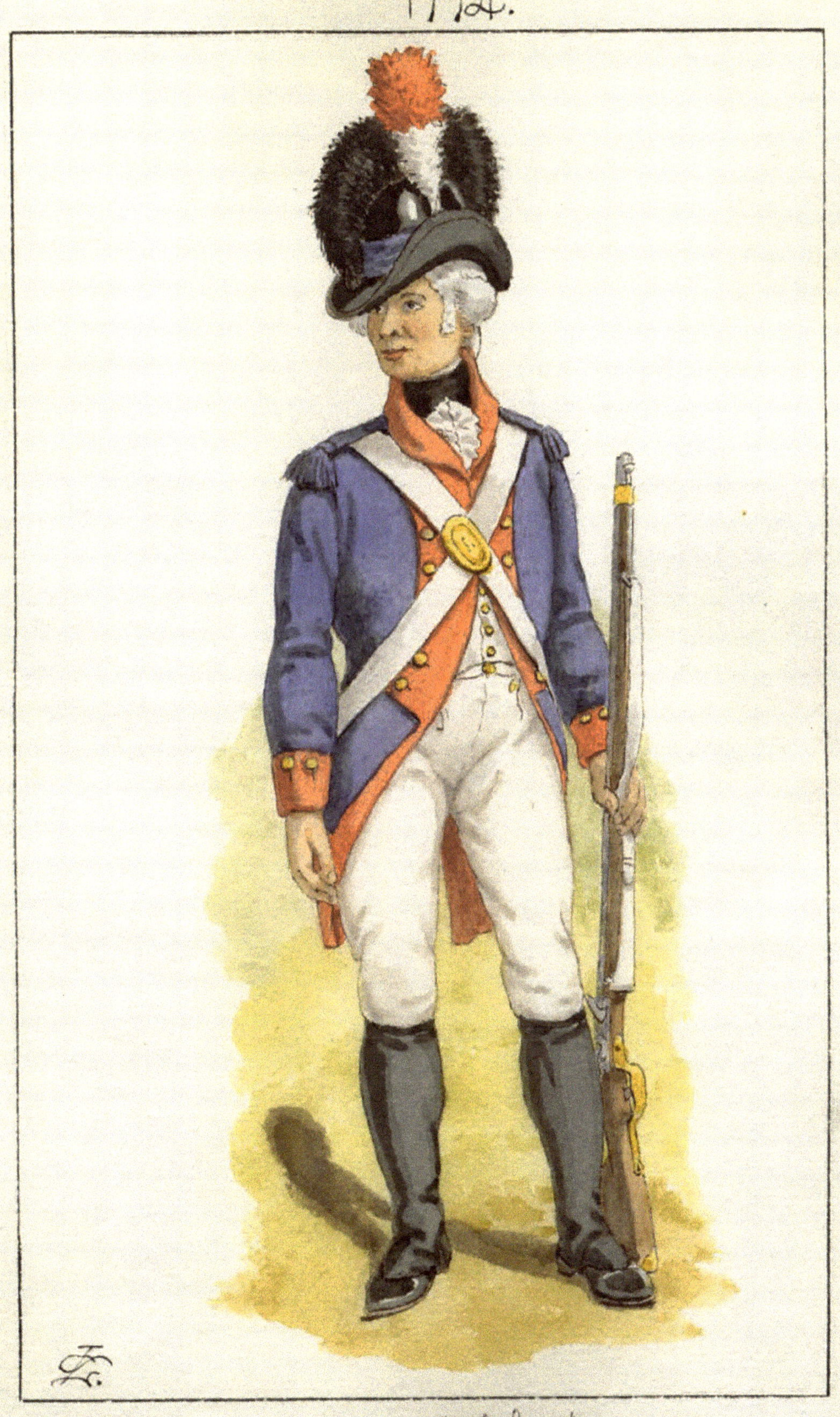

Wandsworth Volunteers.

70 – WESTMINSTER VOLUNTEERS, 1794

This corps was originally formed in the parish of St. Ann's, Soho, which name it bore till the year 1797 when it became the Royal Westminster Volunteers. There were grenadier, light and battalion companies, Charles Lyall's painting representing a member of the latter. The oval cross-belt plates of this corps were engraved with the portcullis from the arms of the City of Westminster.

1794.

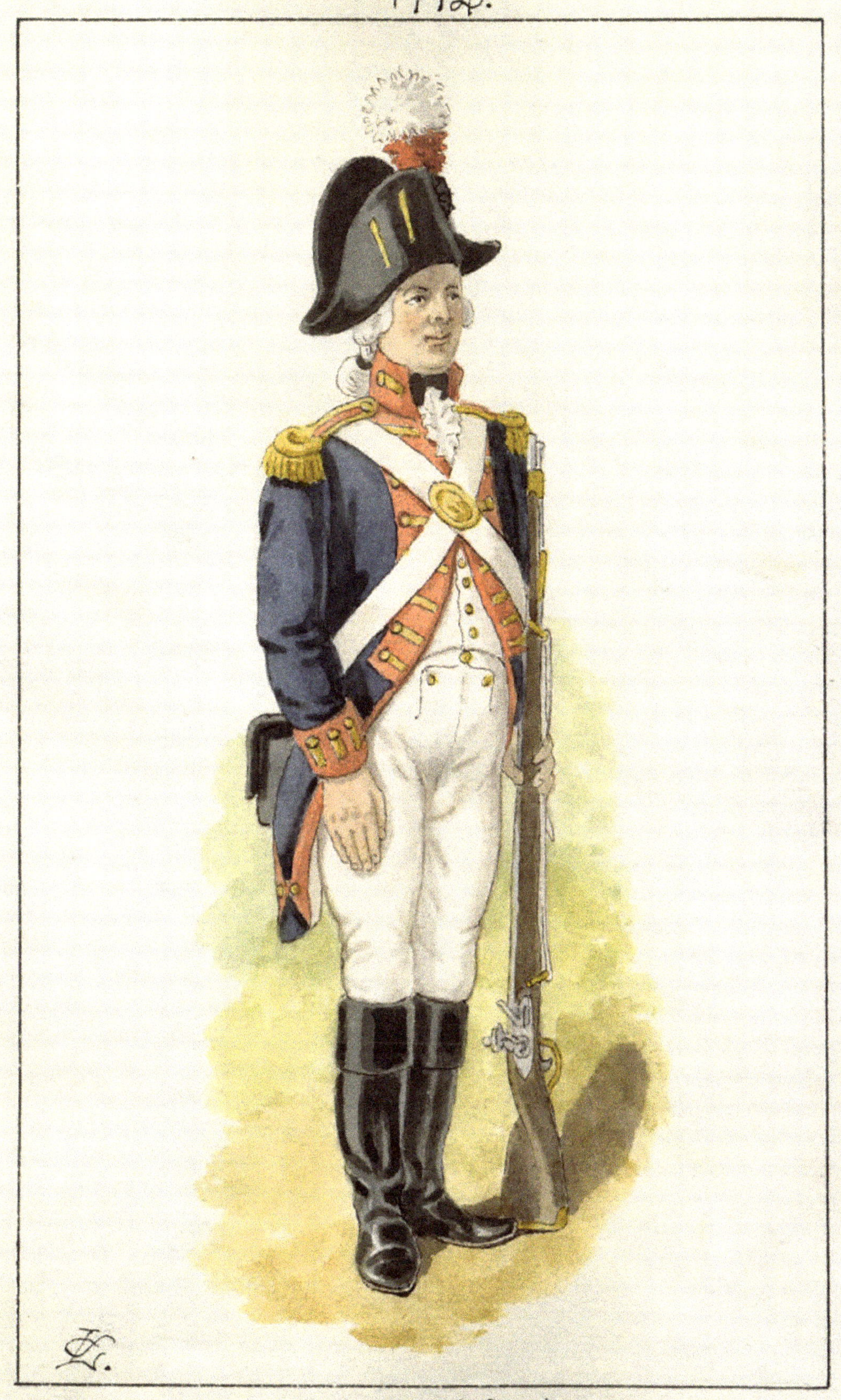

Westminster Volunteer.

71 – WESTMINSTER GRENADIER VOLUNTEER, 1794

A member of the grenadier company, Royal Westminster Volunteers.

1794.

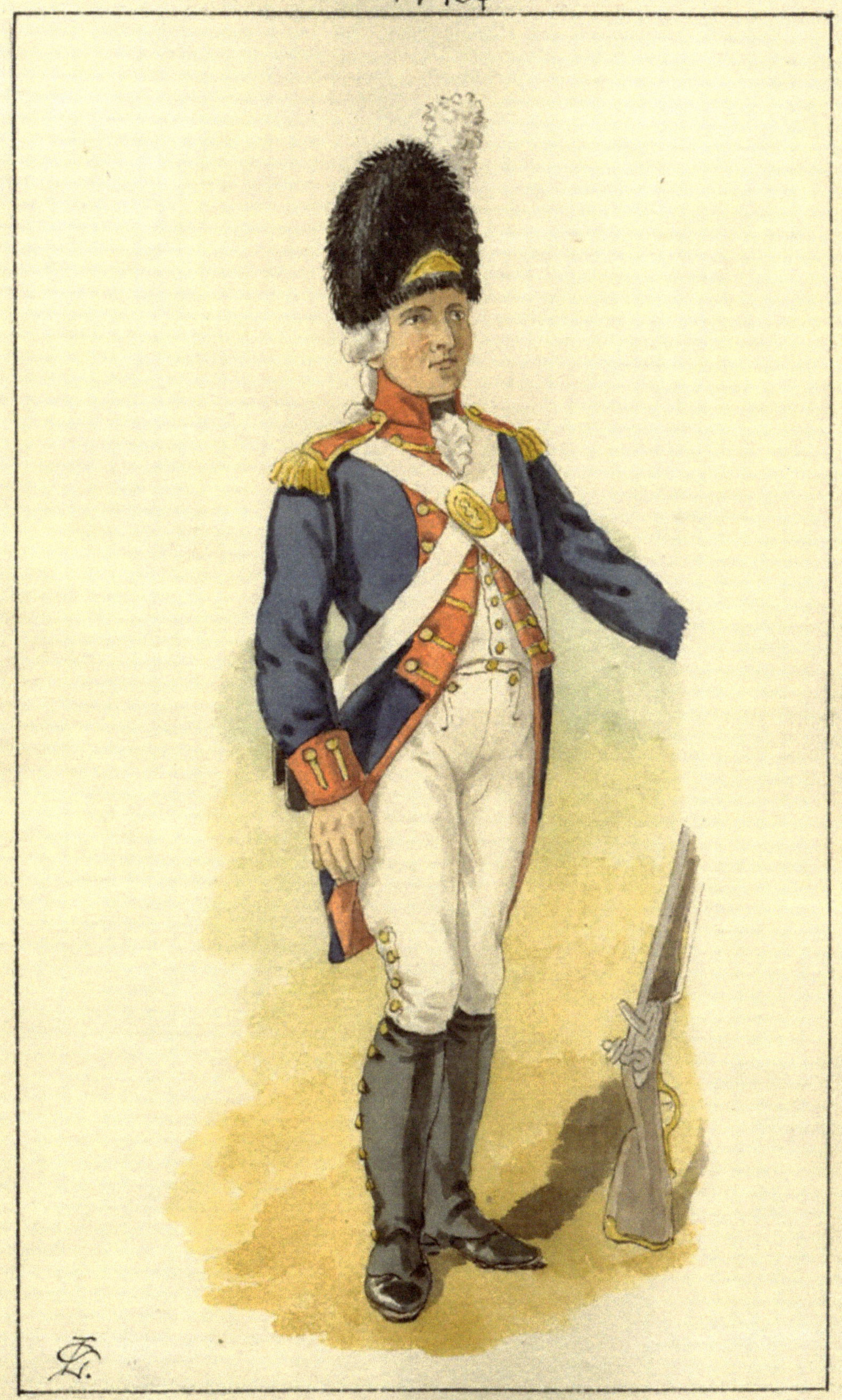

Westminster Grenadier.
Volunteer.

72 – LIGHT DRAGOONS, TRUMPETER 1795

The trumpeter in Charles Lyall's unidentified regiment wears a short yellow jacket with a blue collar, shoulder wings and cuffs. Yellow also for the shabraque, which has a white (or silver) edging and an embroidered crown over star device.

1795.

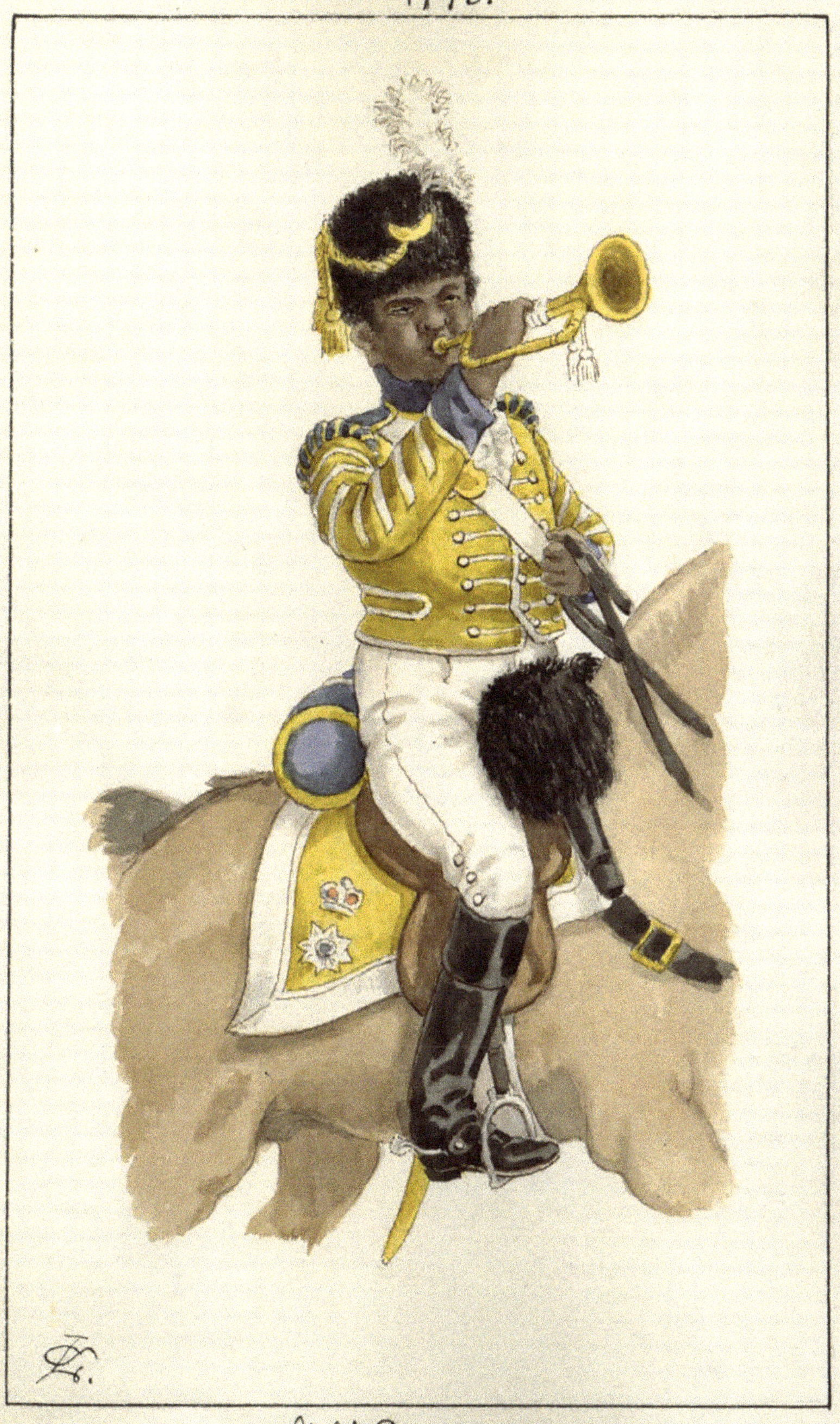

Light Dragoons.
Trumpeter.

73 – 8TH LIGHT DRAGOONS ROYAL IRISH, 1795

Raised as a regiment of dragoons in 1693, numbered as 8th in 1751 and styled as light dragoons in 1775. King's Royal Irish entered the title in 1777 and the regiment became hussars in 1822. Proudly displayed on the helmet is an Irish harp, the badge authorised with the title in 1777. The short coat is blue, following an order of 1784 that directed all light dragoon regiments to change to this colour, and the facings scarlet. Just prior to Charles Lyall's date of 1795 service was seen in Flanders, and in the year after the 8th Light Dragoons took part in the capture of the Cape of Good Hope.

1795.

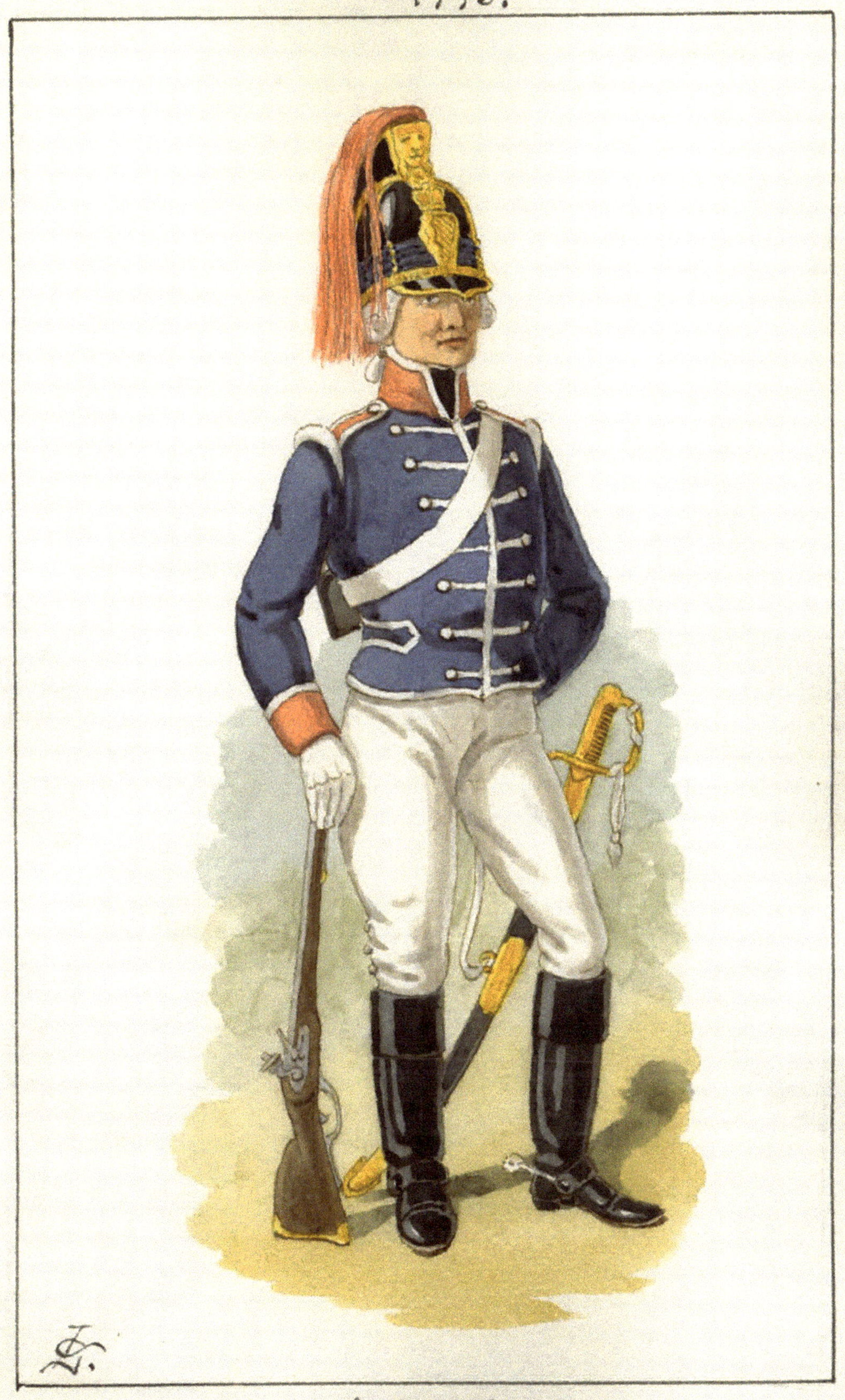

8th. Light Dragoons.
Royal Irish.

74 – HANS TOWN ASSOCIATION, 1796

An all-blue uniform with red cuffs and piping is being worn by this Hans Town Volunteer who is shown demonstrating the 'Stand at Ease Supporting Arms' position. Sir Hans Sloane, before his death in 1753, had done much towards the advancement of London's Chelsea. His daughter Elizabeth would inherit her father's property in Chelsea, this then passing to Lord Cadogan who she married in 1717. Cadogan then, in 1771, leased some eighty-nine acres to Fulham architect Henry Holland for the purpose of building, what Weinreb and Hibbert described as '...plain brick terraces for people of moderate means.' What followed over the next ten years was the building of Hans Town, a collection of spacious three-storied terraces in and around Sloane Street, Sloane Square, Hans Place and Cadogan Place. Charles Lyall has based his painting on one by Thomas Rowlandson who shows a much darker blue.

1796.

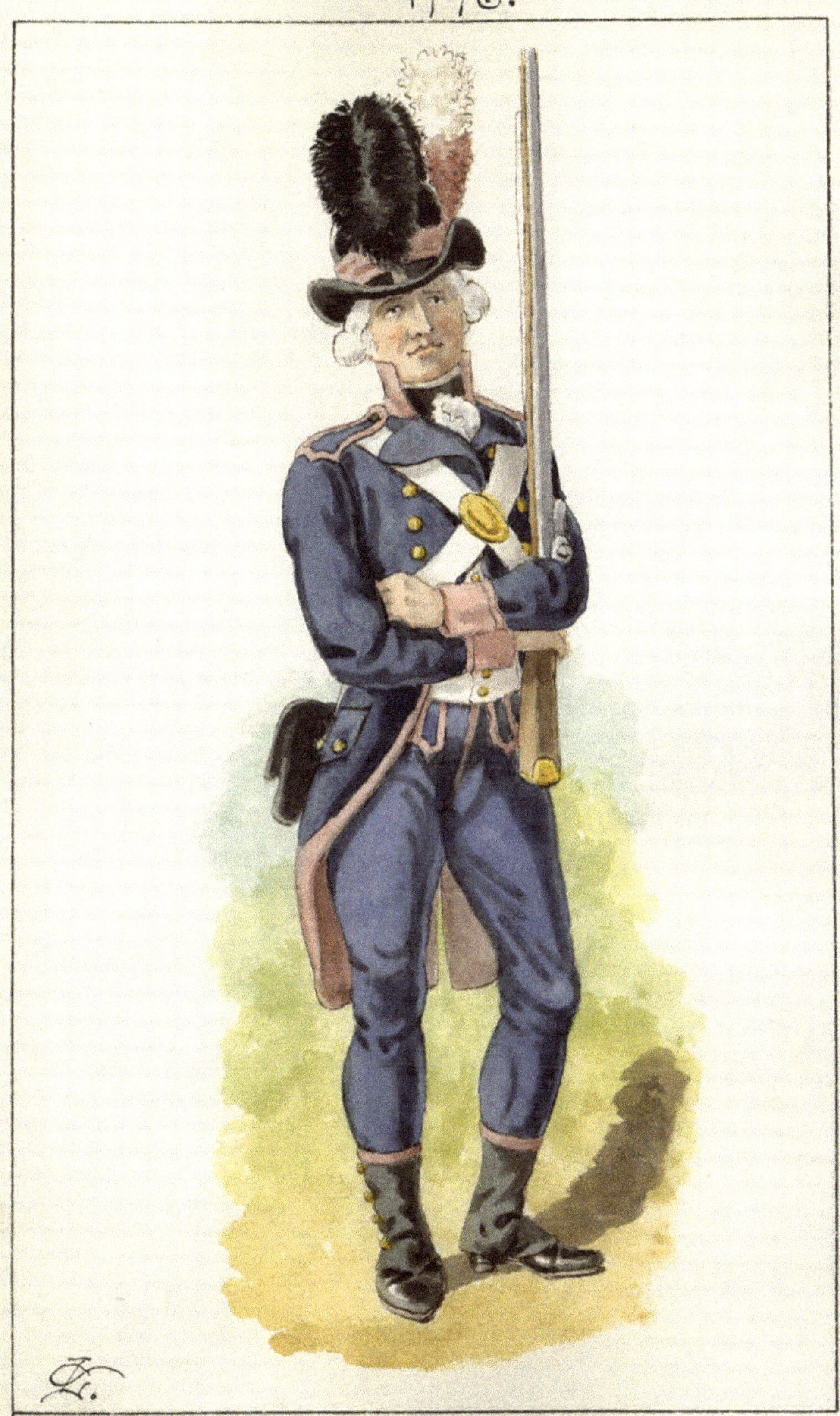

Hans Town Association.

75 – LONDON AND WESTMINSTER DISMOUNTED LIGHT HORSE VOLUNTEERS, 1796

The caption date accompanying this plate predates Plate 83 by just two years and there are a number of differences in uniform. Starting with the helmet, this is now shown with no chains on the blue turban. The collar is without buttonhole loops, the shoulder straps and wings are red instead of blue, and the cuffs are without cord. Also absent is the blue flask cord seen in the 1798 image running through the shoulder belt. There are two shoulder belts, but absent is the waistbelt and its black pouch.

177

1796.

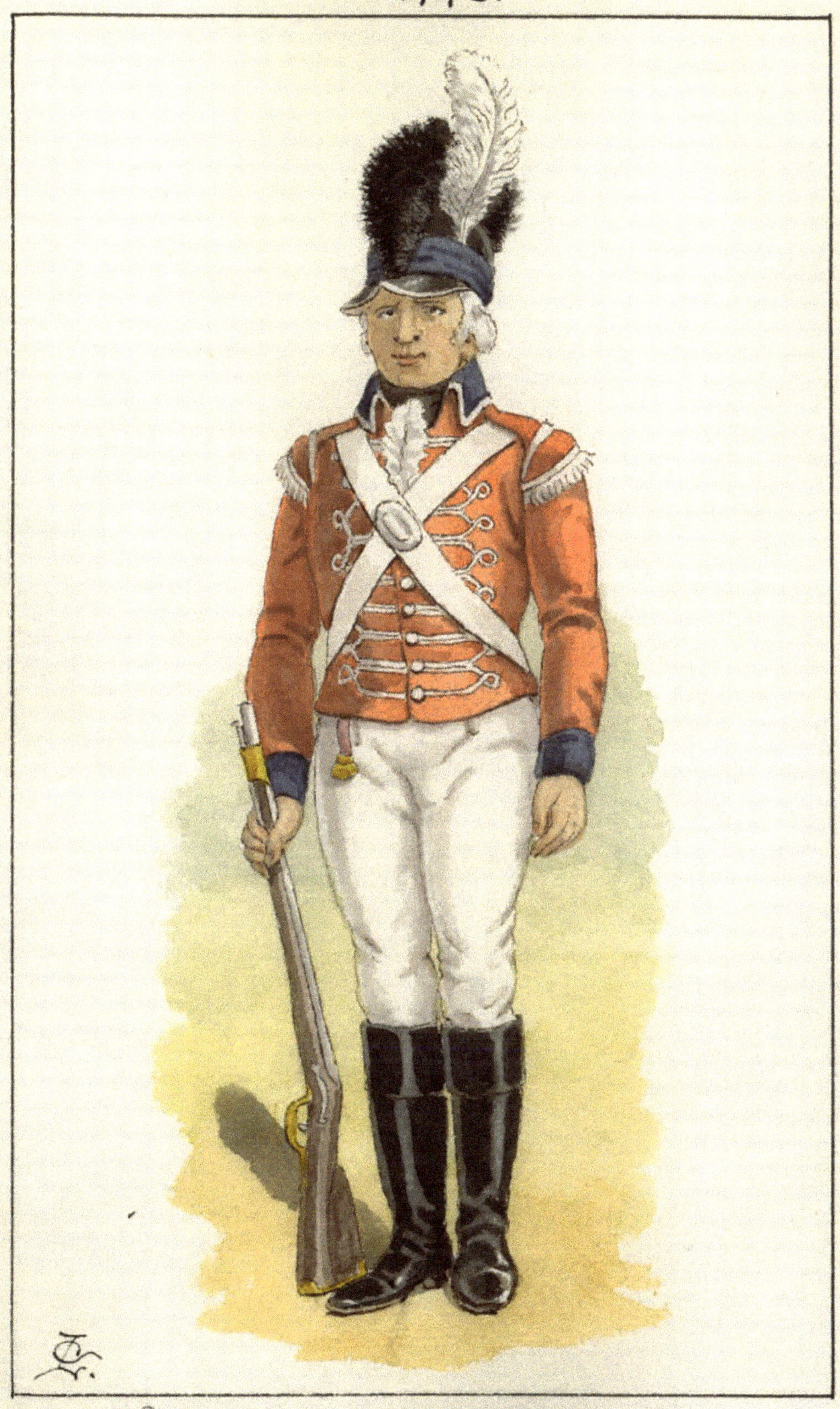

London & Westminster dismounted Light Horse Volunteers.

76 – St JAMES'S VOLUNTEERS, 1796

The white feather worn in the headdress suggests a member of a battalion company. The short scarlet coat has a blue collar, cuffs and lapels, all of which are edged with white piping. Short gold fringes decorate the shoulder wings, the waistcoat is white and the breeches dark blue to match the facings. It was following the building of Wren's St James's Church, Piccadilly in 1684 that the Parish of St James's was established. Part of Oxford Street to the north formed one boundary, to the east was Soho's Berwick and Rupert Streets, St Martin's parish, approximately along Pall Mall, was to the south and to the west and St George's Hanover Square parish, there was a boundary that followed Conduit Street, Old Bond Street and Dover Street. By 1796 the area around St James's Church had developed into probably Georgian London's most fashionable location. The aristocracy of Britain lived there and shops to meet their every need soon sprang up. On Saville Street (later Row), built between 1731 and 1735, army officers and their wives came to live, before tailors had taken over by 1803. Gentlemen's clubs soon appeared, and at No 191 Regent Street there was a wonderful shop selling prints produced by none other than Rudolph Ackermann.

178

1796.

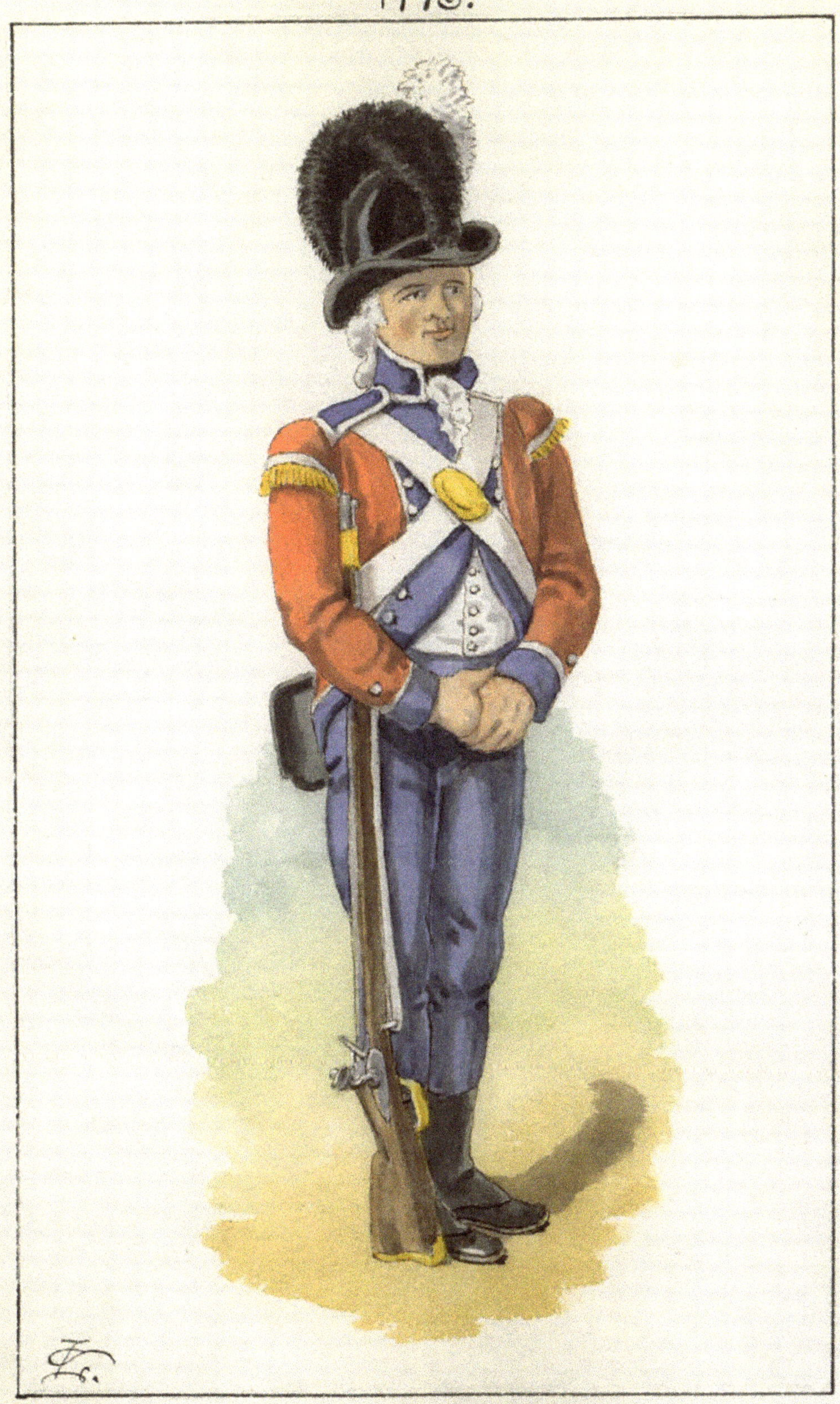

St. James's Volunteers.

77 – THE 72ND HIGHLANDERS, LIGHT COMPANY OFFICER 1798

Charles Lyall's title and date places this regiment as that raised twenty years earlier as the 78th Highlanders (or Seaforth Highlanders) then renumbered as 72nd in 1786. It would become the 1st Battalion Seaforth Highlander in 1881. If so, we must be considering yellow facings, silver lace and buttons, and not the green and gold clearly indicated in Lyall's painting. Could it be that the artist is in fact one regimental number out in his captioning, the 73rd of 1798 certainly having green facings, gold lace and gilt buttons?

183

1798.

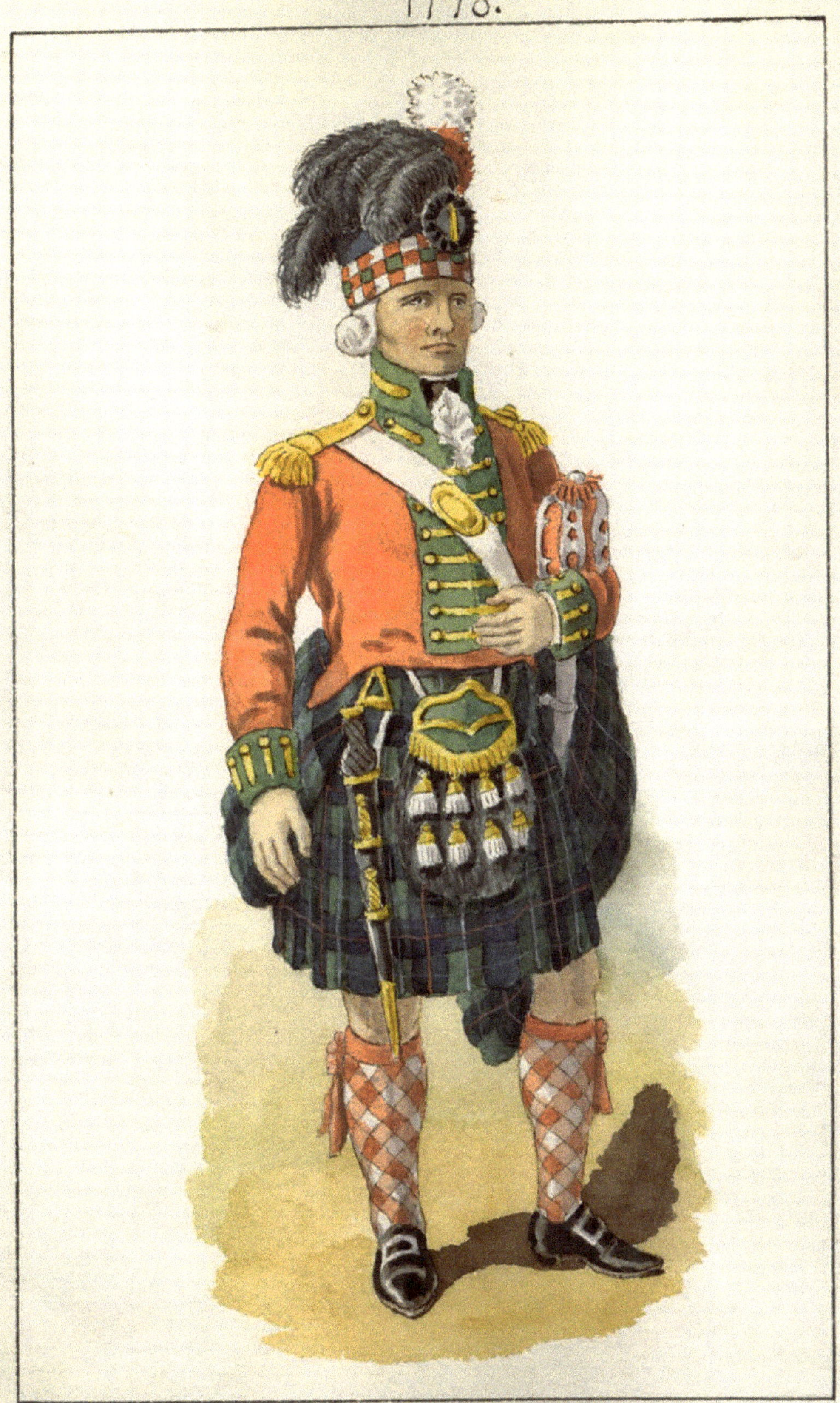

The 72nd Highlanders.
Light Cy. Officer.

78 – THE RIFLE CORPS, OFFICER 1798

Although Charles Lyall's painting is high in detail as a representation of the uniform worn by an officer of the Rifle Brigade, his caption date of 1798 is inaccurate by two years. Willoughby Verner included, in his history of the regiment, a copy of the following letter sent to a number of line infantry regiments dated Horse Guards, 17 January 1800: 'Sir.—I have the honour to inform you that it is His Royal Highness the Commander-in-Chief's intention to form a corps of detachments from the different regiments of the line for the purpose of its being instructed in the use of the rifle....This was the origins of the Rifle Brigade.'

1798.

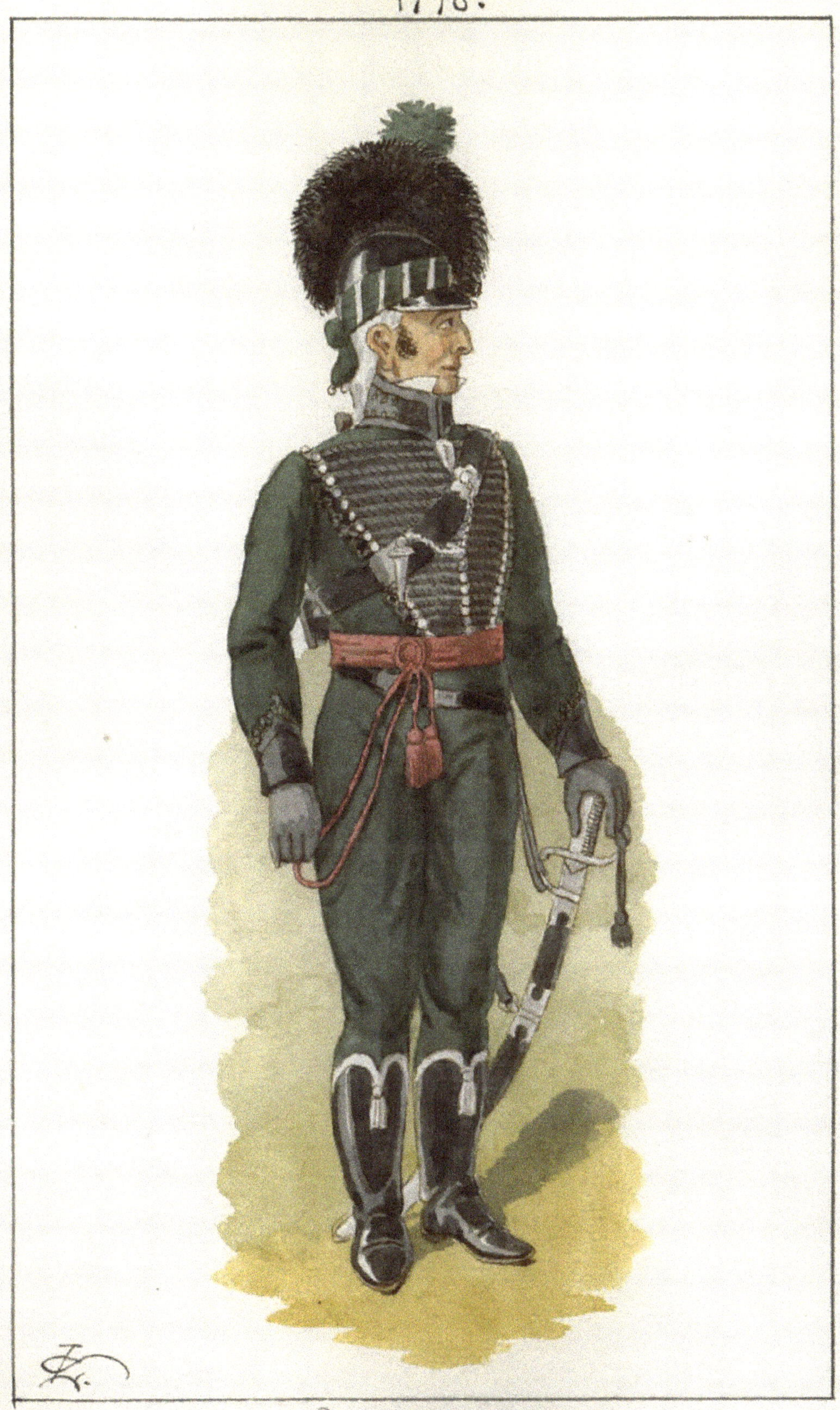

The Rifle Corps.
Officer.

79 – BRIDGE WARD VOLUNTEERS, 1798

A light blue for the collar, cuffs and breeches of this corps, the latter having scarlet cord down the outer and inner legs, down the front and forming points on each side. The jacket, scarlet and without lapels or tails, is ornamented with white lace across the front, bottom edge and around the cuffs. The blue shoulder straps and wings also have white decoration. For the headdress: gilt fittings, a scarlet turban and a white feather on the left side. Bridge Ward in the City of London is so named from its contiguity with London Bridge.

1798.

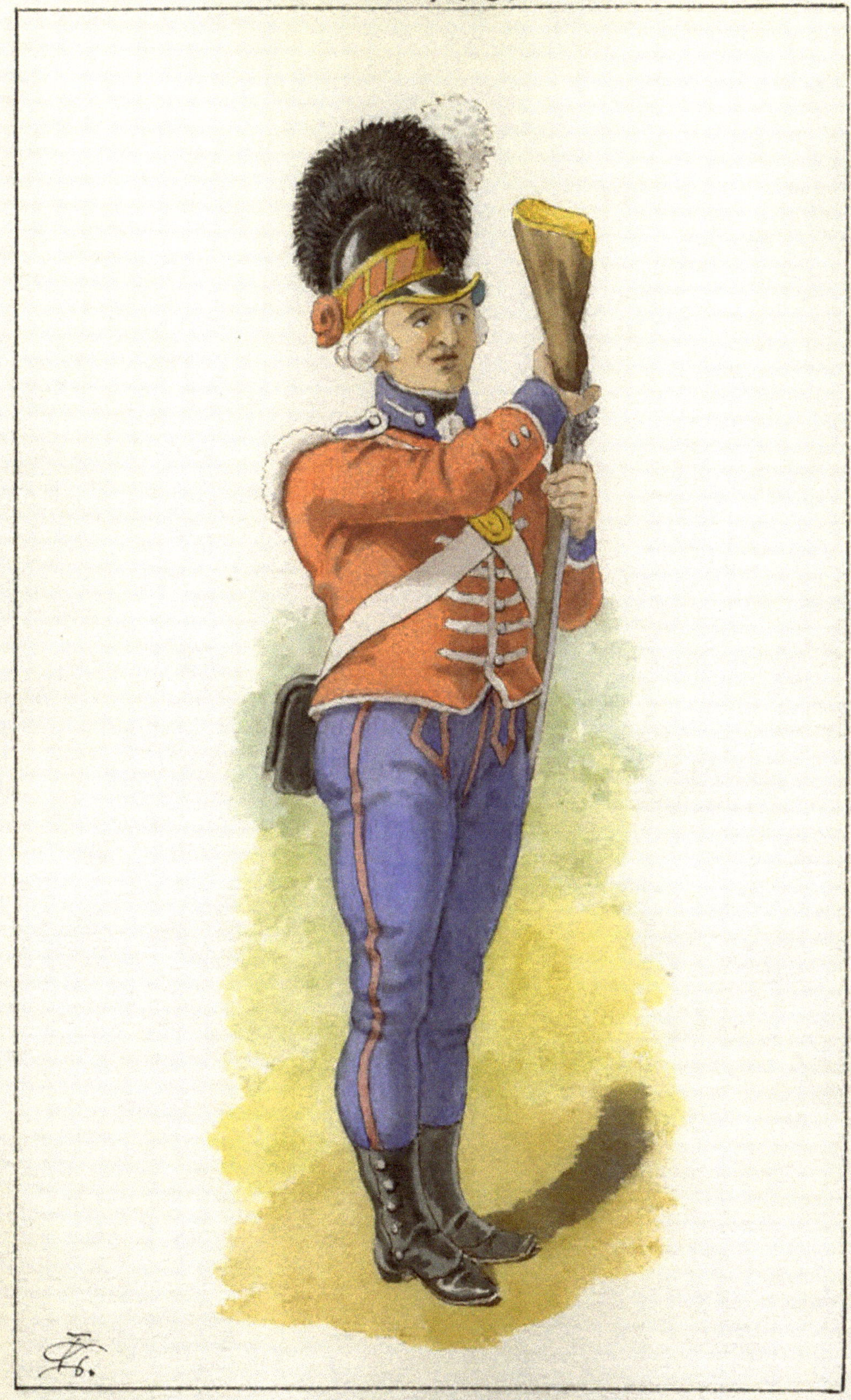

Bridge Ward Volunteers.

80 – CLERKENWELL CAVALRY VOLUNTEERS, 1798

This Clerkenwell Cavalry volunteer wears a short scarlet jacket with a blue collar, cuffs and epaulette, all three being richly decorated with gold lace. There are gold lines and loops at the front, sides and all around the bottom. The fur-crested helmet has gilt fittings, a blue turban and white feather. Charles Lyall has based his image on that which appeared after Thomas Rowlandson in *Loyal Volunteers of London*.

1798.

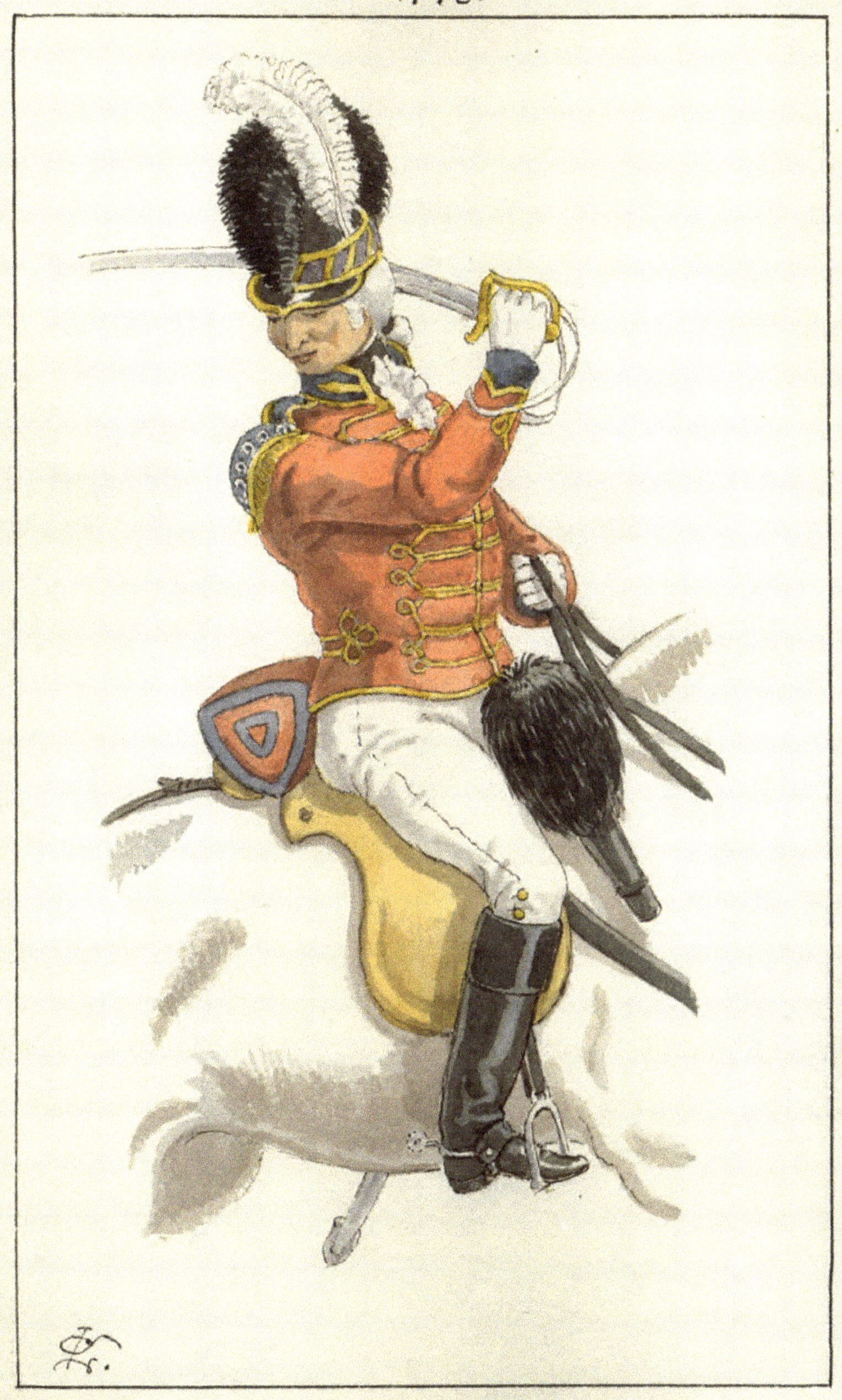

Clerkenwell Cavalry Volunteers.

81 – EAST INDIA COMPANY VOLUNTEERS, OFFICER 1798

Representing the three regiments of the Royal East India Company Volunteers, Charles Lyall shows an officer. From a grenadier company, he wears a bearskin cap with white plume, gilt plate at the front, gold lines and tassels. The coat is scarlet with a blue collar, lapels and cuffs which are edged with gold lace. A gilt gorget is worn, gold lace epaulettes and a crimson sash. For the protection of their London warehouses, the Honourable East India Company raised two regiments in 1796, and a third in 1798. Each consisted of ten companies. The field officers were selected from the company's chairman, deputy chairman and directors, others from India House. NCOs and privates came from the Assistant Elders, Commodores and labourers belonging to the company's warehouses. The Court Minutes of the company dated 24 August 1796 note that the officers' uniforms be scarlet with black facings, buff waistcoats and breeches. Gorgets were worn bearing the HEIC's arms and motto '*Auspicio Regis et Senatus Angliae*' (Under the auspices of the King and Senate of England). The lion crest of the company appeared on the buttons. Cecil CP Lawson in Volume V of his *A History of the Uniforms of the British Army* makes mention of the drummers belonging to the regiment who wore scarlet coats with blue facings and bearskin caps. There is also a reference to a black bandsman with a white turban and red plume, and a trumpeter with a cocked hat and Hessian boots whose blue trumpet banner is embroidered with the company arms.

1798.

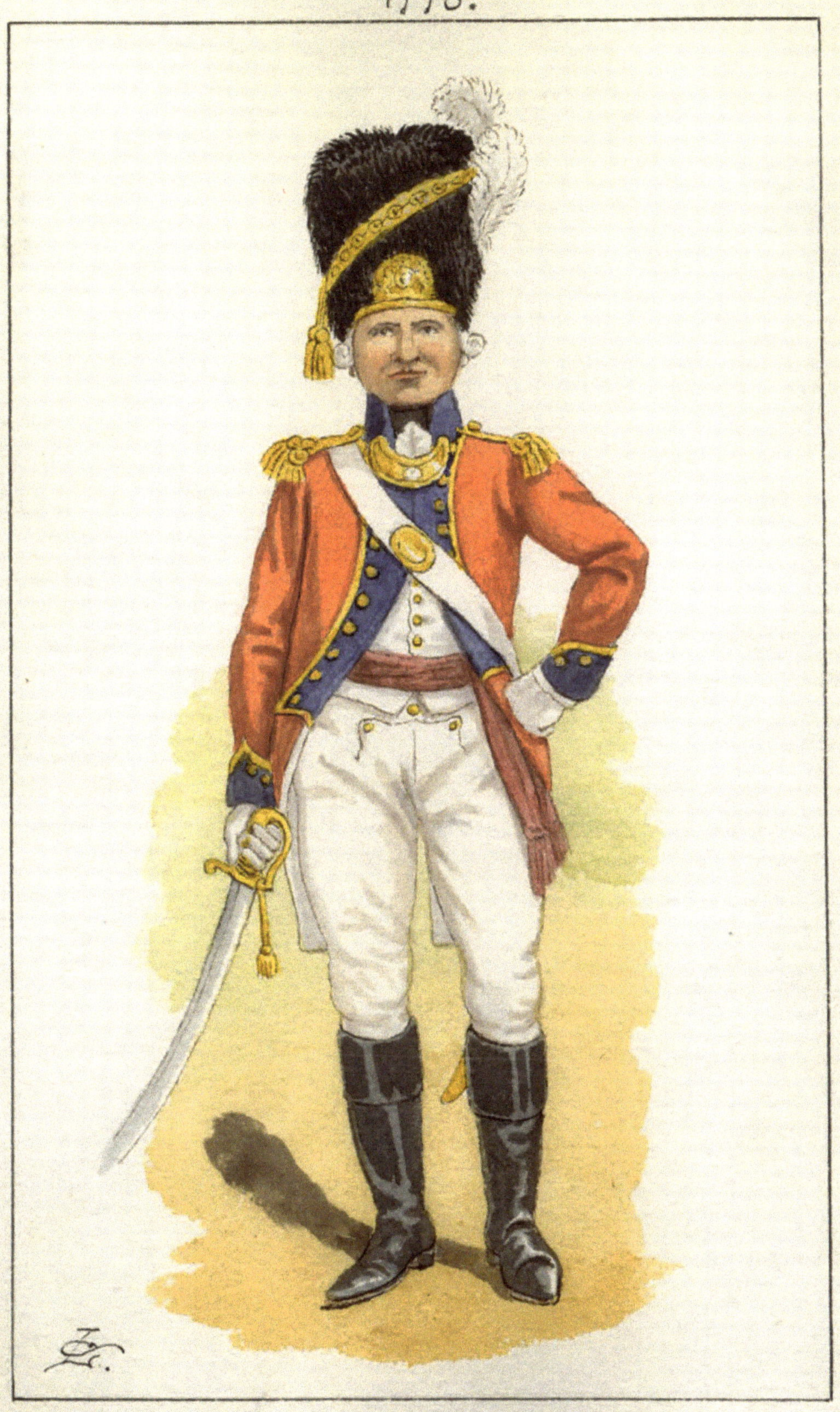

East India Company
Volunteers.
Officer.

82 – GUILDHALL LIGHT INFANTRY VOLUNTEERS, 1798

Here we see a member of the light company in the prosses of drawing a cartridge from his cartouche box. He wears a scarlet coat with epaulettes richly decorated with gold lace. The collar, lapels and cuffs are blue. It seems that the corps was formed to protect the district of Guildhall, and not just the municipal building in the Moorgate area of the City of London which sits more or less in a square with London Wall to the north, Aldermanbury in the west, Colman Street in the east and Gresham Street to the south. Within the square there were several Halls belonging to Livery companies: Coopers, Armourers and Brasiers and Girdlers. Charles Lyall's painting is based on an illustration after Thomas Rowlandson from Ackermann's Loyal London Volunteers.

1798.

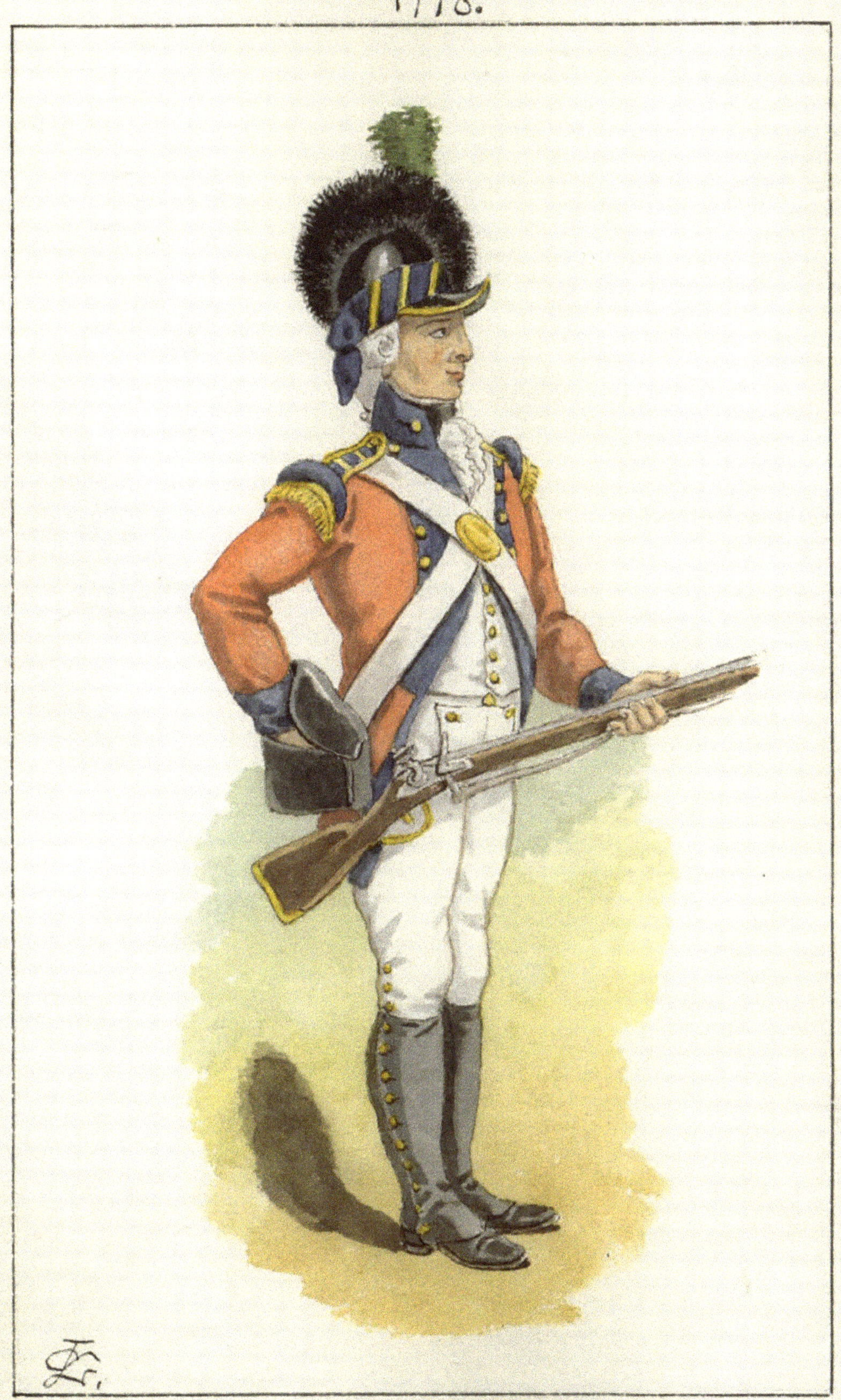

Guildhall Light Infantry.
Volunteers.

83 – LIGHT HORSE VOLUNTEERS, 1798

The scarlet hussar-type jacket and helmet with its blue turban and silver fittings seem to suggest that Charles Lyall's subject is a dismounted member of the London and Westminster Light Horse Volunteers. Commander of the corps was Colonel Charles Herries who died on 3 April 1819 and was subsequently buried in the nave of Westminster Abbey. By the door that leads into the west cloister there is a marble bust of him by Francis Chantrey. Below this there is an inscription which reads: 'In the nave of this church are deposited the remains of Charles Herries, Esquire, Colonel of the Light Horse Volunteers of London and Westminster....he was a chosen commander of a regiment of gentlemen, who, giving an example of voluntary service, were collected under the standard of loyalty, from the ranks, talents, and property of the Empire, in defence of all that was dear and sacred to men and Britons....The suavity of his manners tempered the strictness of his discipline; respect and love ensured obedience to his authority....The Light Horse Volunteers, regarding him as their father, followed him to the grave with filial reverence and, as a lasting tribute of honour to his memory, have raised this record of his virtues and their affection.'

1798.

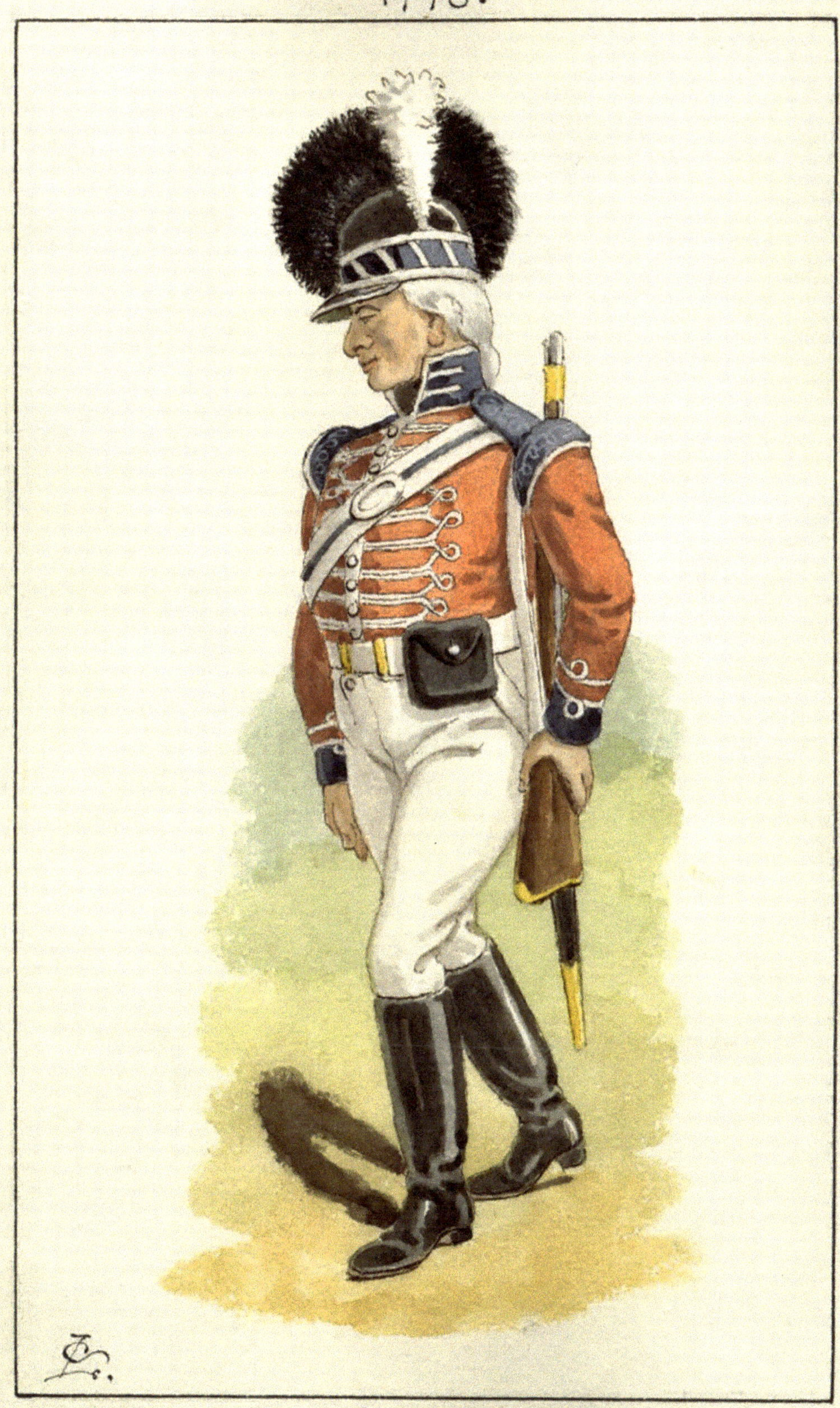

Light Horse Volunteers.

84 – WESTMINSTER CAVALRY VOLUNTEERS, 1798

The helmet has a white feather, gilt fittings and a blue turban matching the colour of the coat. Charles Lyall provides just a hint of a badge on the right side, but this would have been a representation of the portcullis from the Westminster arms. Open to reveal a white waistcoat, the coat is richly decorated with gold lace across the chest. Large gold epaulettes with scarlet fringes are worn and behind the rider, a rolled, blue cloak which has a scarlet lining.

85

1798.

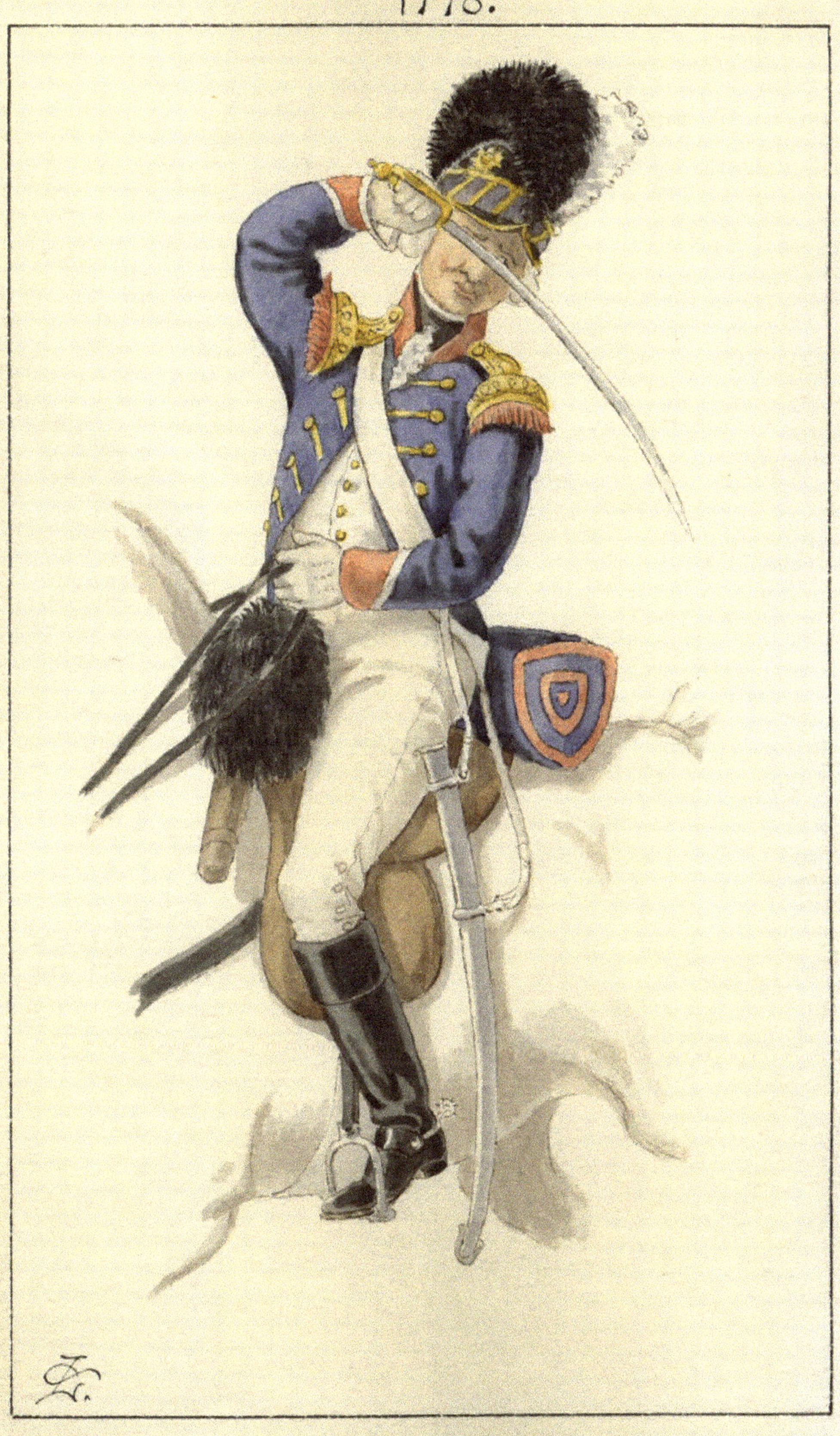

Westminster Cavalry Volunteers.

85 – St George's Hanover Square Light Infantry Volunteers, 1798

This painting of Charles Lyall's is based on Thomas Rowlandson's Plate No 9 from *Loyal Volunteers of London* and features a volunteer demonstrating the first motion of the 'shoulder arms from recover' position. The firelock has been brought up against the left shoulder, the butt is now held firmly by the left hand while the right hand is positioned over the breech pin with the thumb placed between the barrel and stock. The Parish of St George Hanover Square was formed in 1724 and centres around the church designed by John James and built between 1721 and 1725. Taking in fashionable areas of London such as Belgravia and Mayfair, the parish boundary to the north ran from Lancaster Gate, along Bayswater Road, past Mable Arch into Oxford Street as far as Oxford Circus. To the west was the River Westbourne, which fed Hyde Park's Serpentine lake, and in the south, the Thames. North Audley Street, which was laid out in the mid-1720s, and where the corps held its parades, runs northwards from Grosvenor Square to Oxford Street, 'the houses' records Ben Weinreb and Christopher Hibbert, 'were generally small and by 1790 were chiefly occupied by tradesmen.'

1798.

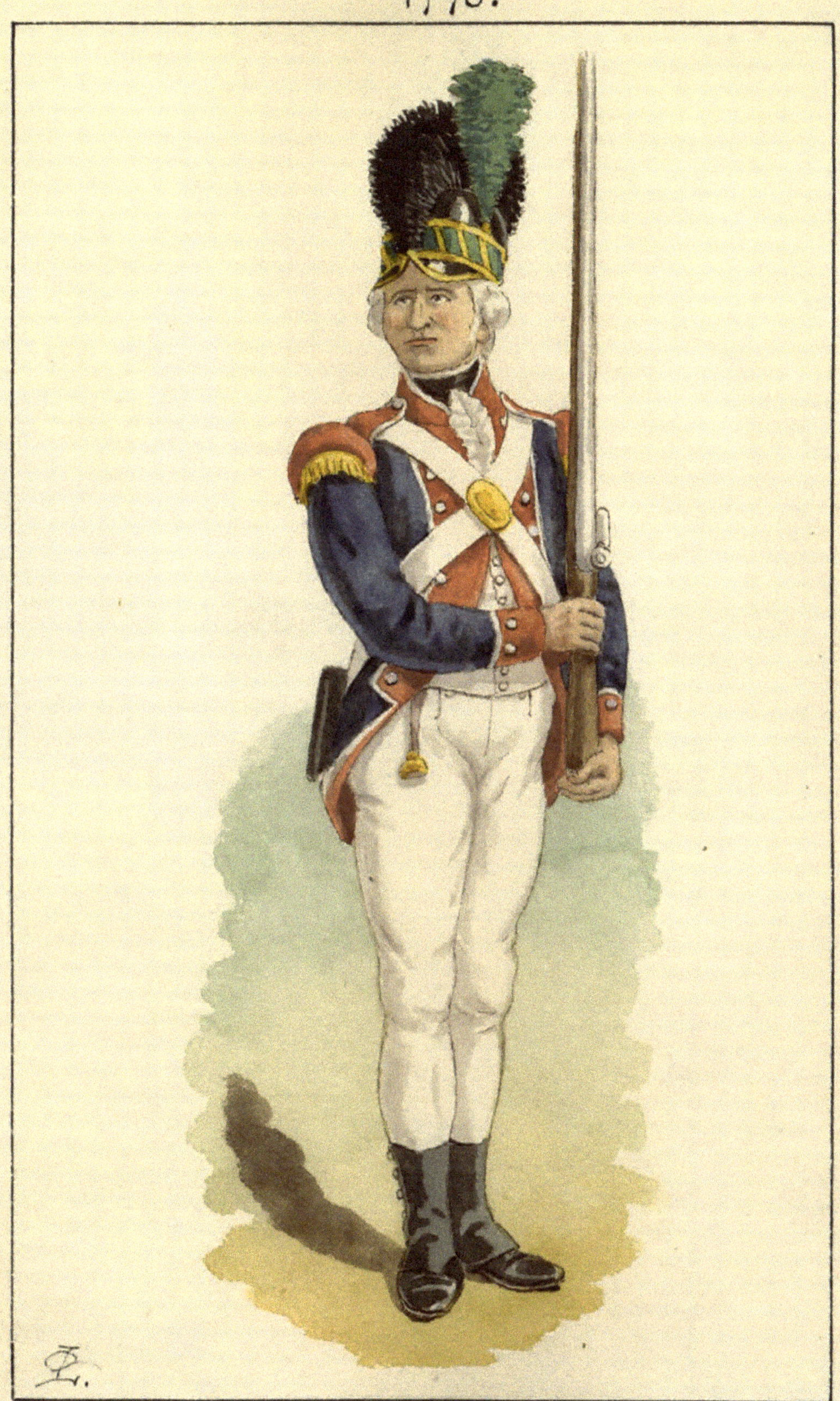

St. George's, Hanover Square.
Light Infantry Volunteers.

86 – ROYAL ARTILLERY, DRIVER 1799

The source for Charles Lyall's painting has clearly been taken from a detailed sketch by Captain RJ MacDonald. Yellow worsted lace across the chest, around the red collar and jacket bottom. The headdress has a black fur crest, gilt fittings, a blue turban and white plume.

1799.

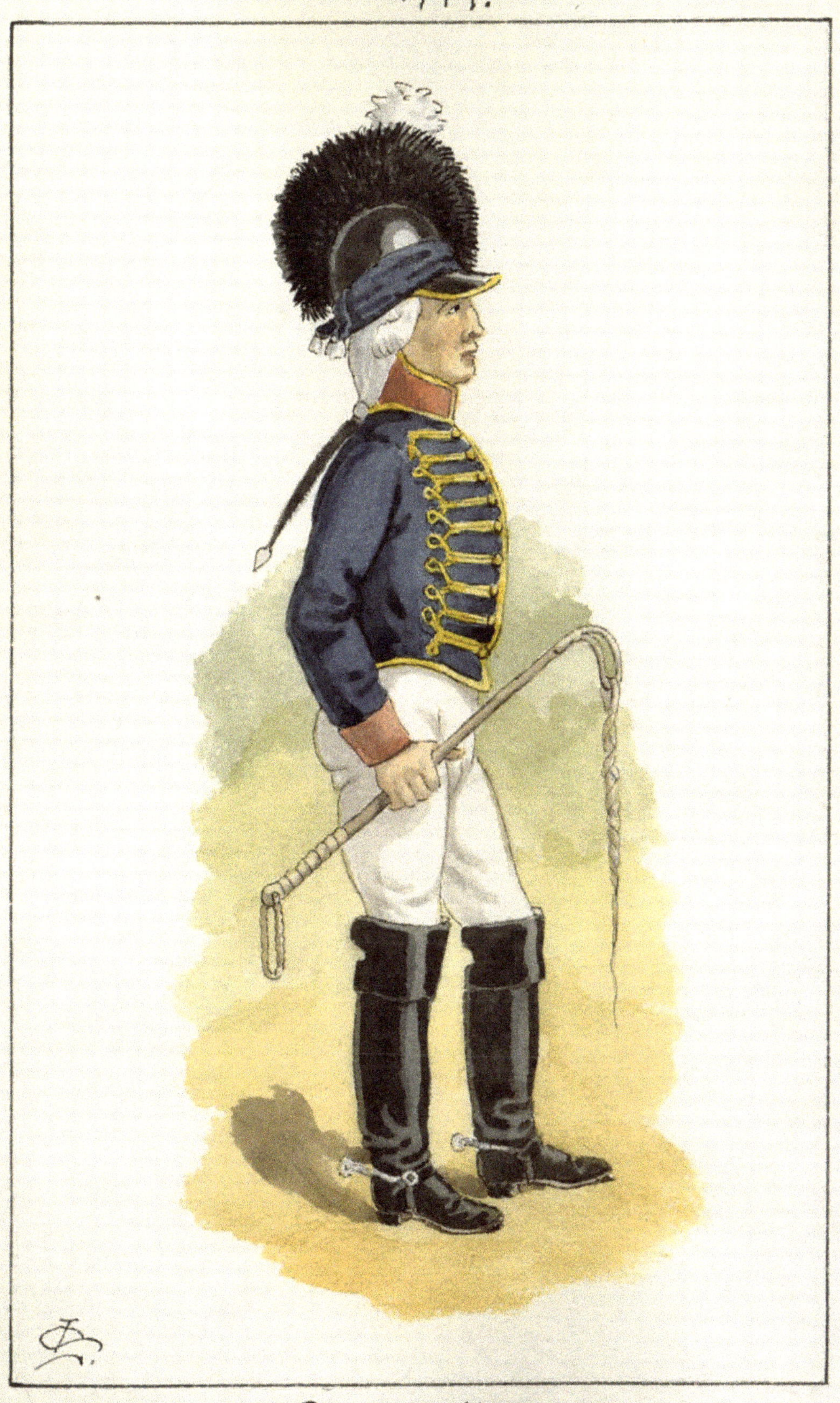

Royal Artillery.
Driver

87 – ROYAL ARTILLERY, OFFICER 1799

Another inspiration from Captain MacDonald. A field officer this time with scarlet collar, lapels, cuffs and gold piping, although MacDonald has the latter in red.

1799.

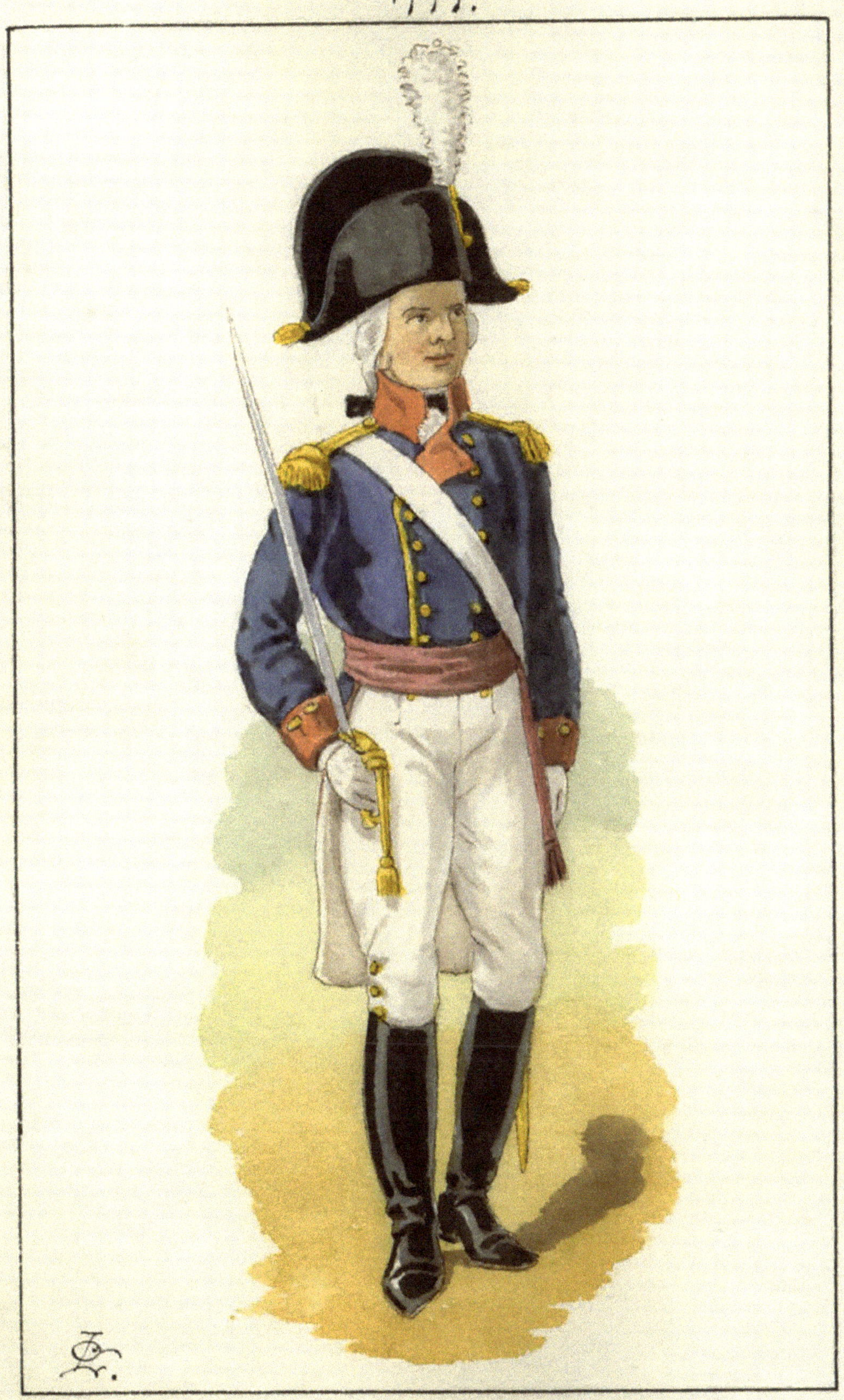

Royal Artillery.
Officer.

88 – ROYAL ARTILLERY, PRIVATE 1799

For a similar image to Plate 87, same uniform, same date, Captain MacDonald includes the following text: 'The gunners had left off the long-tailed coats, and taken into wear single-breasted, short-tailed ones.' Charles Lyall, however, shows the pouch as black, not white as in the MacDonald picture.

1799.

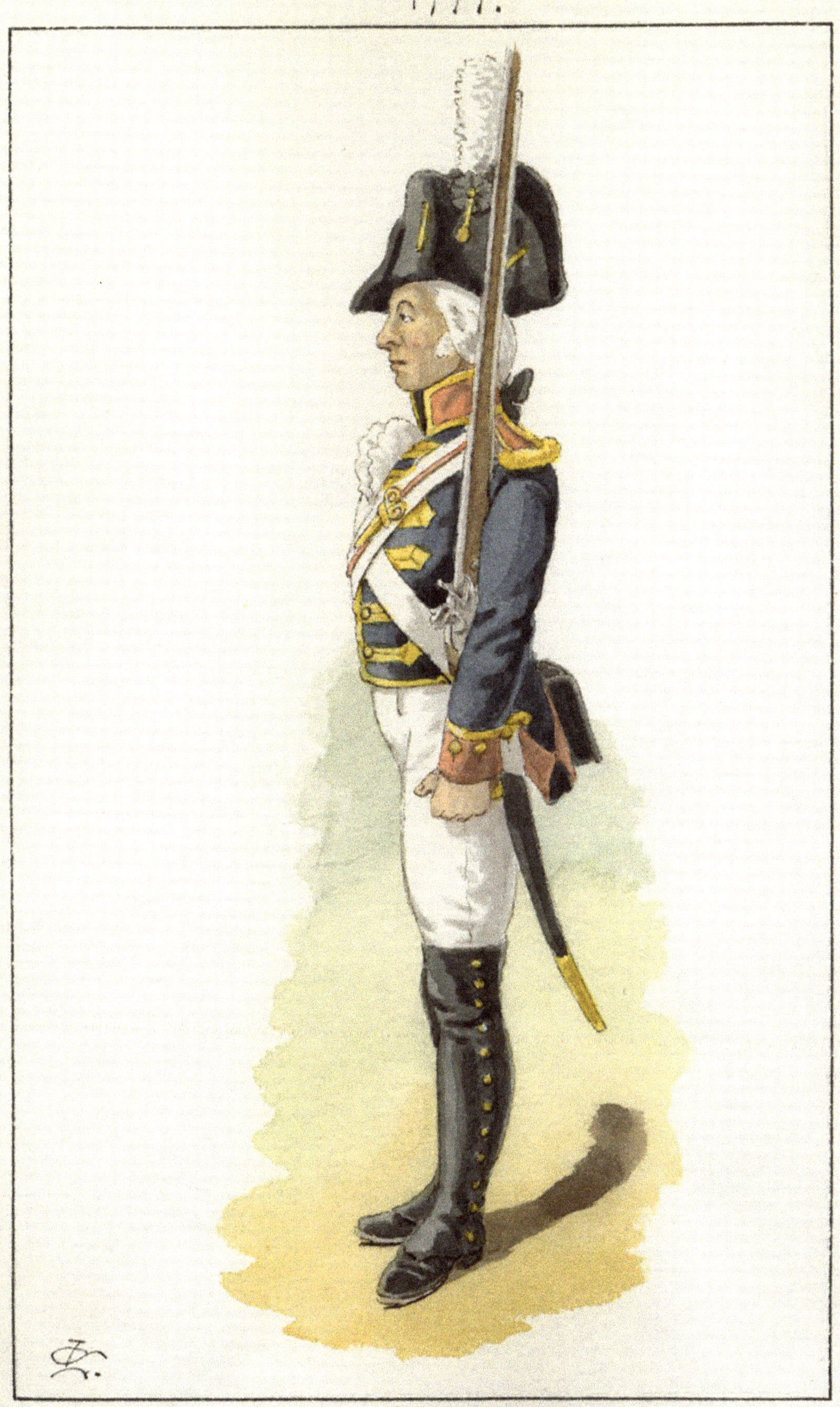

Royal Artillery
Private

89 – 8th LIGHT DRAGOONS IN INDIA, 1804

Chichester and Burges-Short note how 'On proceeding to India, the regiment appears to have adopted the light blue, or cavalry grey, uniform prescribed for King's regiments of cavalry serving in that country, the lace being silver, and the facings and horse-furniture red.' While in India, 1804-5, the regiment had distinguished itself during the capture of Agra, the battle of Leswarree, was present at Aurungabad and Furruckabad, the capture of Deig and during the pursuit of the enemy to Sutlej. The 8th Light Dragoons returned home in 1822.

204

1804.

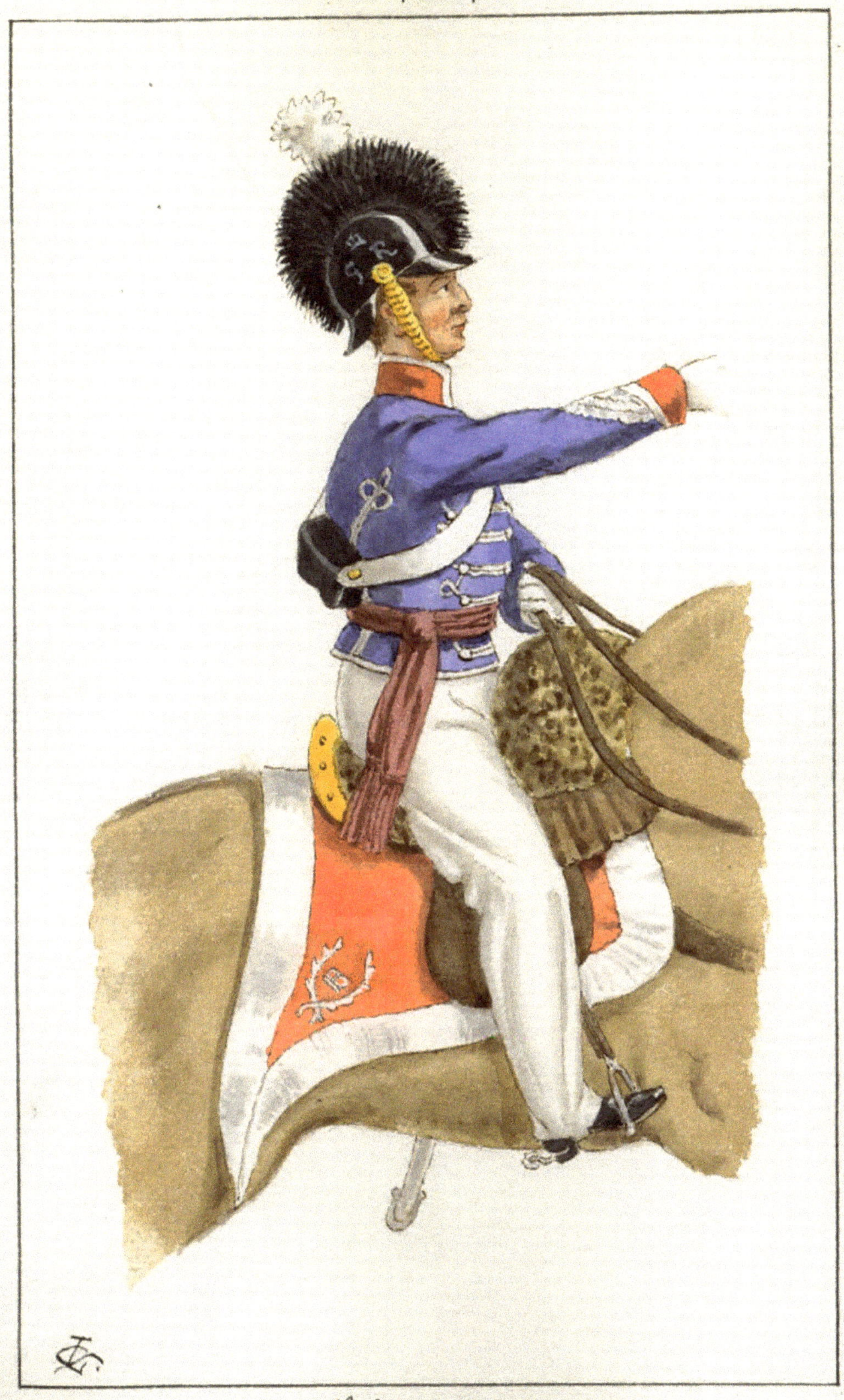

8th. Light Dragoons.
In India.

90 – BANK VOLUNTEERS, 1804

The Bank of England Volunteers had six battalion companies, a light infantry company and one of grenadiers. Here we have a member of the latter who wears a tall fur cap with gilt plate at the front and a tall white plume at the side. Since 1734 the Bank of England, as it is today, can be found in London's Threadneedle Street. This Corps had been formed by the Governors of the Bank from their own managers and employees in April, 1798 to protect the bank and its property. The oval brass cross-belt plate was engraved with the figure of Britannia.

1804.

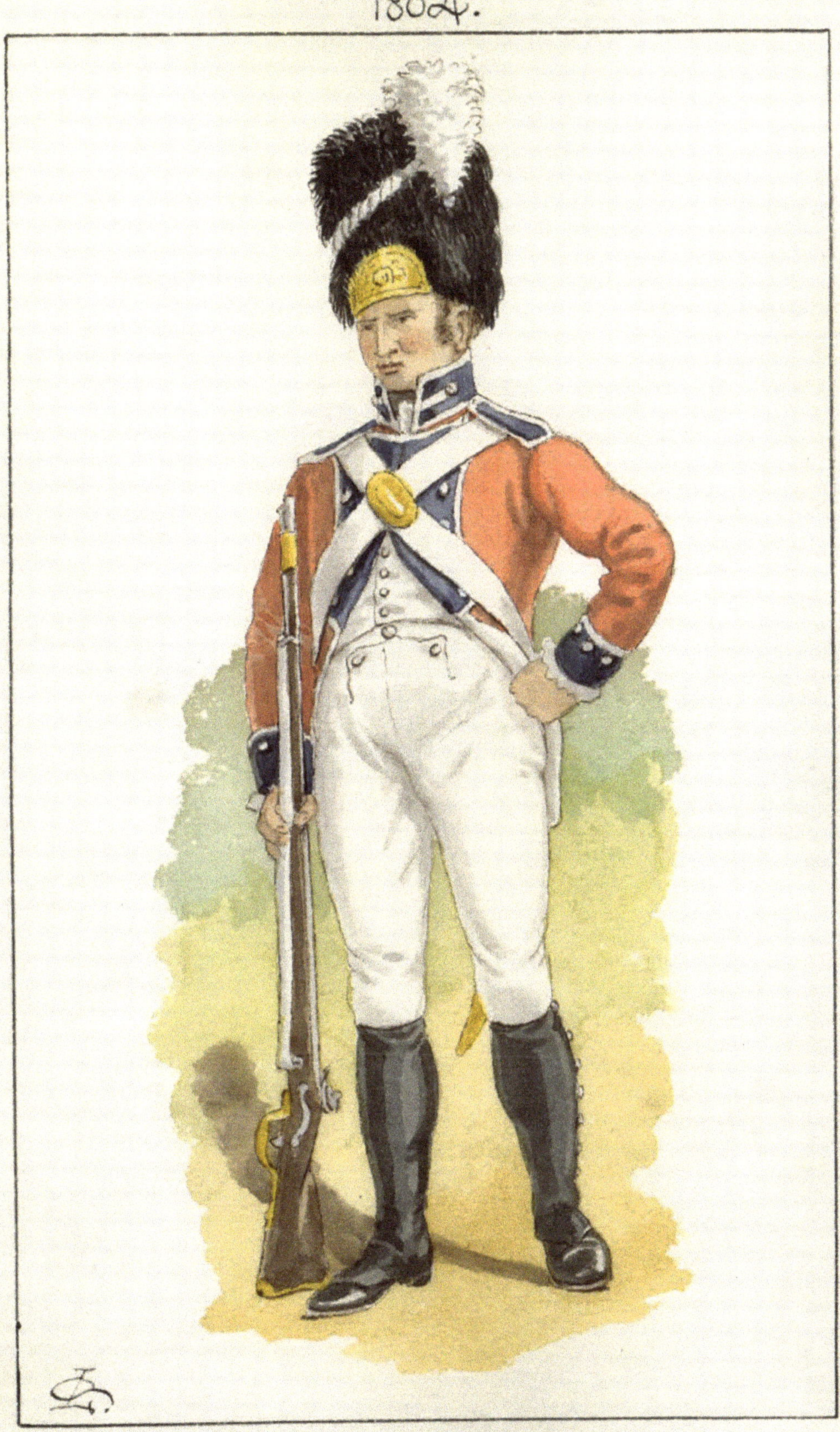

Bank Volunteers.

91 – THE HONOURABLE ARTILLERY COMPANY, 1804

Charles Lyall shows a private of the corps wearing a scarlet coat with blue facings, the collar edged all around with white piping. The buttons are white metal, the shoulder straps and wings blue with white piping and fringes. The helmet has a leopard-skin turban, gilt fittings and a tall white-over-red feather. It is not without good reason that the Honourable Artillery Company is thought of as a corps of great antiquity, having been established in Henry VIII's time by a Royal Charter dated 25 August 1537. This of course predates by centuries any other volunteer corps of the Napoleonic period. Although the HAC includes an artillery section, the use of the word 'Artillery' in its title is in the ancient sense and meaning a projectile such as an arrow shot from a bow.

225

1804.

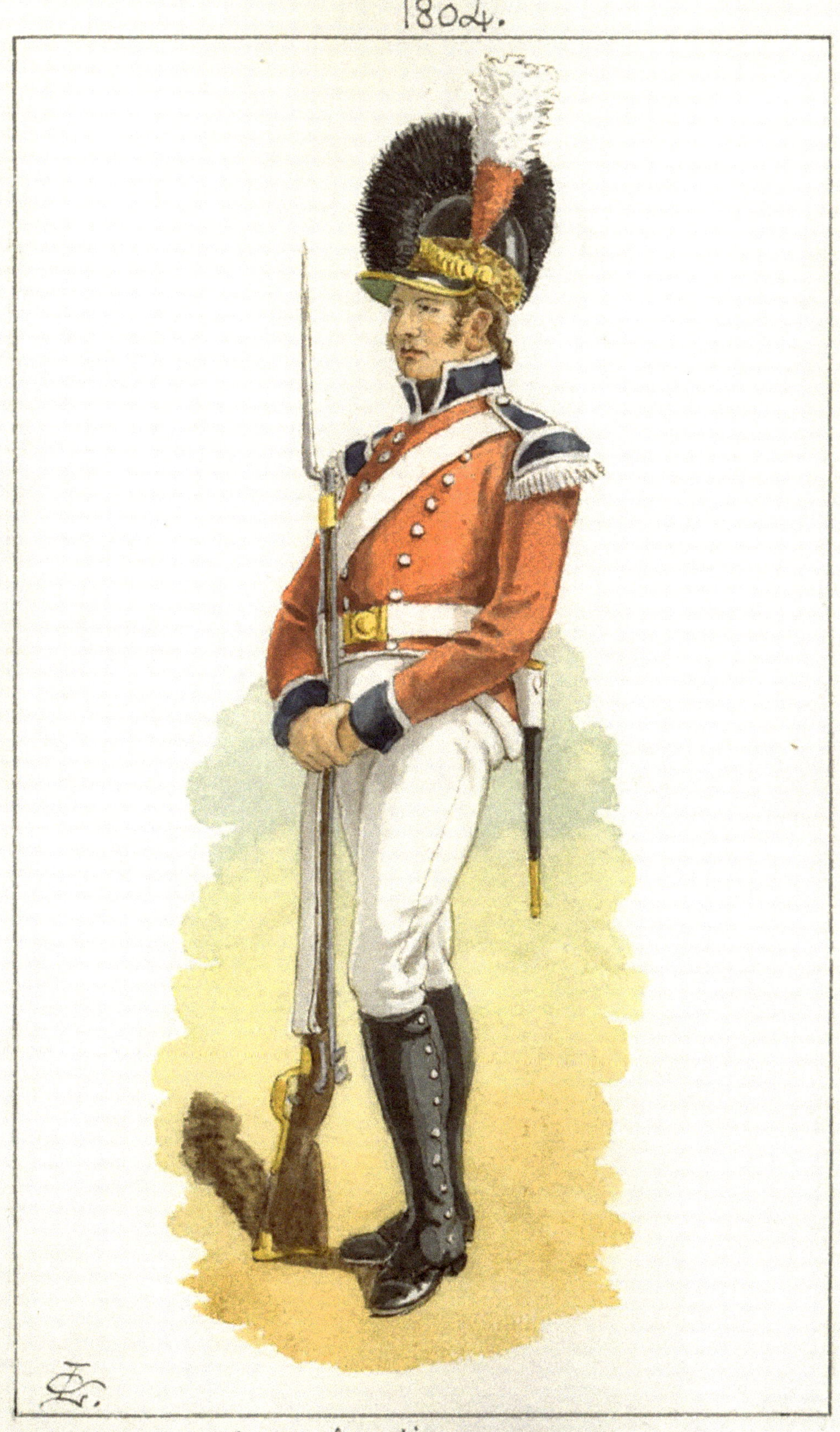

The Honble. Artillery Comp^y.

92 – HORSE GUARDS, BLUES 1806

Charles Lyall shows a closed coat, cut away at the front to make long tails at the rear. A black stock can be seen behind a high red collar, the same colour also for the jacket front and lining. Two belts are worn, one having a red flask cord, and the hat (soon to be replace by a helmet) has a tall white-over-red plume and generous gold lace.

307

1806.

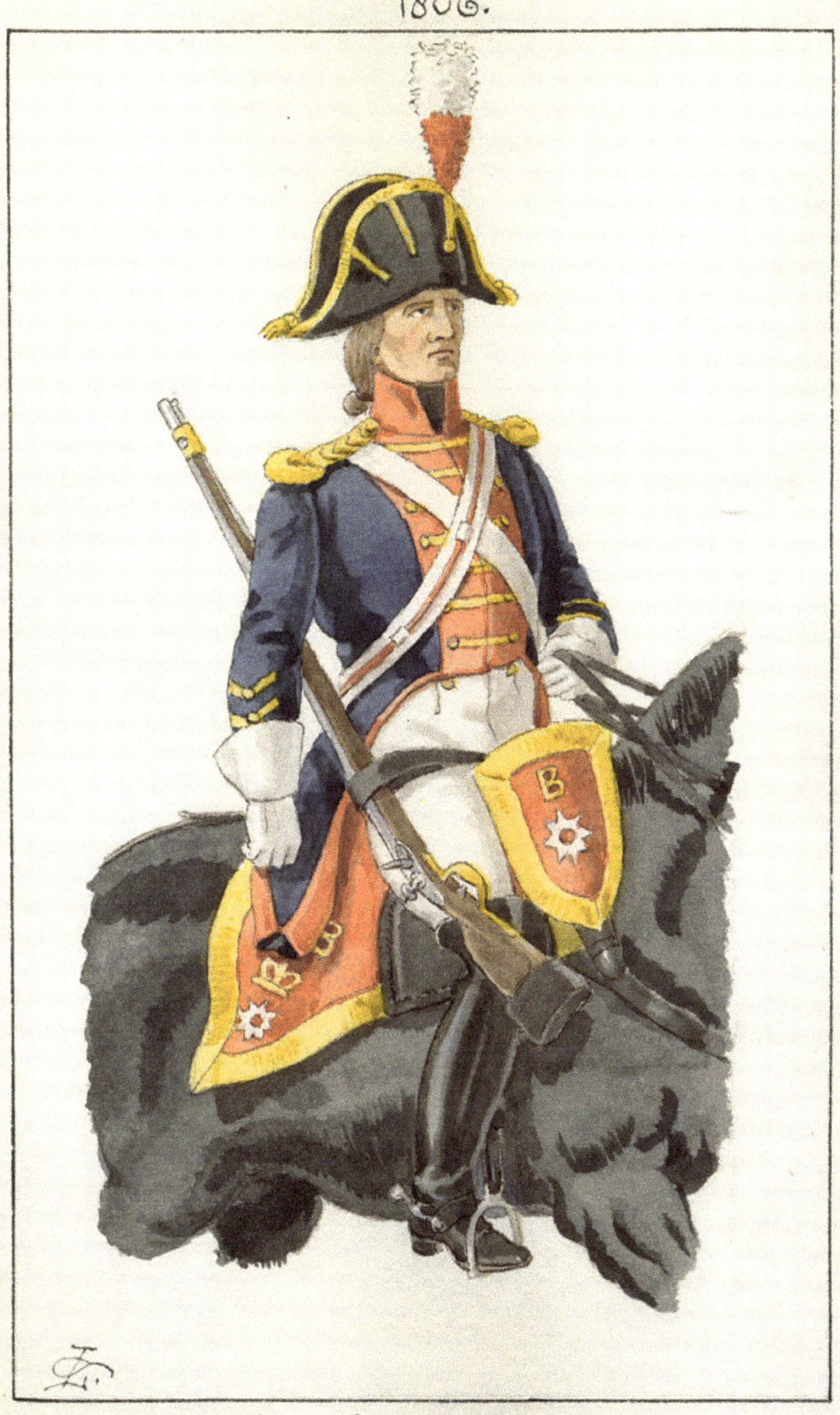

Horse Guards, Blues.

93 – LIGHT DRAGOONS, 1807

From the time of George III, an unusual rear view of a light dragoon wearing a blue coat with red facings and blue, buttoned at the sides, overalls, the latter fitted with leather attachments at the bottom to cut down on wear. The image allows us to see how the cap lines encircled the shako, and also the lace arrangement at the back of the jacket. A rolled blue cloak can be seen at the front of the rider and at the rear, a brown blanket secured by two white leather straps.

1807.

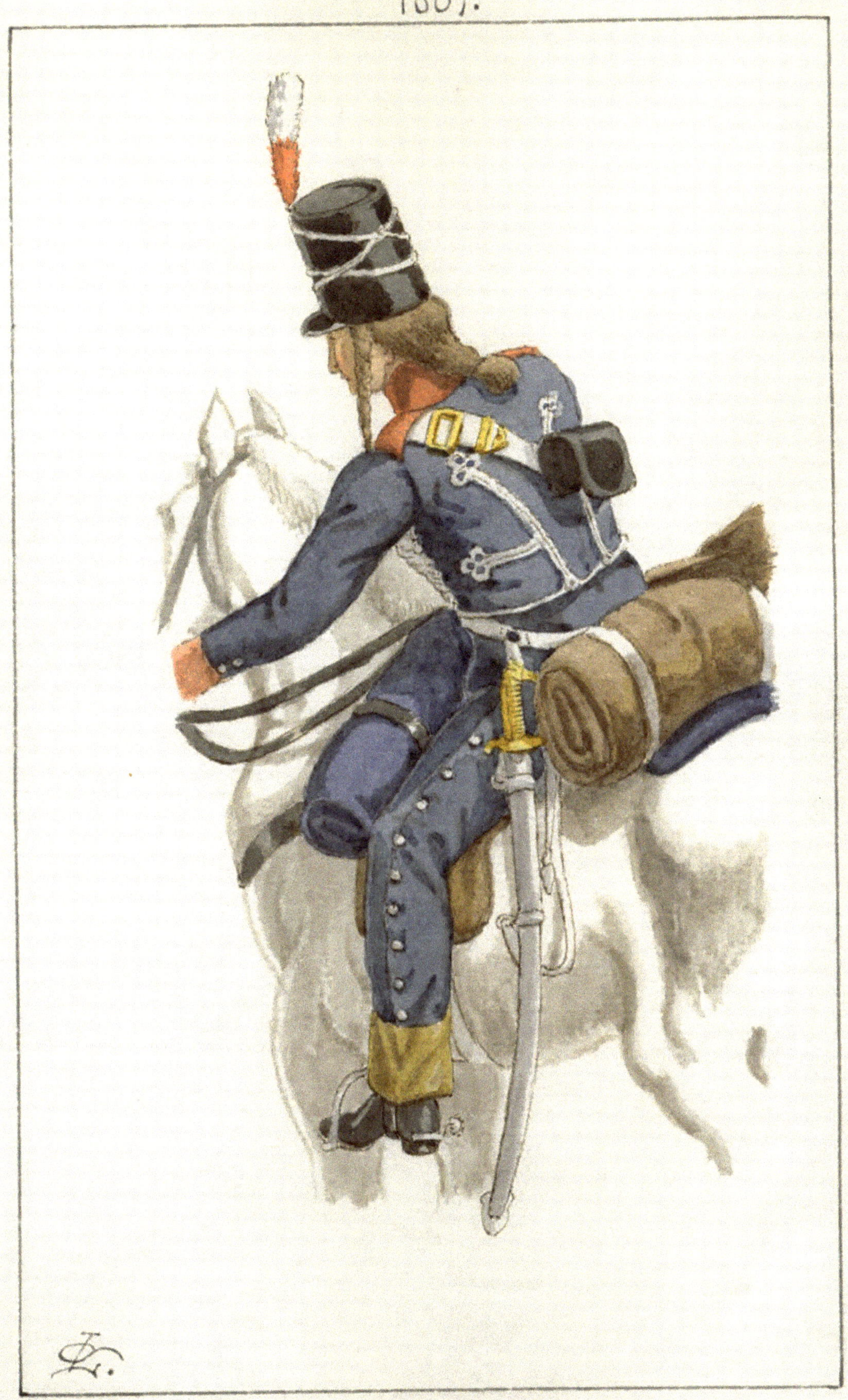

Light Dragoons.

94 – TROOPS WATERING HORSES, 1807

A young cavalryman mounted on a horse with no saddle wearing stable dress comprising a soft cloth cap, short red jacket with plain blue collar and overalls buttoned from the waist down to the ankle.

1807.

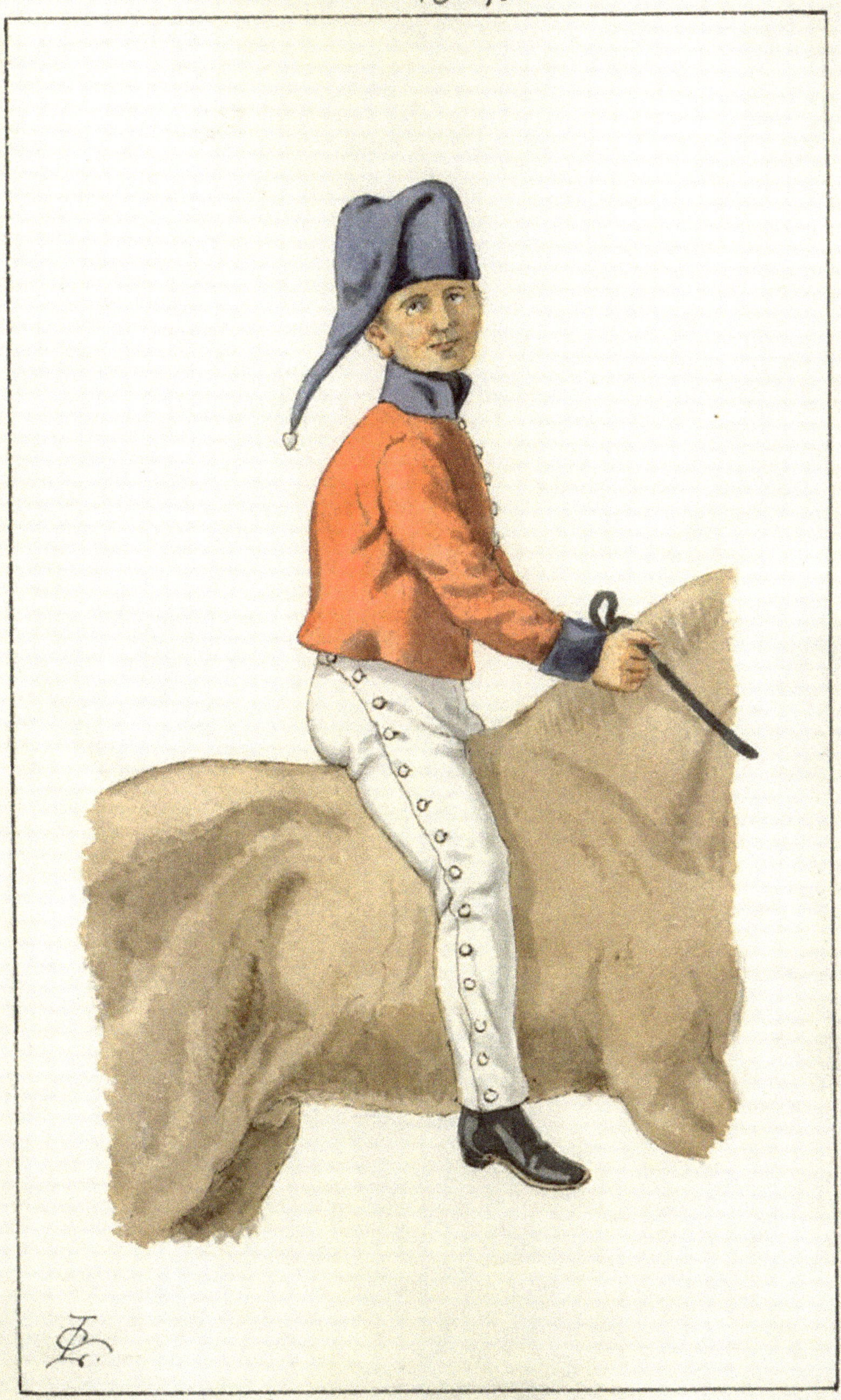

Troops watering Horses.

95 – LIFE GUARDS, 1807

An interesting and unusual rear view from Charles Lyall of a member of the Life Guards during the time of George III. There is plenty here not normally seen in military paintings: the heavy brass fittings of one cross belt and bayonet frog of another, the ammunition pouch with its rolled cover, the buttonhole loops of the tails, and rolled cloak with its three leather straps.

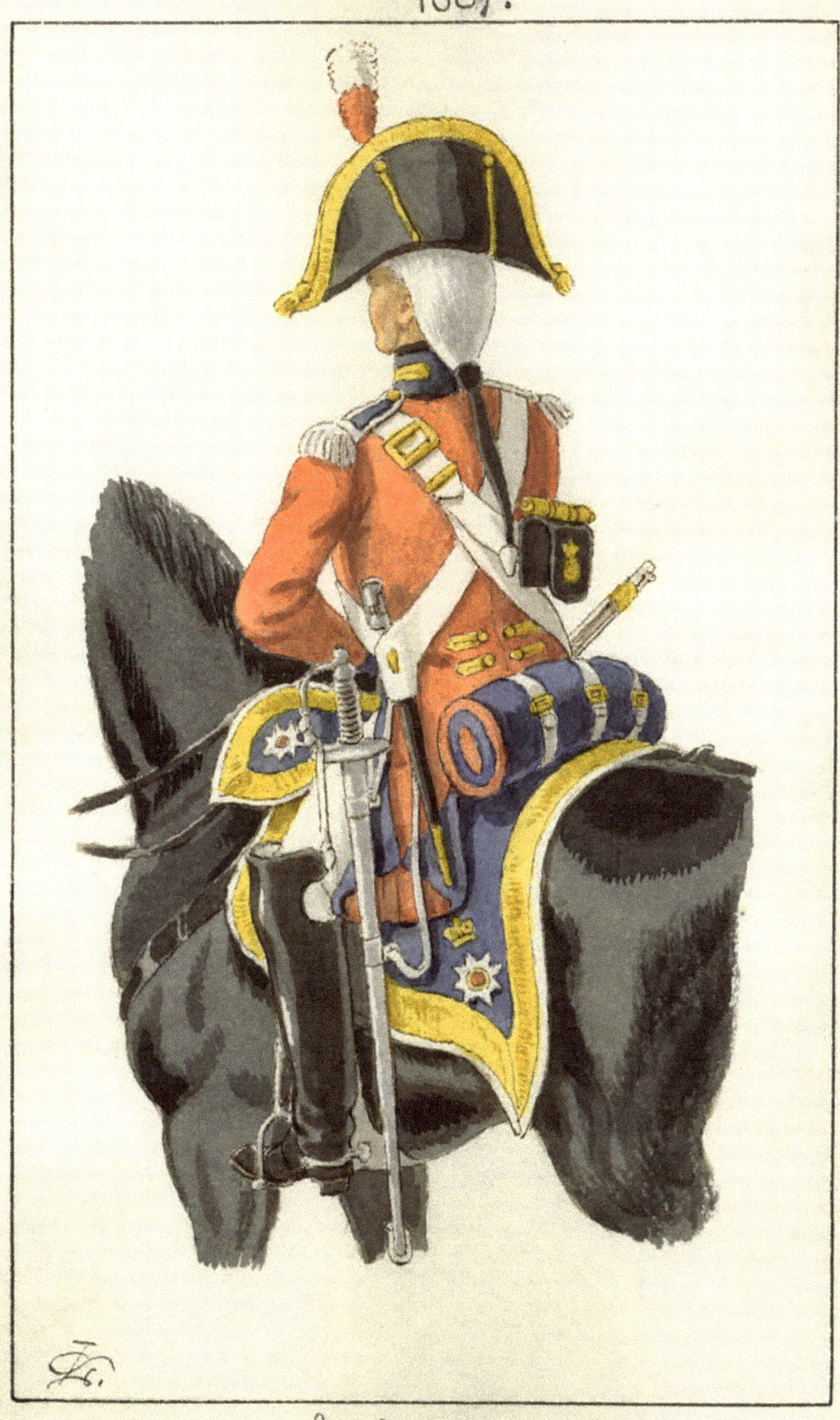

1807.

Life Guards.

96 – ROYAL ARTILLERY, 1807

In this, the first of two Royal Artillery plates for 1807, we see a gunner wearing the so-called 'Stove-pipe' shako introduced into the British Army around 1800. Arthur Kipling and Hugh King illustrate a specimen of the actual shako plate worn at this time which they describe as the usual infantry style with the exception that the Garter is replaced by a strap inscribed with 'Royal Reg. of Artillery'. Below this is a representation of a mortar with piles of shot either side. On the coat, the yellow braid of the loops terminates into bastion or spear-headed shapes. There is a white belt worn over the left shoulder which has a red flask cord running through its centre and passing behind an oblong brass plate. The red shoulder straps and cuffs are also decorated with gold braid.

1807.

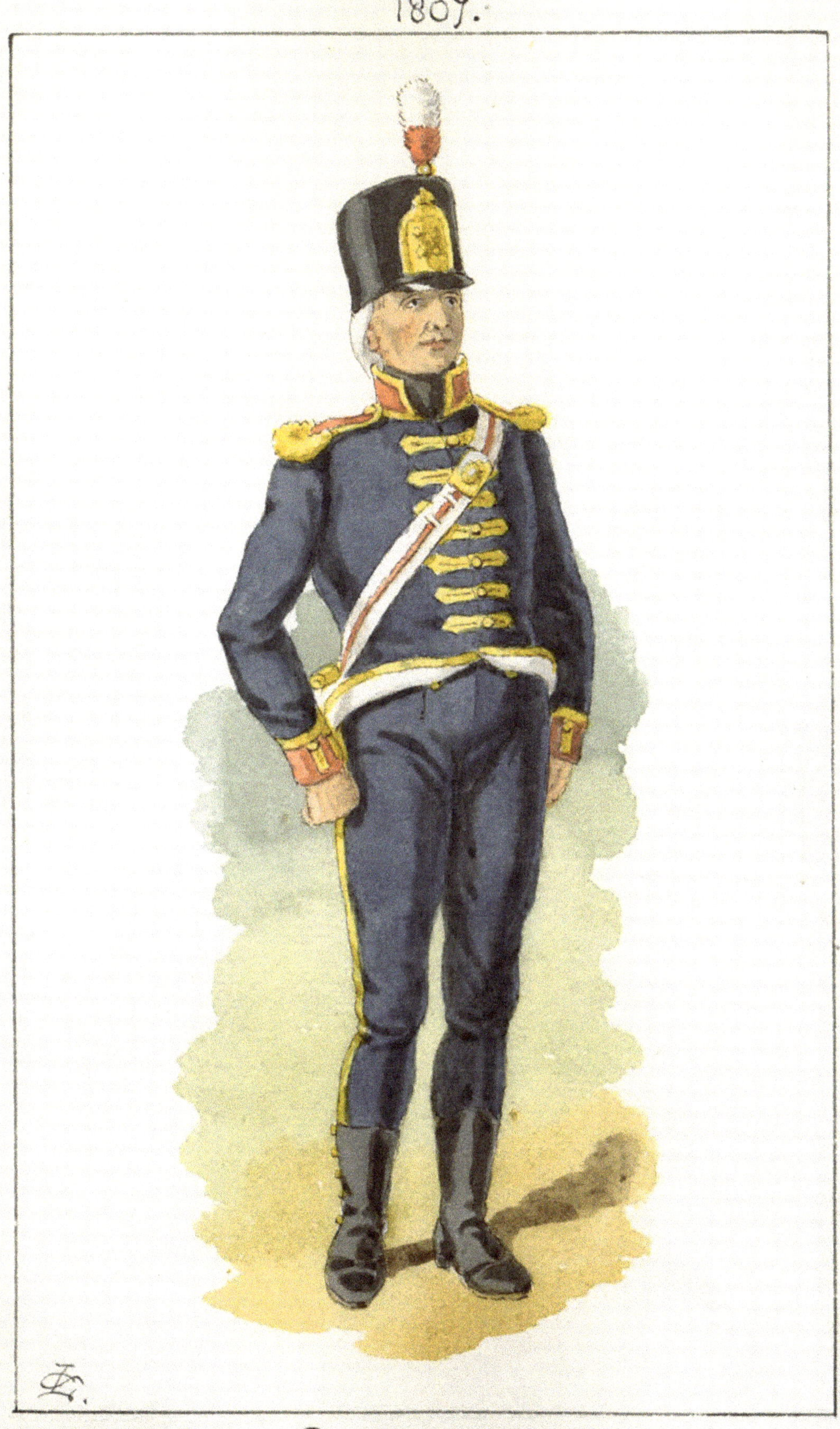

Royal Artillery.

97 – ROYAL ARTILLERY, 1807

Charles Lyall has provided a detailed rear view of a gunner. The powered hair is queued all the way down to the middle of the back. Gold braid can be seen forming edging to a rear pocket and carrying on around the short skirts to form an arrowhead. Carried in the hand is a white pouch-belt with brass fittings and badge.

271

1807.

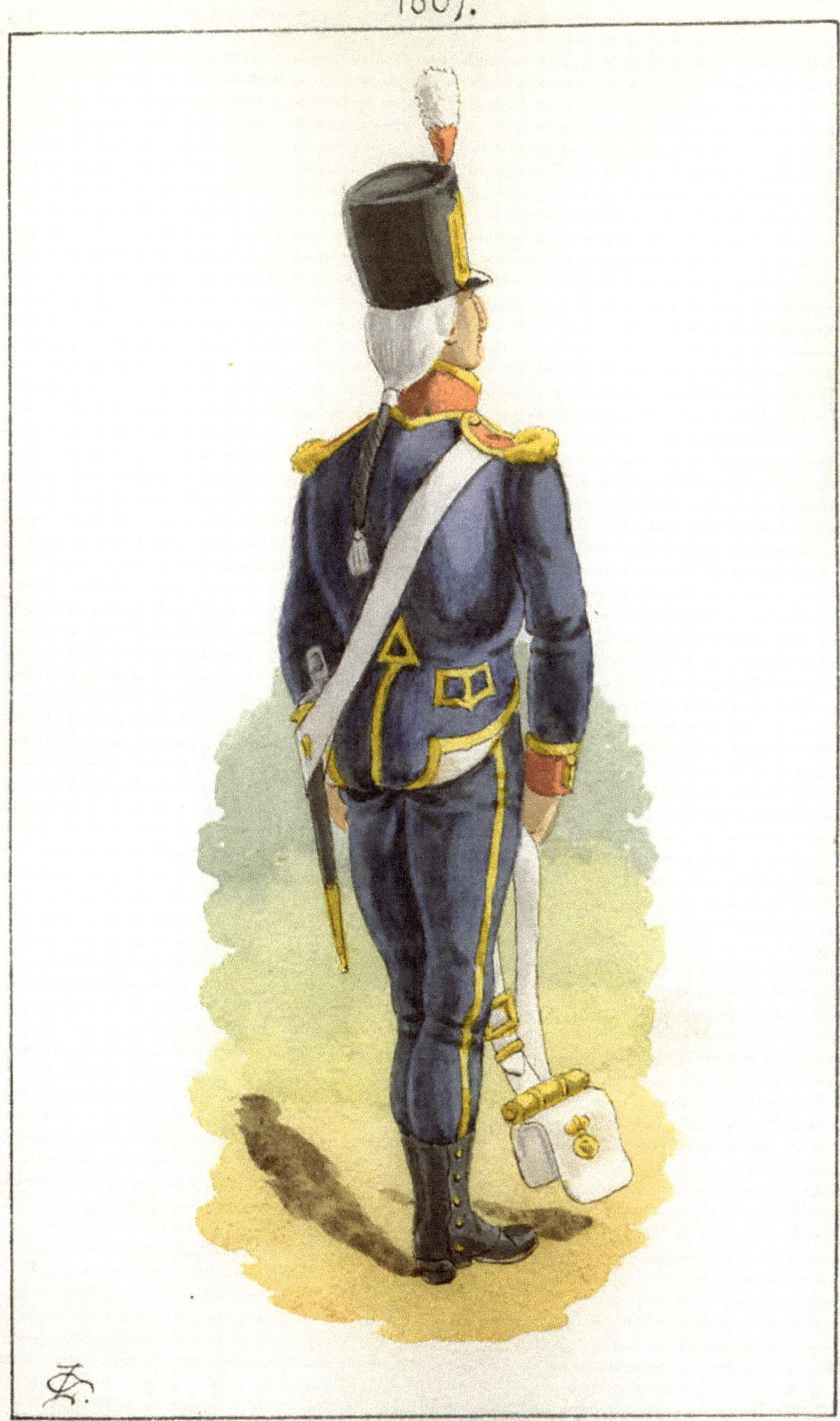

Royal Artillery.

98 – 93rd HIGHLANDERS, 1807

This regiment dates from 1800 and the formation by Major-General Wemyss of a regiment mainly from members of the 3rd Sutherland Fencibles. As we can see from Charles Lyall's painting the facings were yellow, and they would remain so right up to 1881 when the 93rd became the 2nd Battalion Princess Louise's (Argyll and Sutherland Highlanders).

1807.

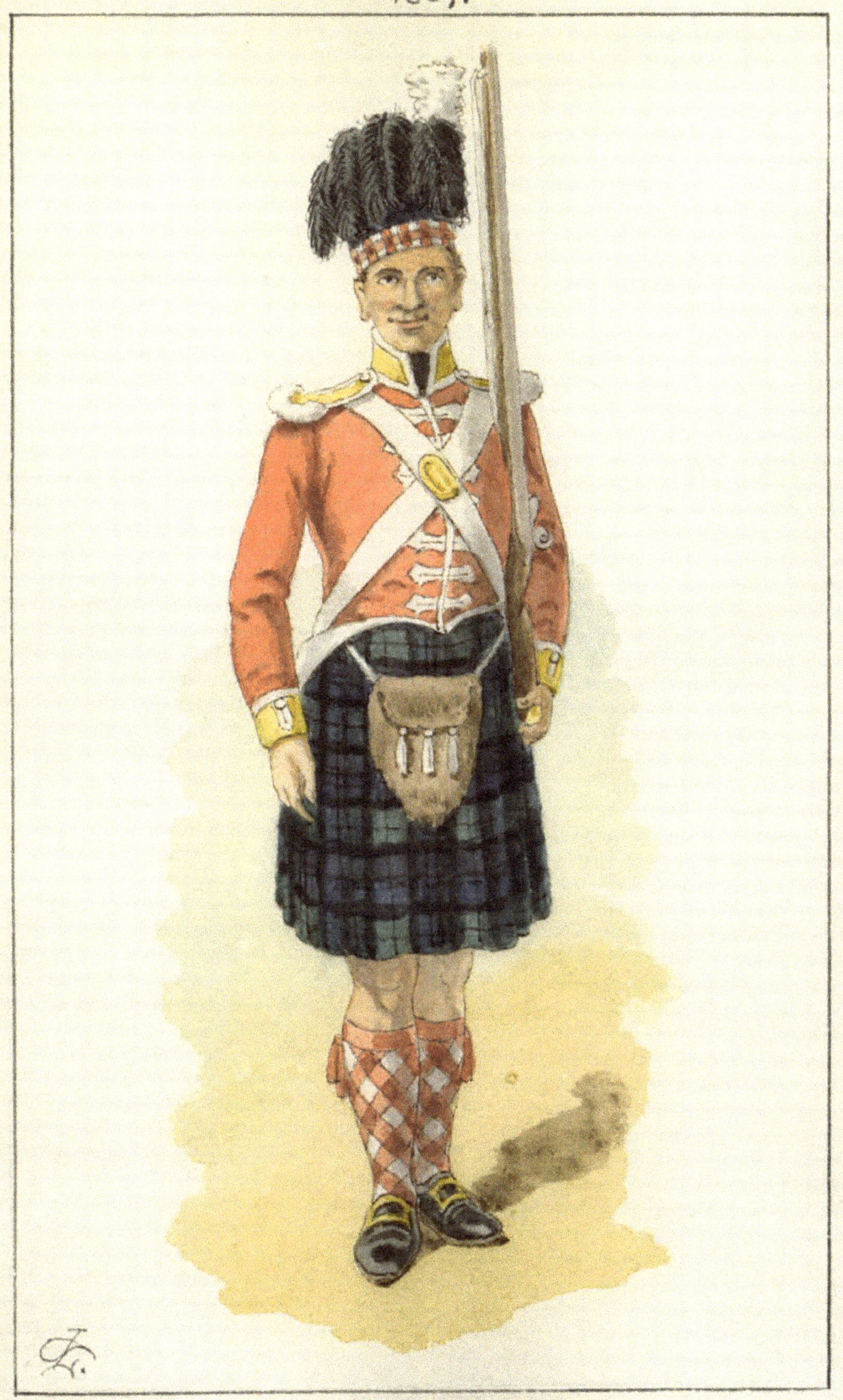

93rd Highlanders.

99 – 95TH RIFLES, 1807

The Rifle Brigade was known as the 95th Regiment between 1803 and 1816. In 1807 the regiment had taken part in the expedition to Buenos Aires and the siege of Copenhagen under Sir Arthur Wellesley before its involvement throughout the Peninsular War.

1807.

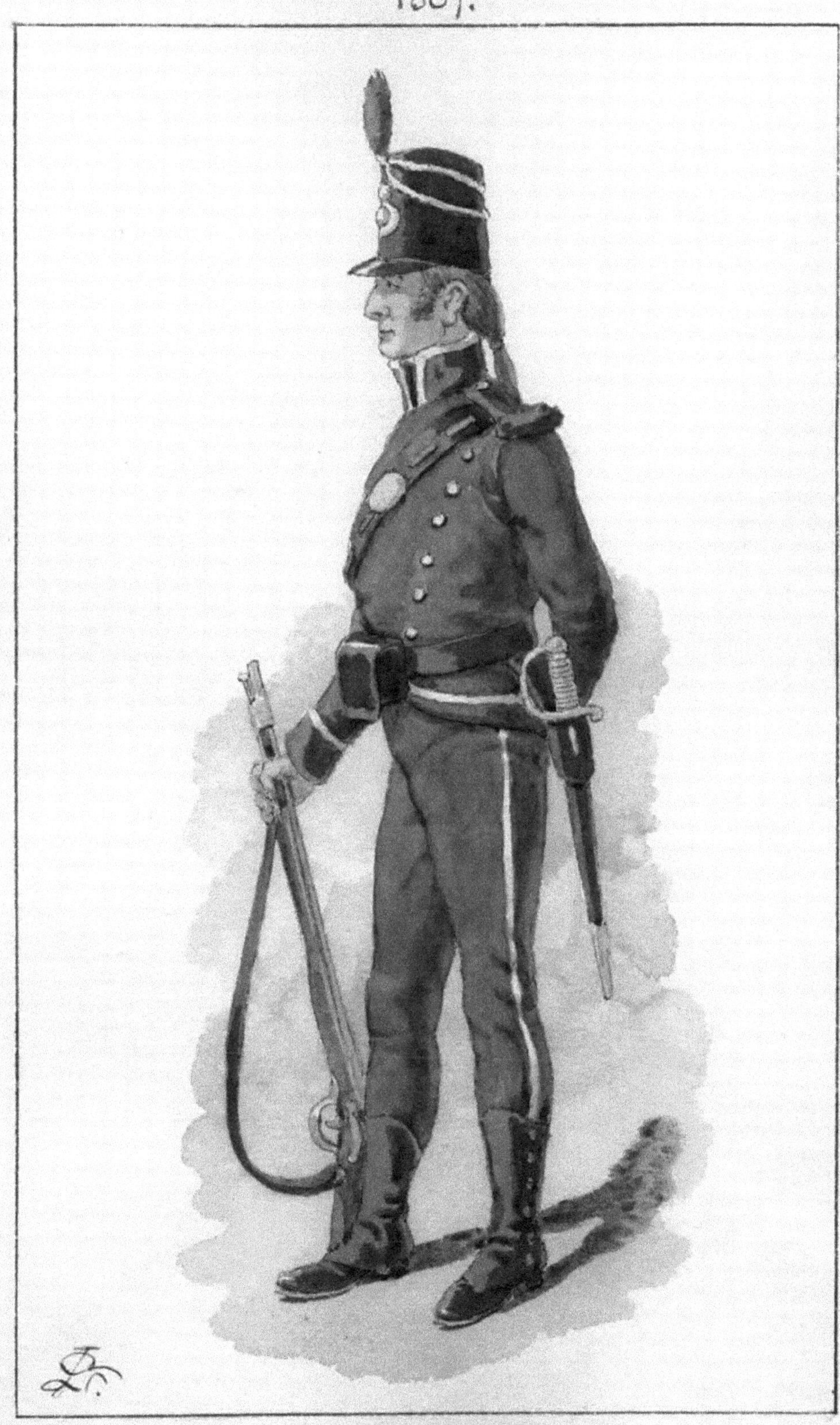

95th Rifles.

100 – HEAVY DRAGOONS, 1812

No clue as to regiment in Charles Lyall's caption, but the red valise behind the saddle is clearly marked for 1st Royal Dragoons. The year 1812 had seen cocked hats replaced by helmets, uniform historian WY Carman also noting the introduction of grey overalls at this time and jackets with wide braid on the front that went all the way up to the collar. The regiment had embarked at Cork for Portugal in September 1809, subsequently serving in the Peninsular campaign until returning home in July 1814.

1812.

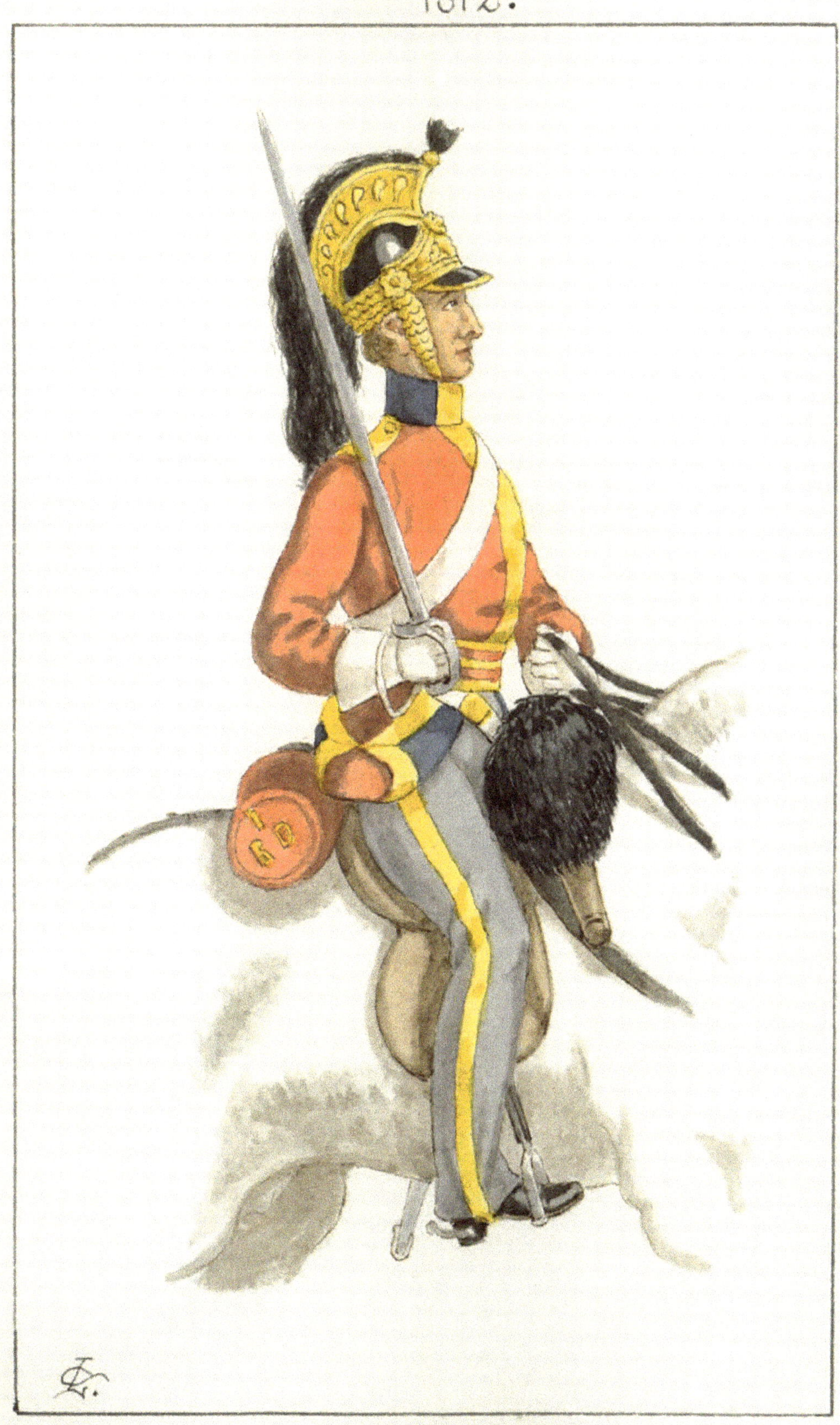

Heavy Dragoons.

101 – FIRST LIFE GUARDS, OFFICER 1812

Charles Lyall shows us an officer of 1812, the year that two squadrons each of the 1st and 2nd Life Guards had been despatched to Portugal towards the end of October. Both regiments returned to England on 22 July 1814. Lyall's officer's coat is richly decorated with thick gold lace. He has been painted with one gauntlet glove off allowing us to see a blue cuff with two rings of gold. Wide belts for sword and pouch are worn, both with a blue edging, together with a crimson sash. On the bicorn hat, a crown above a representation of the Star of the Order of the Garter.

1812.

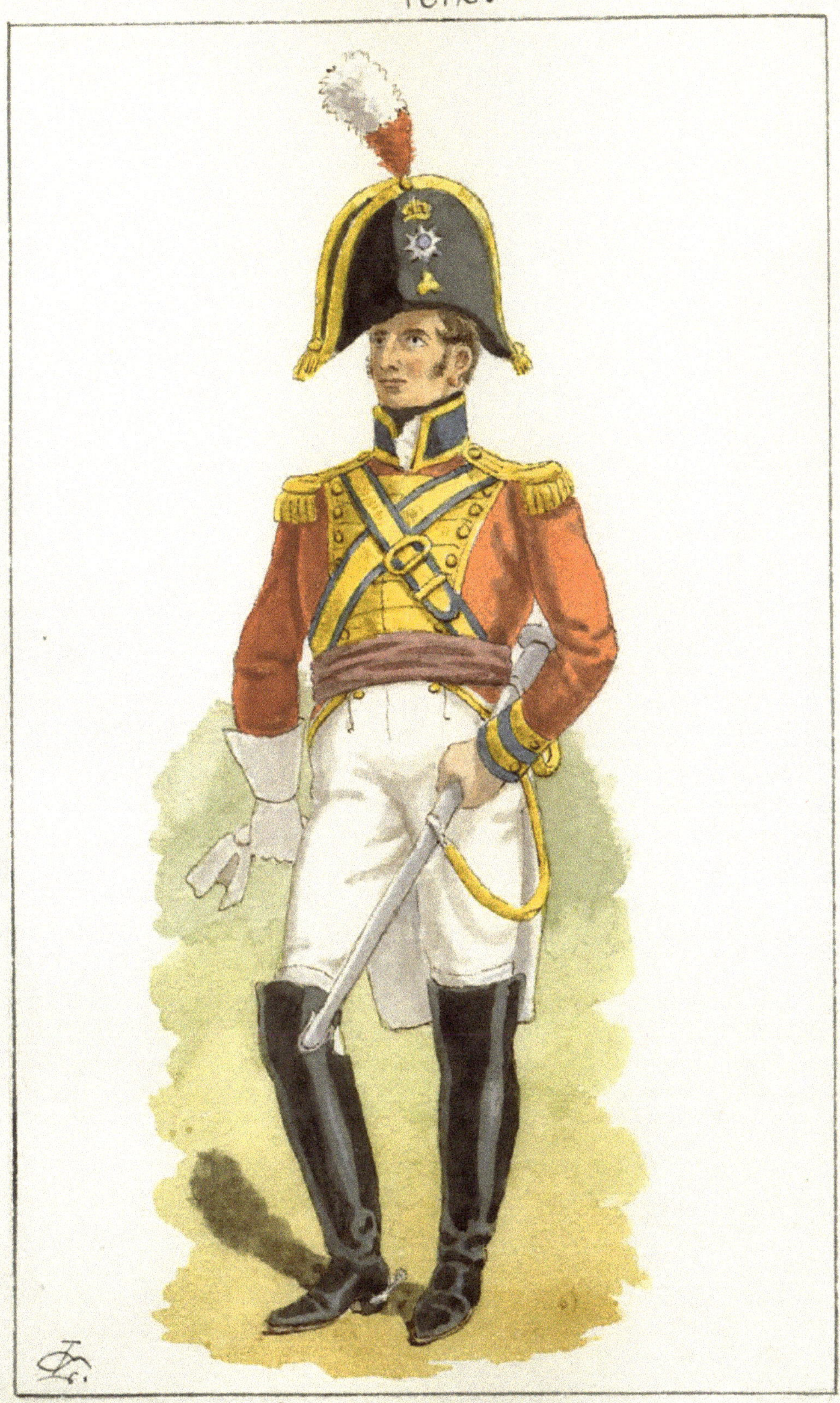

First Life Guards.
Officer.

102 – 2nd Life Guards, Service Uniform 1812

Here we see a heavy cavalry helmet with brass comb supporting a horsehair aigrette at the front and a long falling mane at the rear.

239

1812.

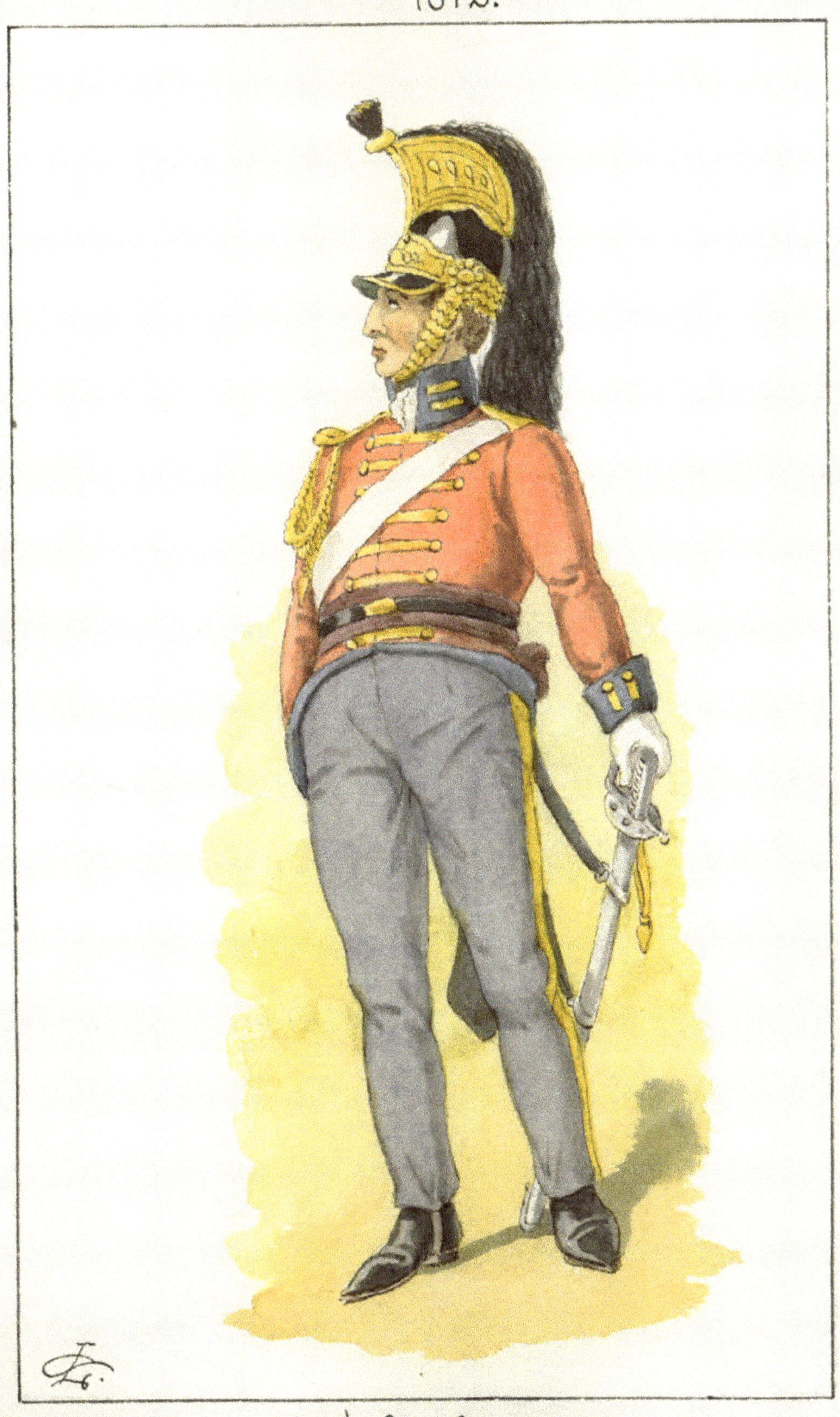

2nd Life Guards.
Service Uniform.

103 – ROYAL HORSE GUARDS, 1812

Charles Lyall shows an officer, his headdress being edged all around with gold lace and sporting a white-over-red plume. One glove has been removed, enabling us to clearly see the gold lace and buttons of the lower arm.

1812.

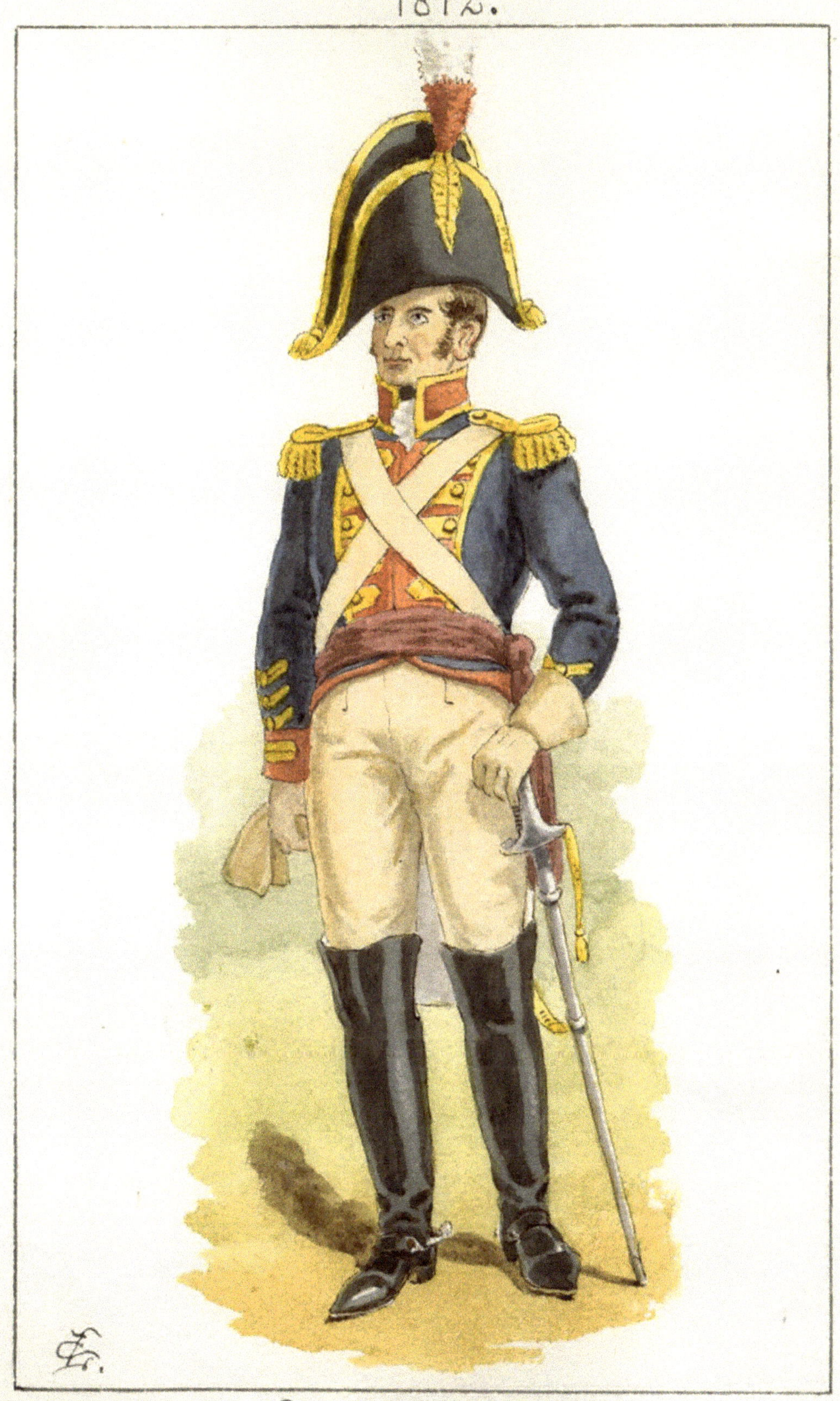

Royal Horse Guards.

104 – 12TH LIGHT DRAGOONS, 1812

Chichester and Burges-Short record how, in 1811, the regiment had proceeded to the Peninsular where it was to win '...a high reputation in the subsequent campaigns.' Ciudad Rodrigo, Badajos, Burgos and San Sebastian are mentioned, along with the battles of Salamanca and Vittoria. Charles Lyall shows an officer wearing a blue jacket with yellow facings and silver lace. After Waterloo, the 12th Light Dragoons were converted to lancers.

243

1812.

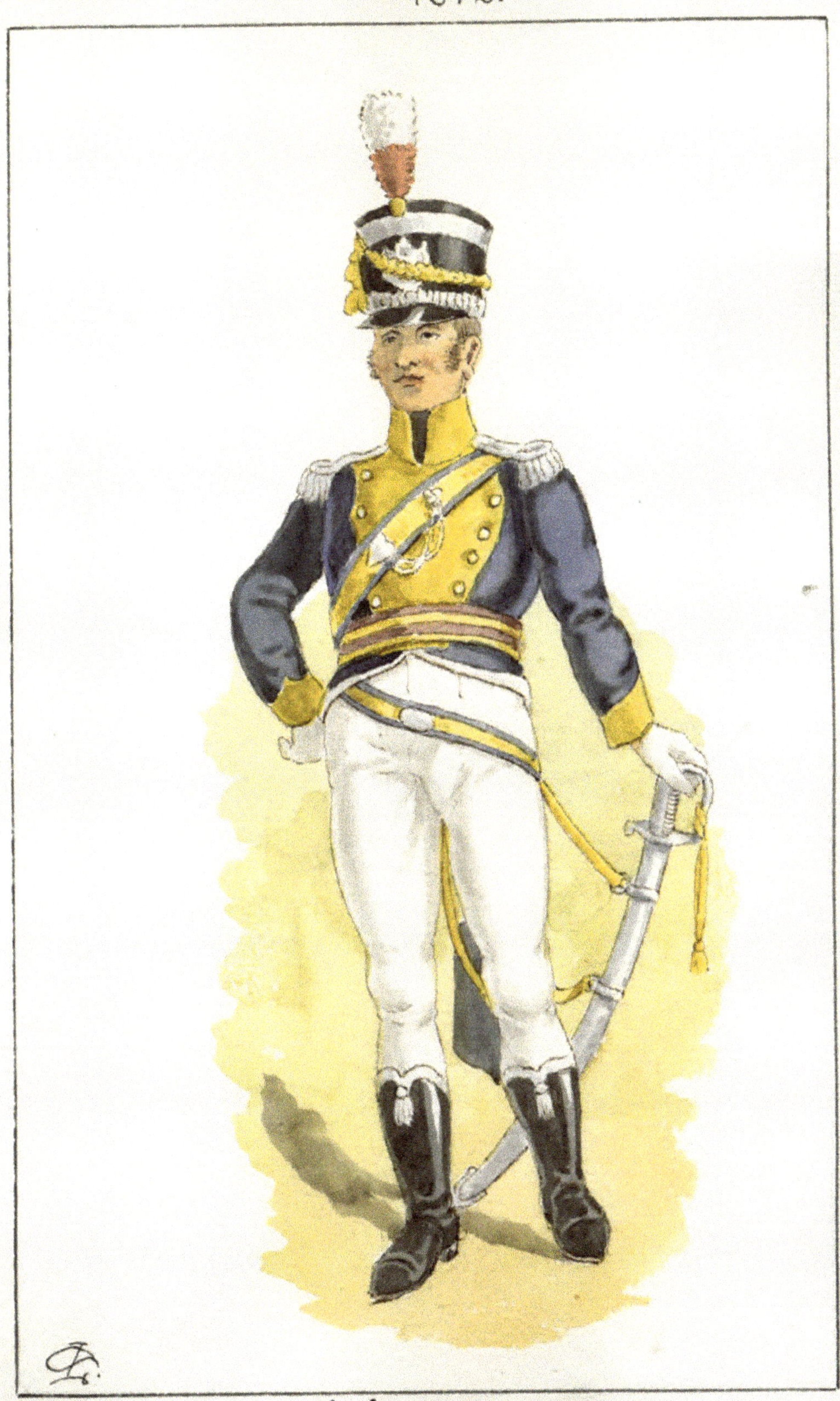

12th Light Dragoons.

105 – 13th LIGHT DRAGOONS, 1812

After landing at Lisbon in February 1810 the 13th Light Dragoons would gain its first honour of the Peninsular war at Albuera on 16 May 1811. Action was later seen at Ciudad Rodrigo, Badajoz, Salamanca, Vittoria and Orthes. At the close of the war the regiment embarked for England, arriving at Ramsgate on 7 July 1814. Charles Lyall shows an officer, his blue jacket having a white collar and cuffs and heavily decorated with gold lace and cord. A fur-crested helmet, soon to be replaced by a shako, with gilt fittings, a blue turban and white-over-red plume is worn, the belts seeming to be crimson with a wide yellow or gold central lines.

1812.

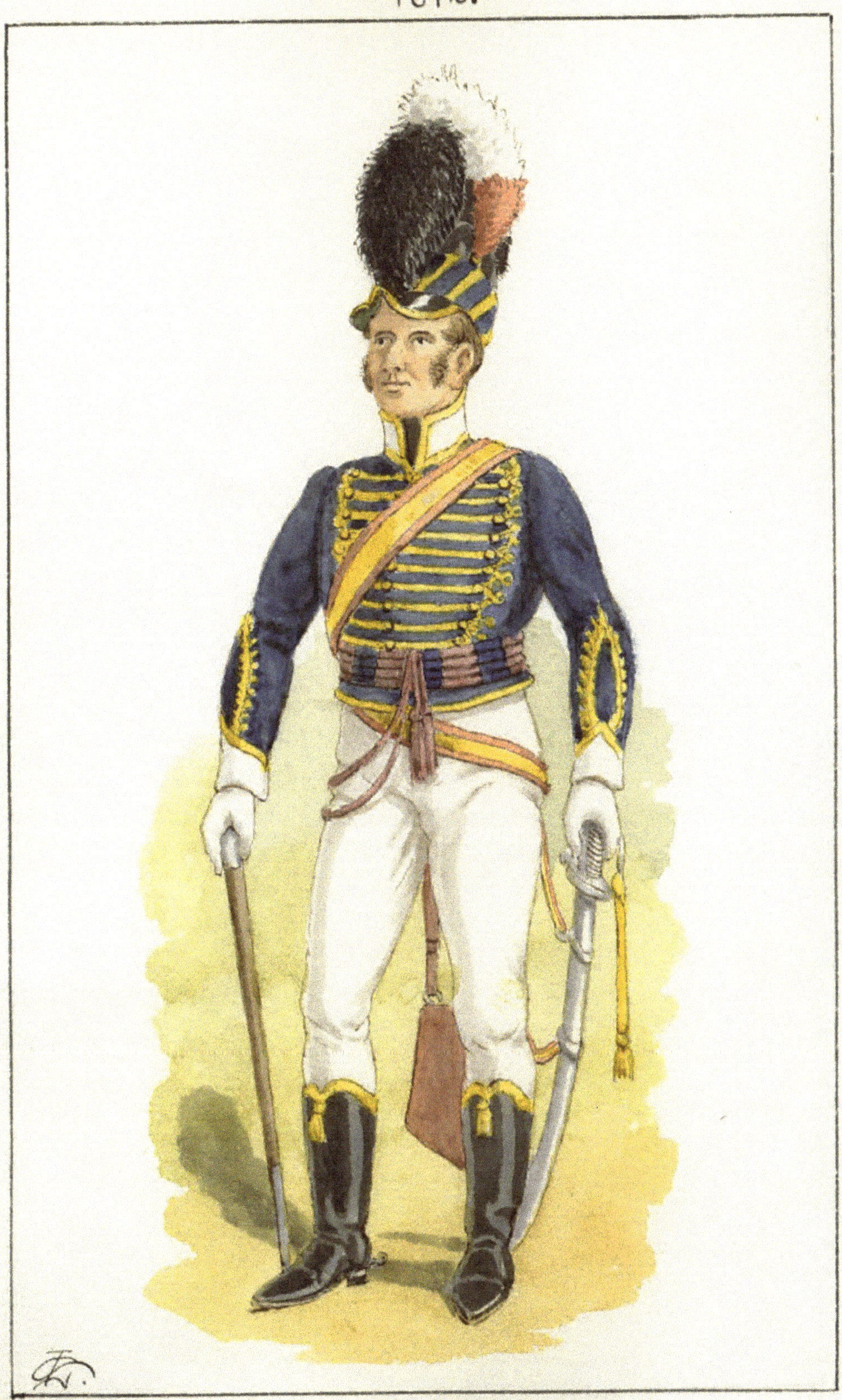

13th Light Dragoons.

106 – 17th LIGHT DRAGOONS, 1812

Here we have the regiment that would become lancers in 1822, their familiar skull and crossbones badge seen here on the sabretache. The same device, which had been adopted in memory of General Wolfe, was also worn at the side of the helmet, but indistinguishable, however, in Charles Lyall's painting. Scarlet coats were originally worn, these later changing to light blue and then dark blue. White facings were on all three. The regiment had gone to India in 1808, where it would remain until 1822.

1812.

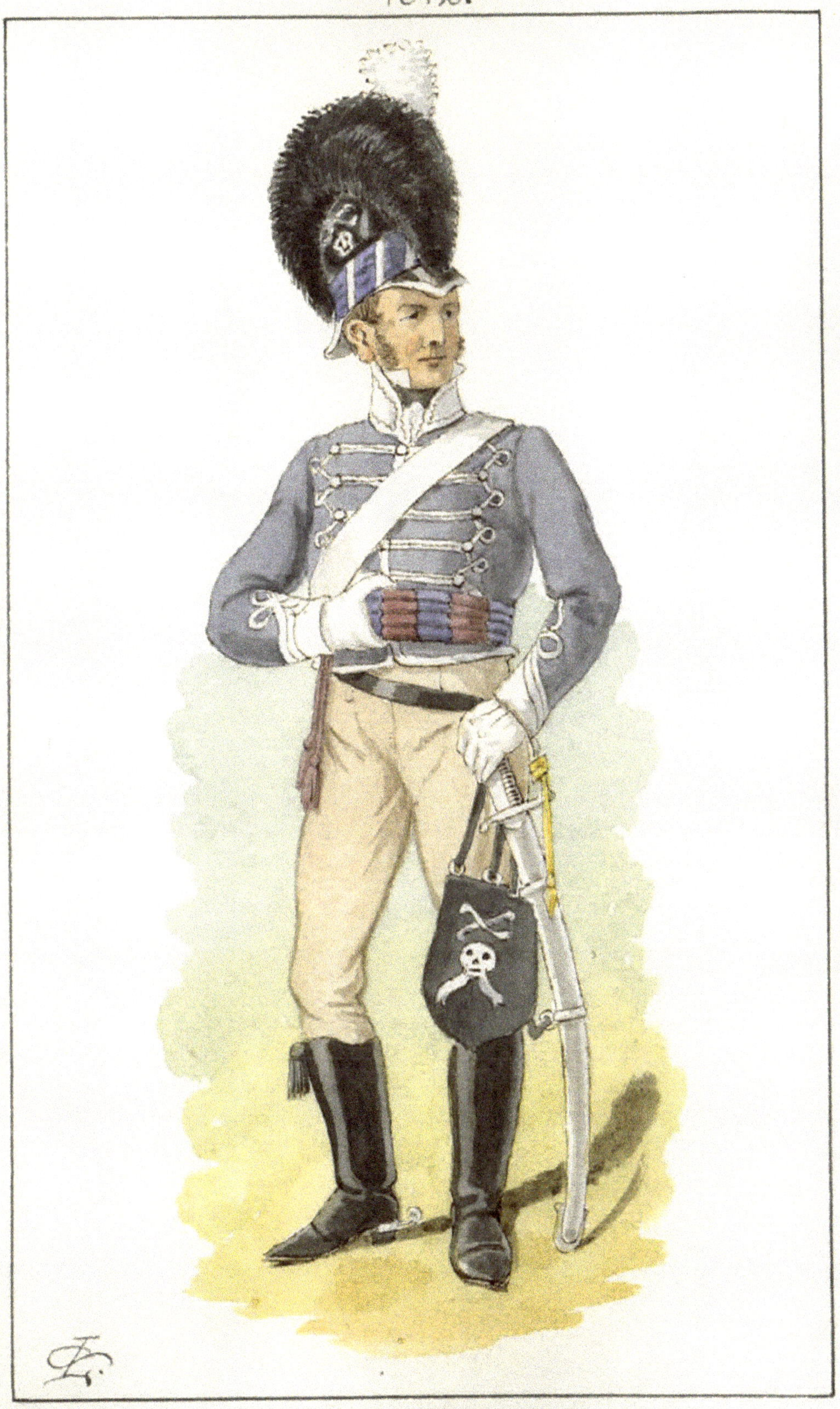

17th Light Dragoons.

107 – 18TH HUSSARS, MUSICIAN, 1812

Charles Lyall's painting of a clarinettist is based on a colour plate after R Wymer included in Colonel Harold Malet's book, *The Historical Memoirs of the XVIIITH Hussars*, published by Simpkin & Co Ltd, London, 1907. That same history tells how in 1805 permission had been obtained to form the regiment (then light dragoons) into a hussar regiment and how in 1812 the 18th was stationed in England. Orders, however, were received on 1 January 1813 to proceed to Portsmouth and embarkation for Portugal.

1812.

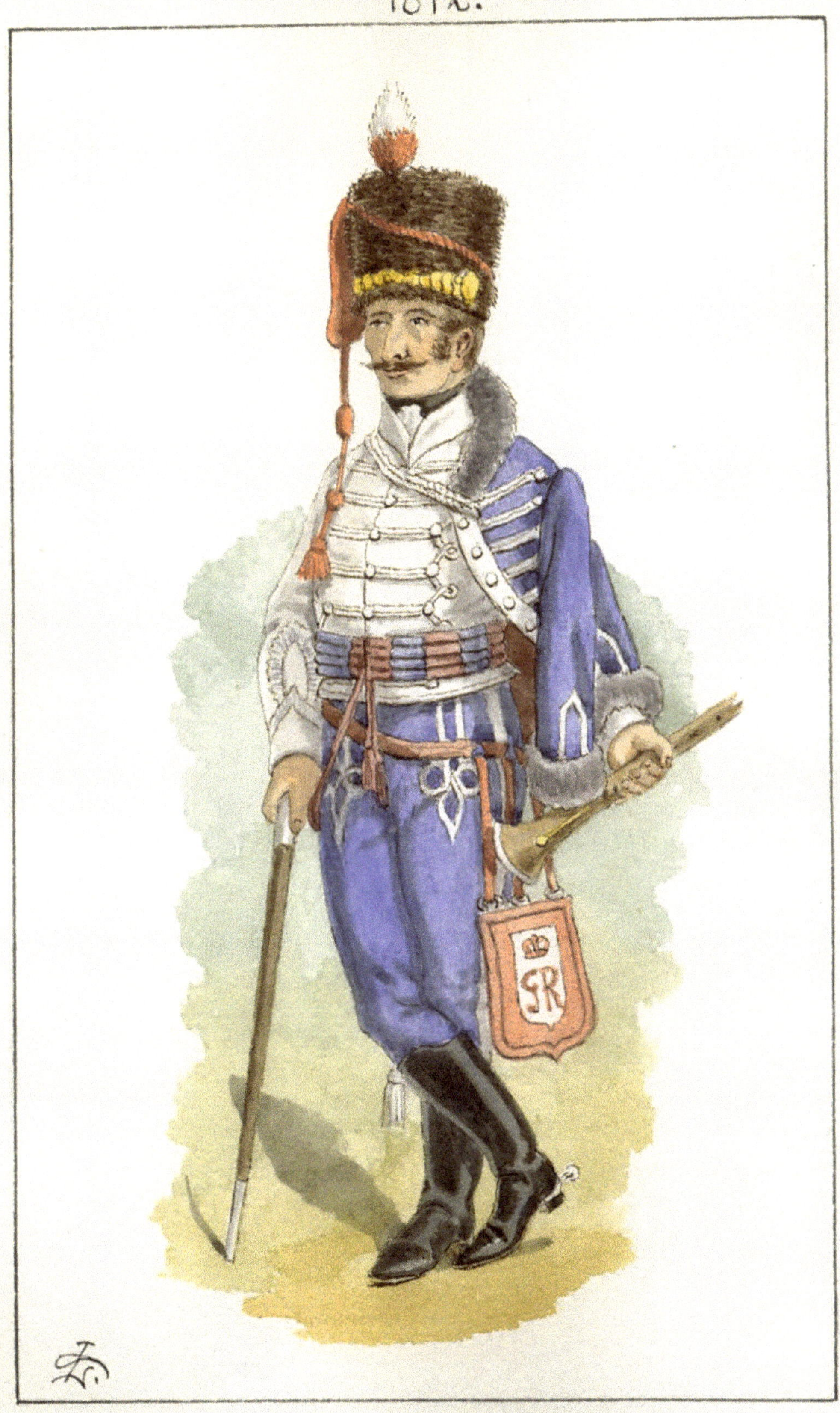

18th Hussars. Musician.

108 – 18th HUSSARS, OFFICER REVIEW ORDER, 1812

The 18th Hussars of this period dates from 1759 when it was raised in Ireland by Charles, 6th Earl of Drogheda. At first known as 19th Light Dragoons—although commonly called Drogheda's Light Horse— re-numbering as 18th came in 1763. Red uniforms with white facings were originally worn, the change to blue taking place in 1782. After service in Portugal, and with the Earl of Drogheda still in command after sixty-two years' service, the regiment was disbanded back in Ireland in 1821.

1812.

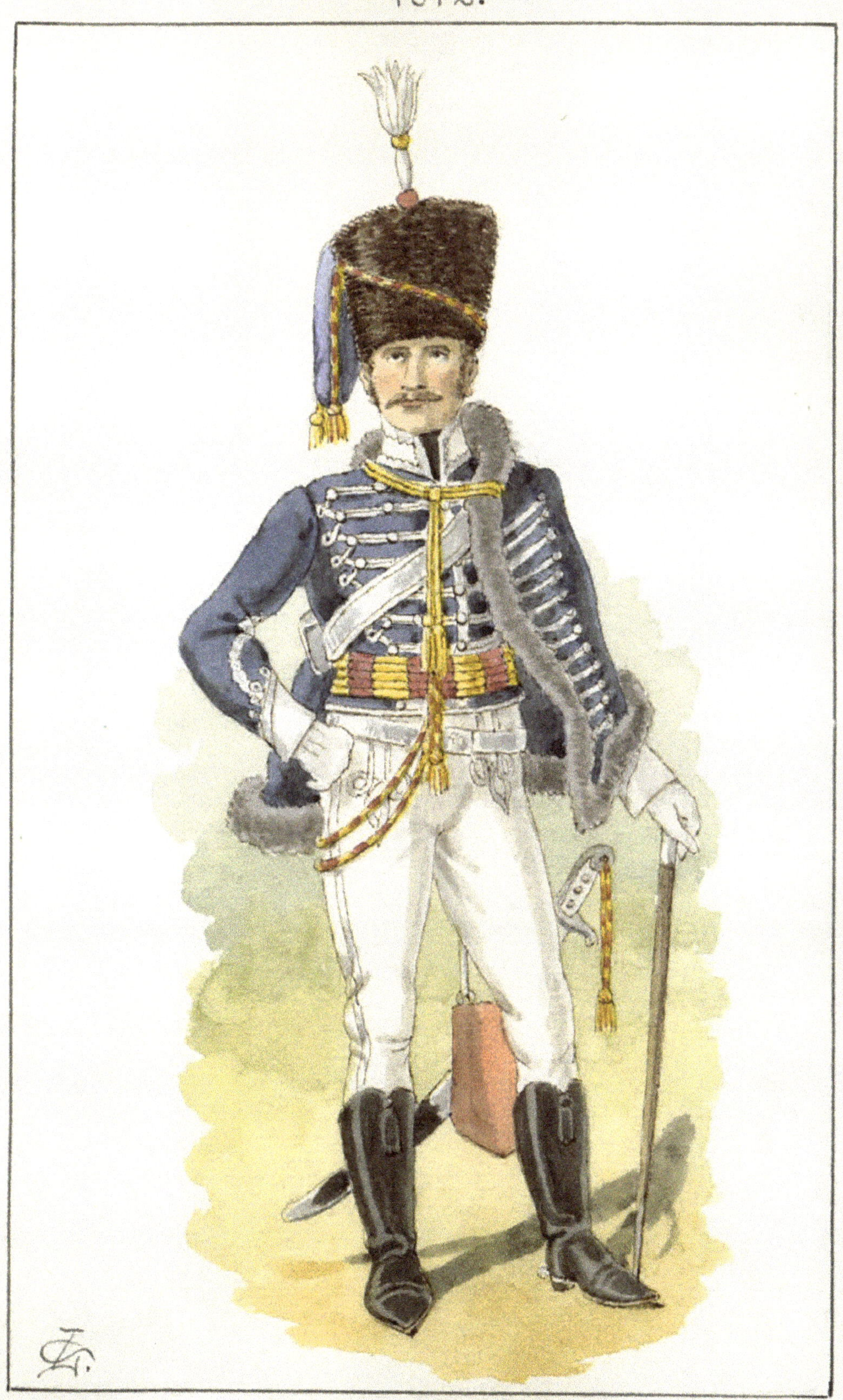

18th Hussars. Officer.
Review order.

109 – 18th HUSSARS, 1812

Charles Lyall shows a private of the regiment enjoying a pipe. The artist's inspiration, a colour plate after R Wymer included in Colonel Harold Malet's book, *The Historical Memoirs of the XVIIITH Hussars*, published by Simpkin & Co Ltd, London, 1907.

1812.

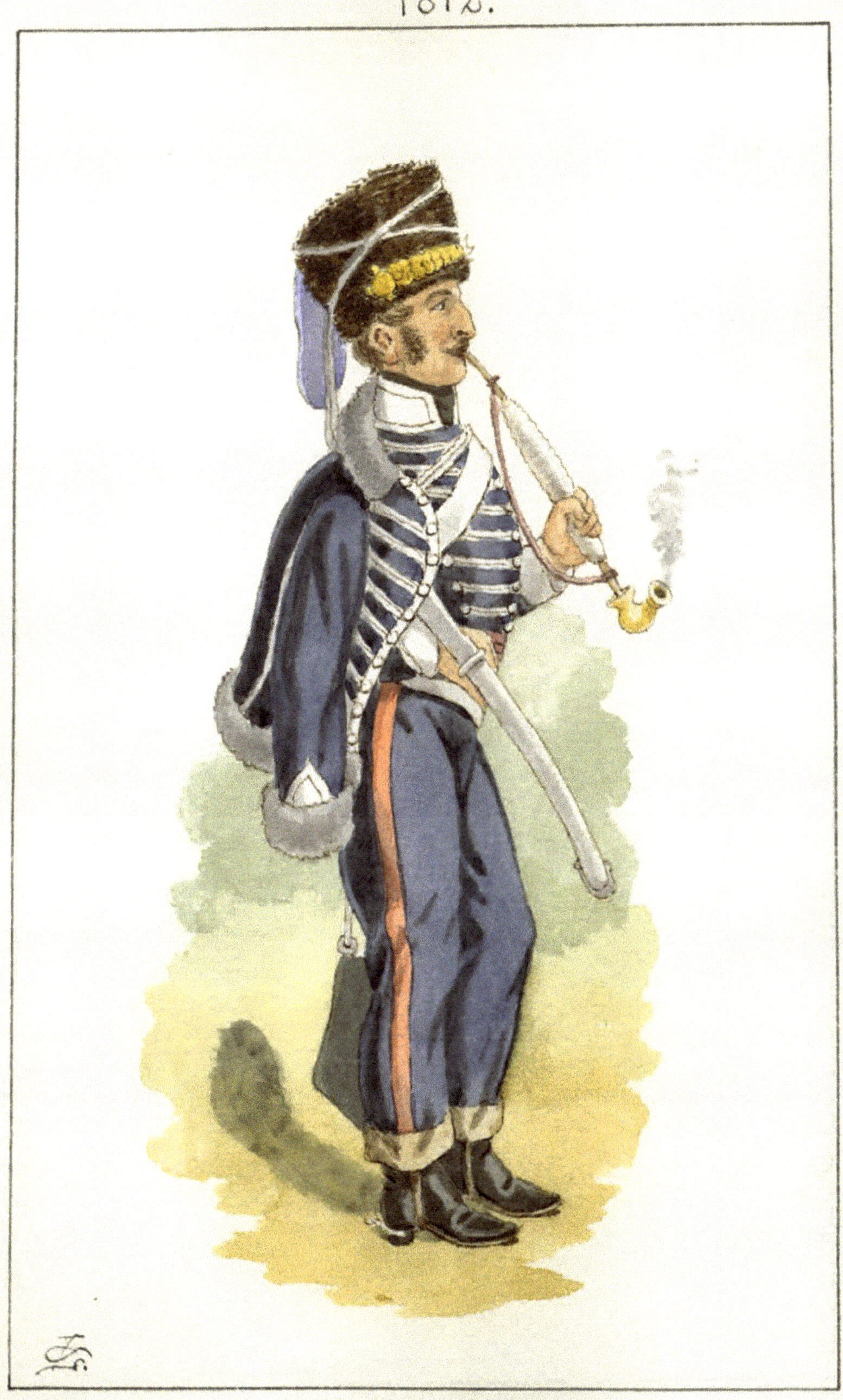

18th Hussars.

110 – ROYAL HORSE ARTILLERY, 1812

Charles Lyall shows an officer of 1812 wearing a fur-crested helmet which has a blue turban, gilt fittings and a tall white-over-red plume on the left side. Captain RJ MacDonald makes the observation that this uniform represents that which was worn for home service. Sword-belts, he notes, were worn by the officers under the jacket, and attached to the sword by slings.

1812.

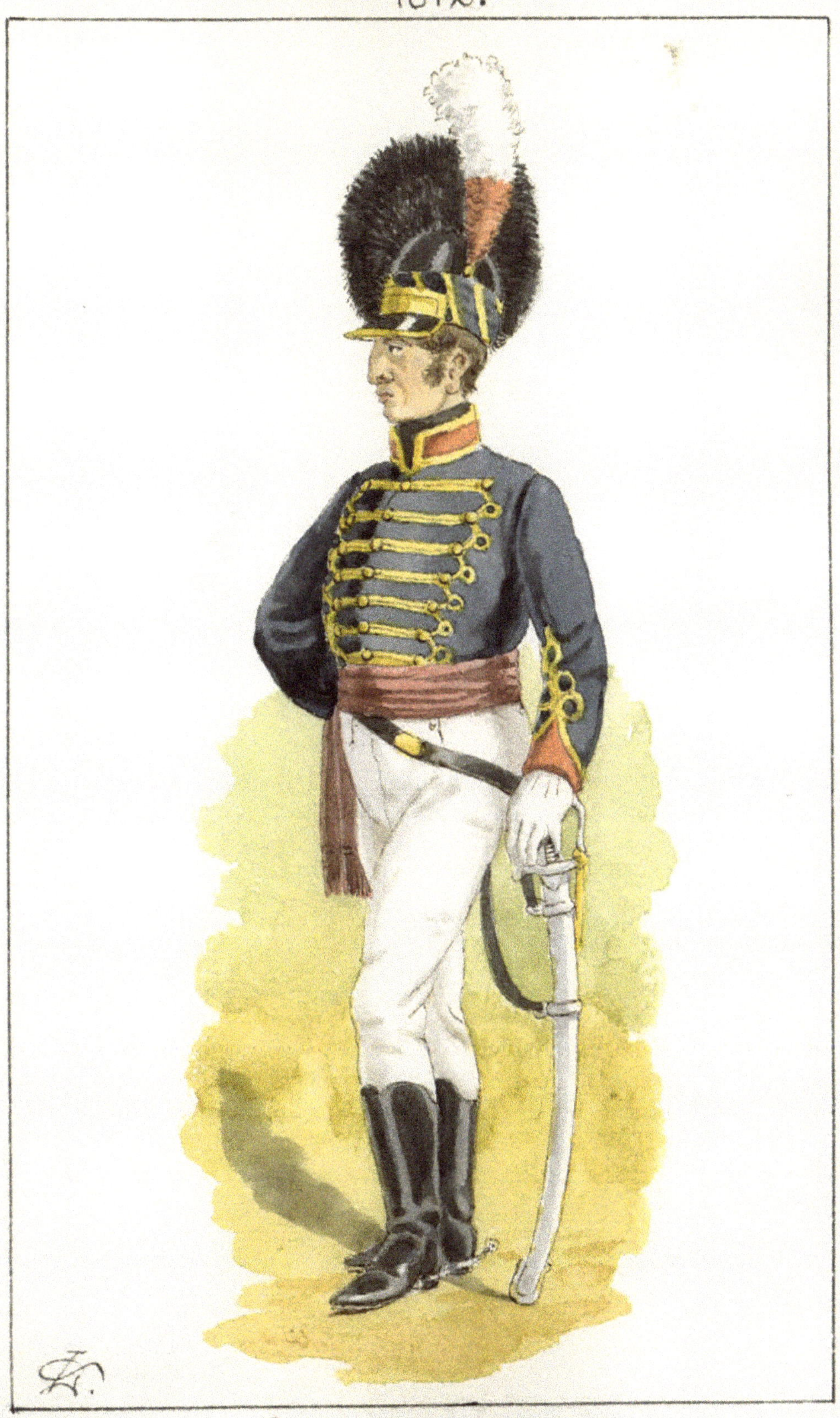

Royal Horse Artillery.

111 – THE FIRST REGIMENT OF FOOT GUARDS, 1812

The year 1812 saw the 1st Foot Guards fighting in the Peninsular campaign and in Holland. Charles Lyall's painting shows an officer, his scarlet jacket being double-breasted with round cuffs and a collar with a 'V' opening. Gold epaulettes are worn with bullion fringes. Note how the white gaiters rise above the knees and are tied with black tapes to hold them in place.

1812.

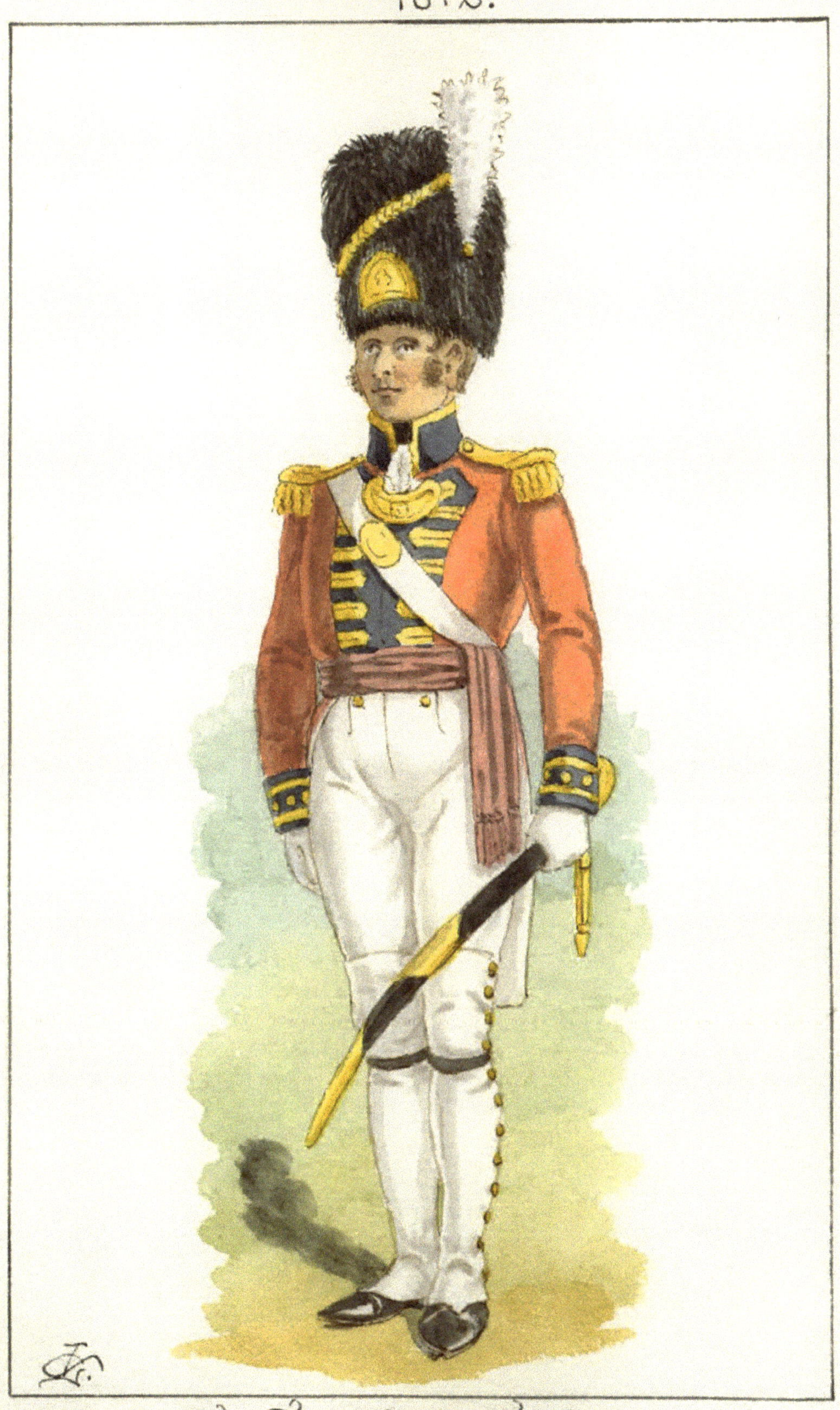

The First Regt. of Foot Guards.

112 – 2nd Coldstream Regiment Foot Guards, 1812

Here we have an officer of the regiment, his double-breasted jacket open at the top to reveal blue lapels edged with gold lace. Worn 'fore and aft', officers had retained their cocked hats although the men were in 1812 wearing the shako.

252

1812.

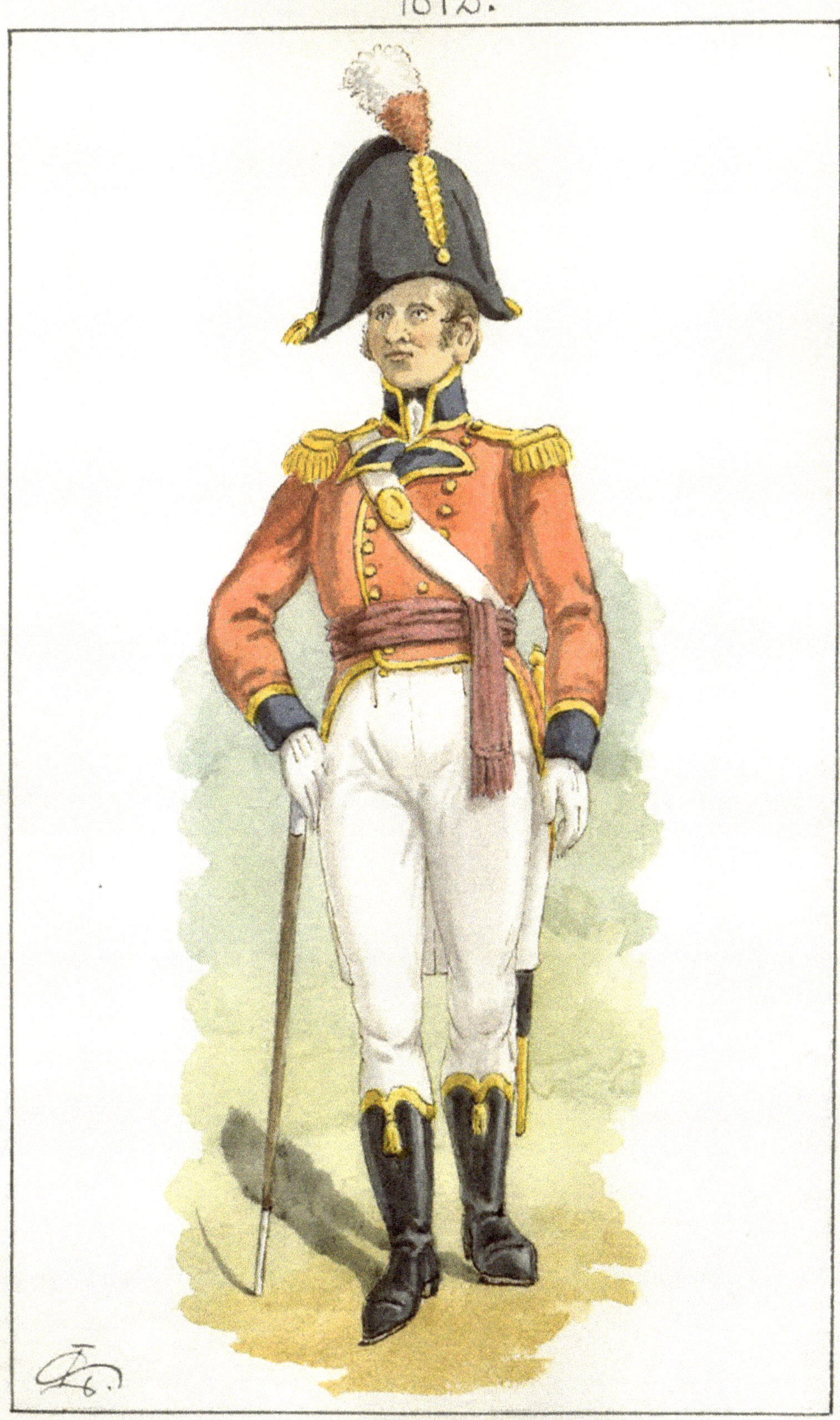

2nd Coldstream Regt. Foot Guards.

113 – 4TH KING'S FOOT, GRENADIER 1812

The regiment was serving in the Peninsular campaign at the time captioned in Charles Lyall's painting. A member of the grenadier company is shown who is identified by his white plume.

1812.

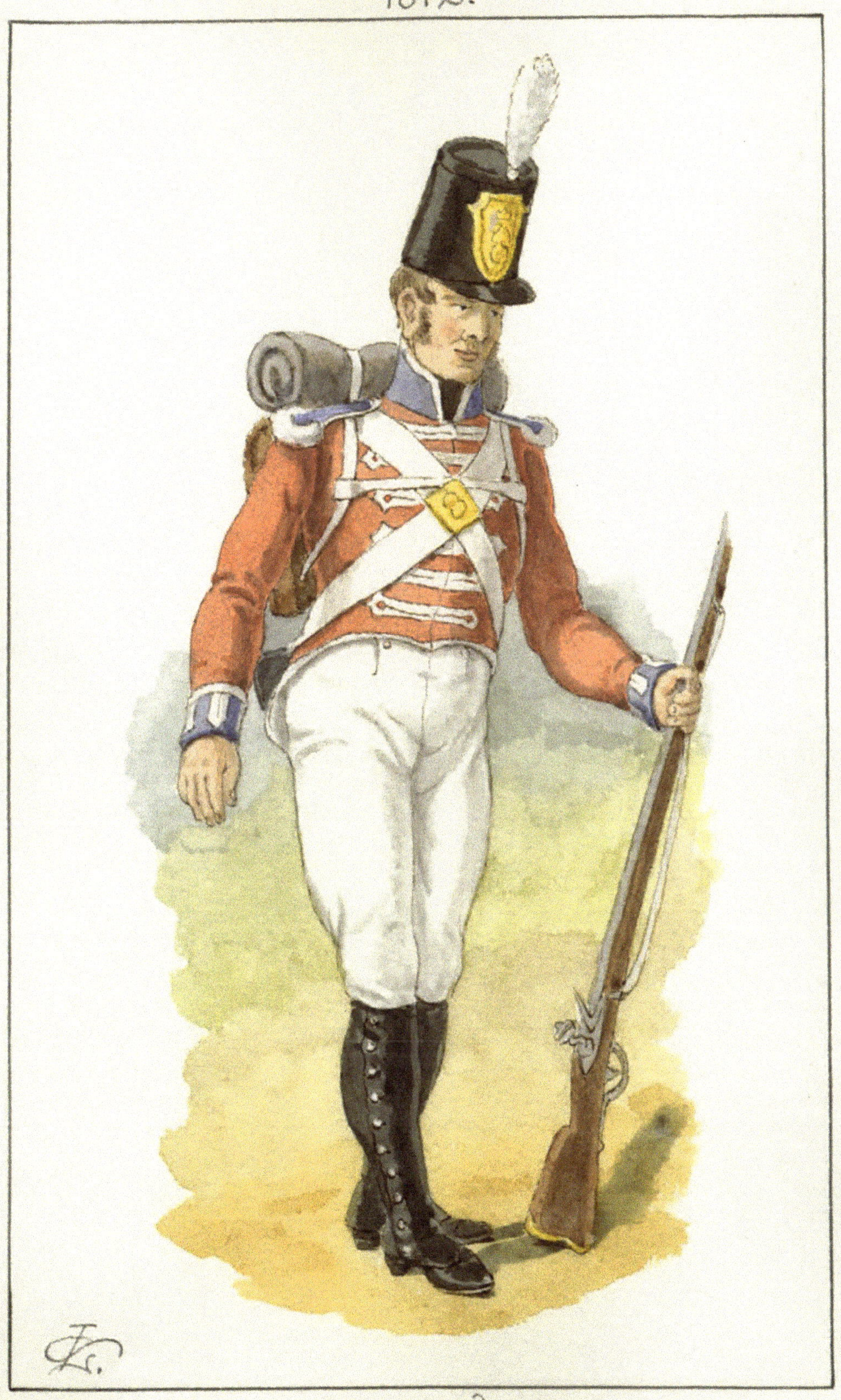

4th King's Foot.
Grenadier.

114 – 9TH BRITANNIA REGIMENT, OFFICER 1812

The officer's headdress here is the shako introduced into the British Army via a Circular Letter dated 18 March 1812 and often referred to as the 'Waterloo' shako. Although special badges were permitted, such as the Britannia device of the 9th Regiment, these would have usually appeared within a standard crowned, shield-shape, plate and not alone as depicted by Charles Lyall. The 9th were present during the siege of Badajoz in March and April 1812 and saw action at Salamanca on the following 22 July. The winter of 1812-13 was spent on the Portuguese border.

1812.

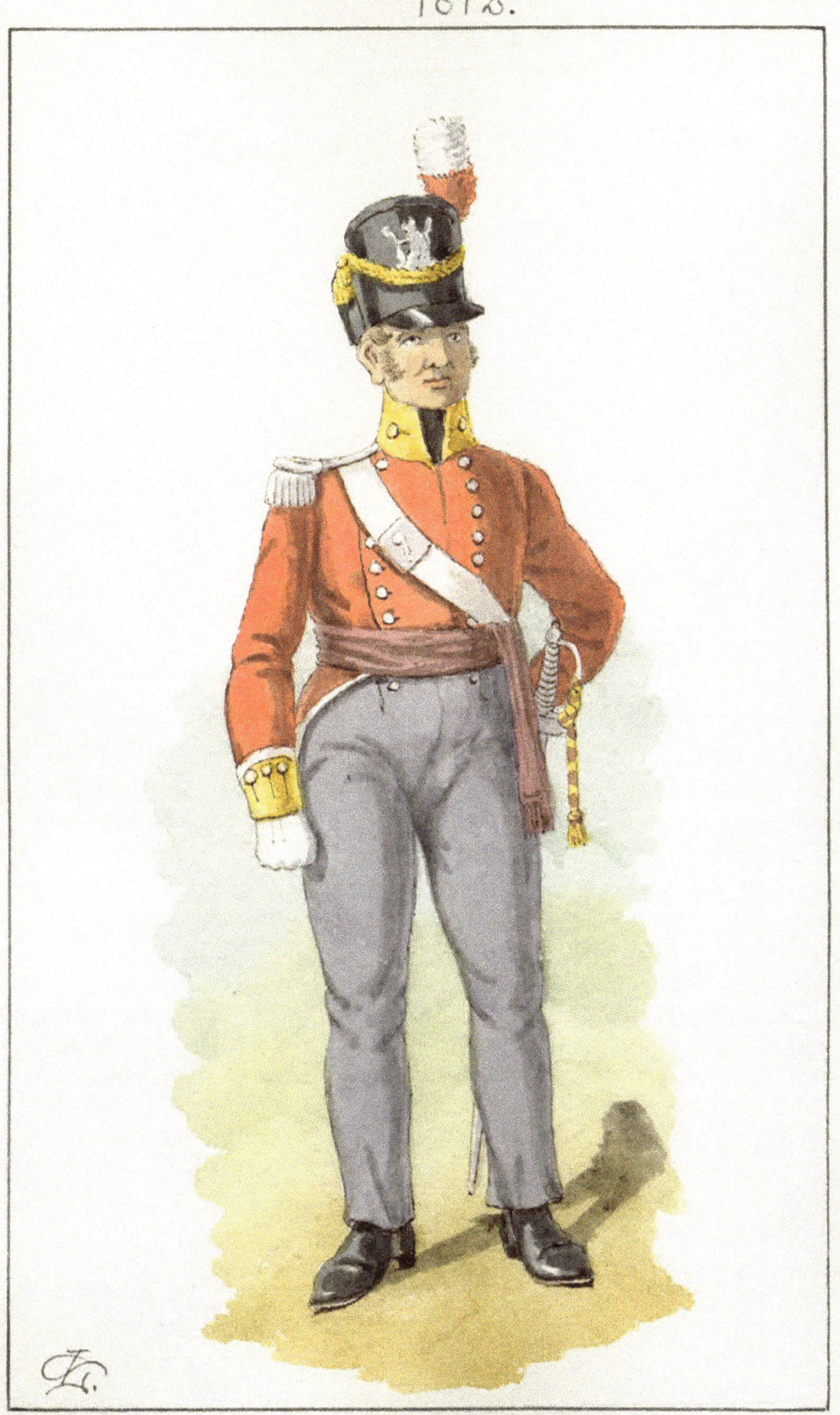

9th Britania Regt.
Officer.

115 – 25TH REGIMENT KING'S OWN BORDERERS, OFFICER 1812

Authorised in 1805 was the title 25th (The King's Own Borderers) Regiment of Foot and with this royal association came the blue facings seen in Charles Lyall's painting of an officer. A deep yellow had been worn since the regiment's formation in 1689. In 1812 the 25th was stationed in the West Indies.

1812.

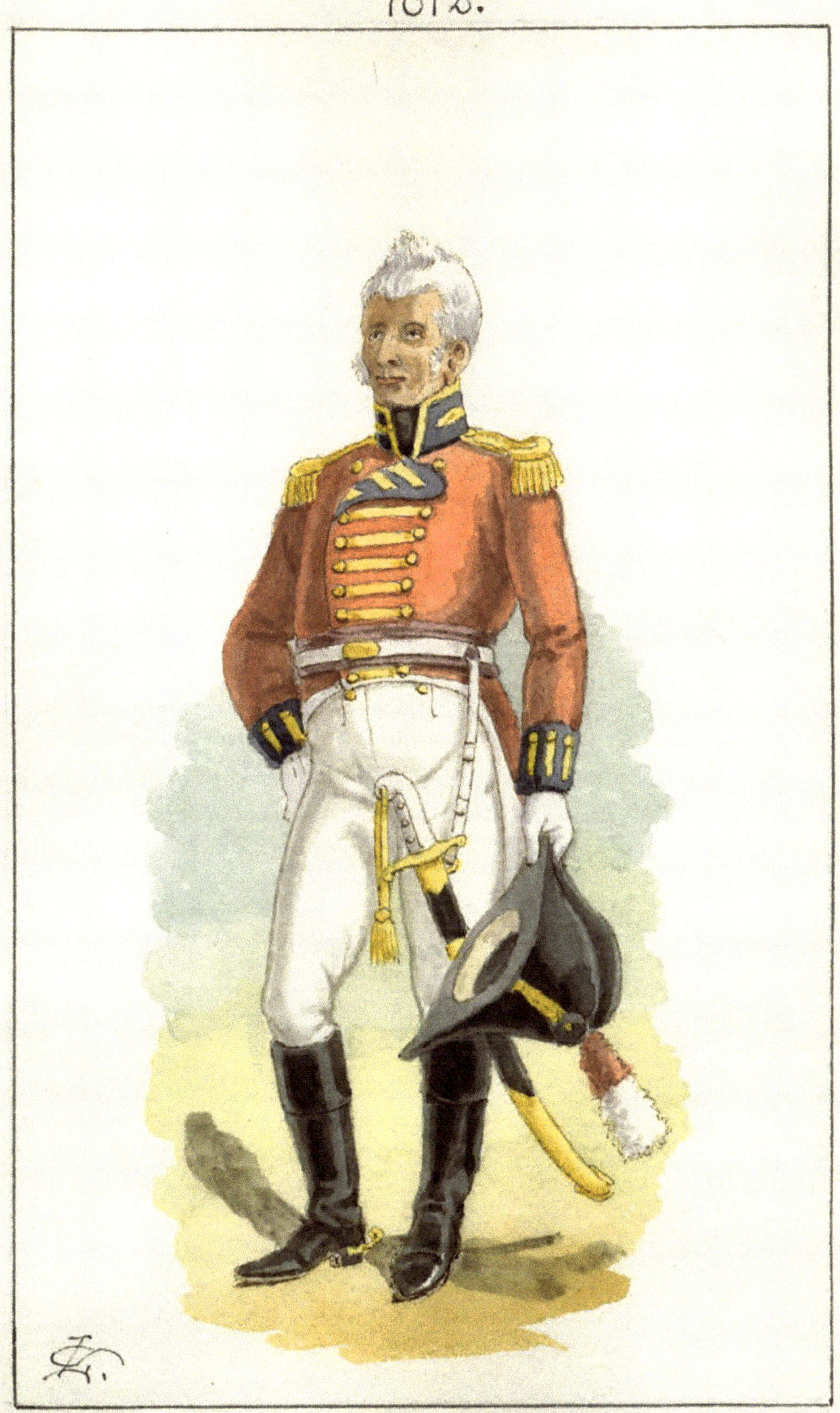

25th. Regt. King's Own Borderers.
Officer.

116 – 43RD REGIMENT LIGHT INFANTRY, 1812

The full title of the regiment in 1812 was the 43rd (Monmouthshire Light Infantry), a designation that was held until becoming the 1st Battalion of the Oxfordshire Light Infantry in 1881. Ian Fletcher records in his book *Wellington's Regiments The Men and Their Battles 1808-1815* how the 1st Battalion of the 43rd had arrived in Portugal just in time to take part in the battle of Vimeiro on 21 August 1808. The 2nd/43rd, raised at Worcester in November 1804, had also arrived in the Peninsular and both battalions were to serve under Sir John Moore.

257

1812.

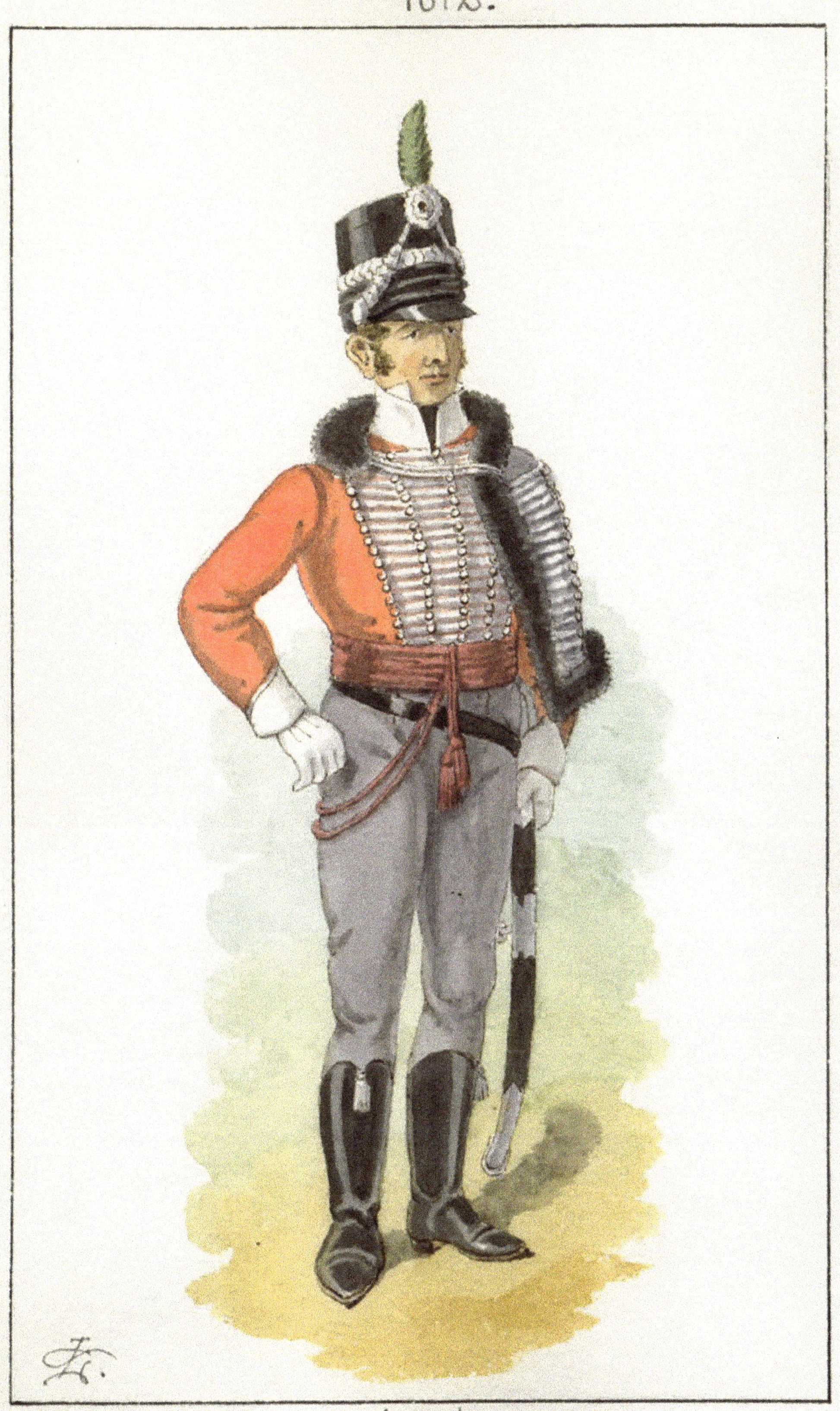

43rd. Regt.
Light Infantry.

117 – 79TH CAMERON HIGHLANDERS, 1812

The 79th dates from 1793, Charles Lyall showing an officer of the regiment around the time of the Peninsular War. The green facings worn had been in use since formation, changing only when a royal connection was established in 1873, the regiment that year changing its title to 79th Queen's Own Cameron Highlanders. Lyall's figure is shown with a dirk at his right side which hangs from a special belt. The two gilt bands at the centre of the weapon cover holders for a small knife and fork. In the left hand, a traditional Scottish basket hilted broadsword.

1812.

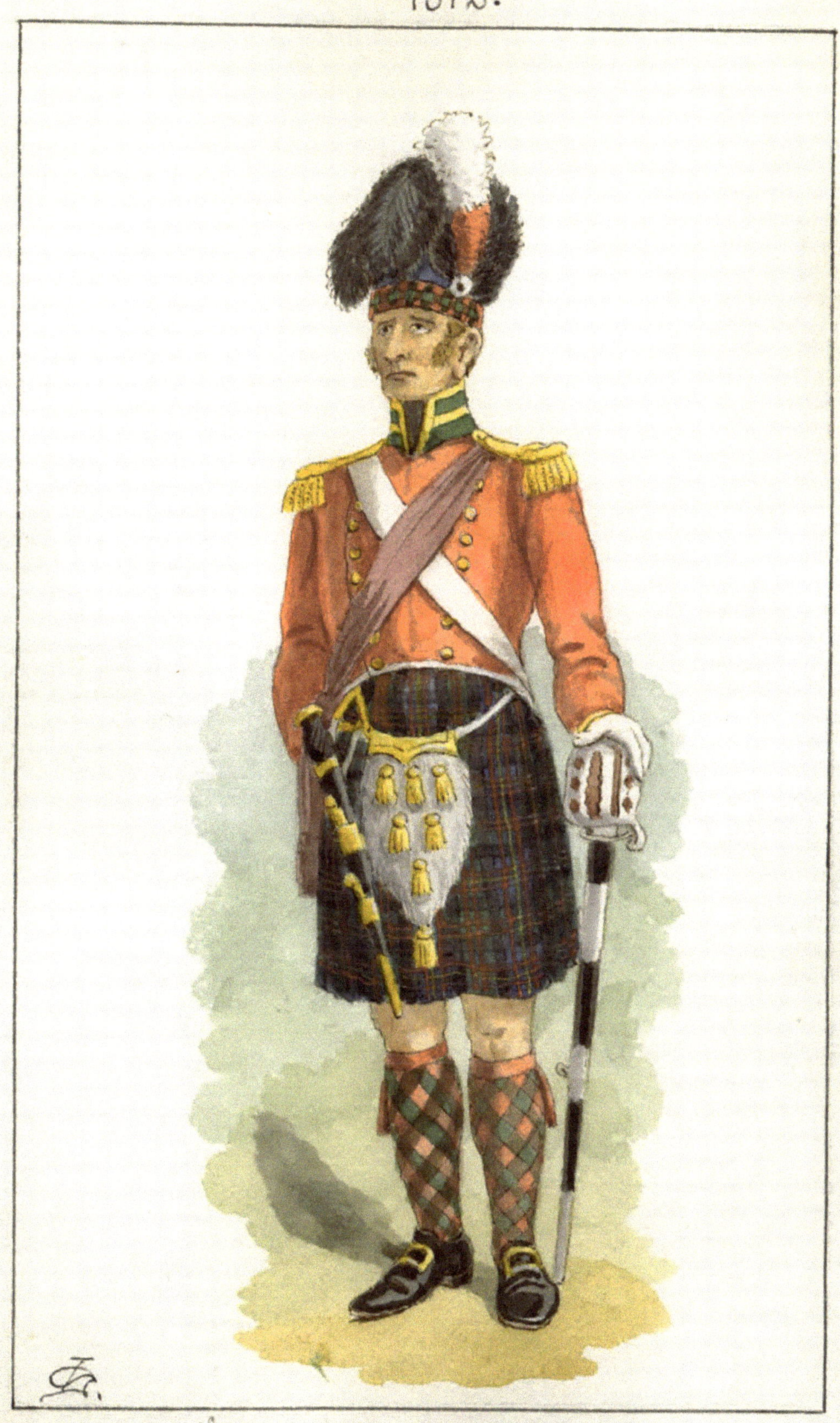

79th Cameron Highlanders.

118 – 87TH OR PRINCE OF WALES'S OWN IRISH REGIMENT, OFFICER 1812

The 87th comprised two battalions in 1812, the 1st at the time being part of the garrison on the island of Mauritius. Raised in 1804 from Irish recruits, the 2nd Battalion left England for Guernsey in 1807 where it remained until returning in 1808. Having been ordered overseas, the 2nd/87th arrived at Lisbon on 12 March 1809, serving during the Peninsular Campaign until returning home on 7 July 1814. Charles Lyall is content to illustrate the officer's sword-belt plate with a simple '87'. Major HG Parkyn, however, records that in about 1812-1815 an oblong plate was introduced which had the design in silver of an eagle surmounted by the Prince of Wales's coronet, plume and motto. The new plate also included the numerals '87', a harp and the recently authorised battle honour 'Barrosa'.

1812.

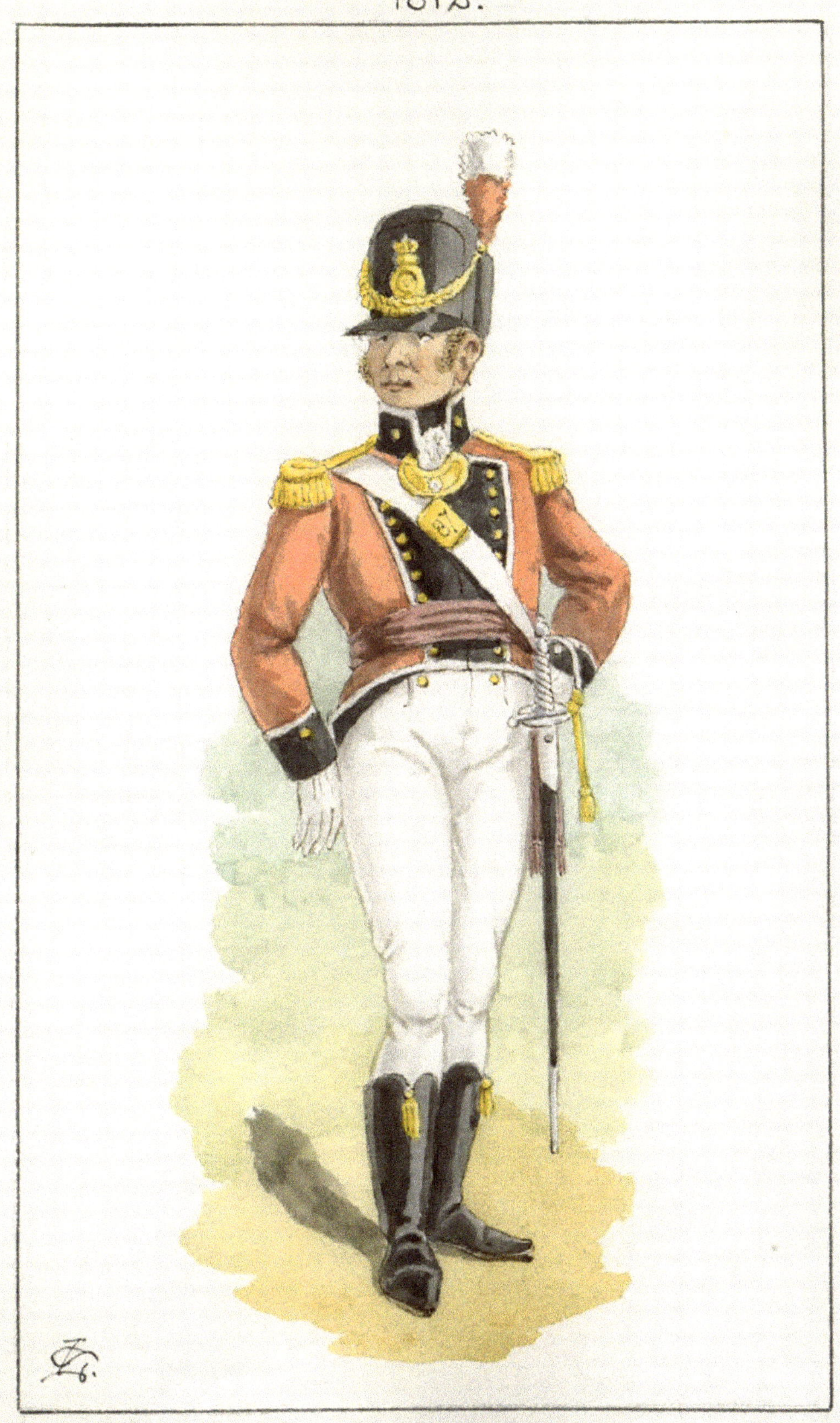

87th or Prince of Wales's own Irish Regt.
Officer.

119 – RIFLEMAN, 95TH REGIMENT 1812

It would not be until 1816 that this regiment exchanged the numerical designation assigned to it in 1803 for the title Rifle Brigade. Ian Fletcher reminds us that the 95th was 'Perhaps the most famous British regiment of the period,' and that it had '…served throughout the entire Peninsular campaign, fighting in almost every major battle from Roliça to Toulouse.' Charles Lyall's painting clearly shows the stringed bugle horn badge worn by the regiment on its shakos. And of course, the famous green jackets with their black facings.

1812.

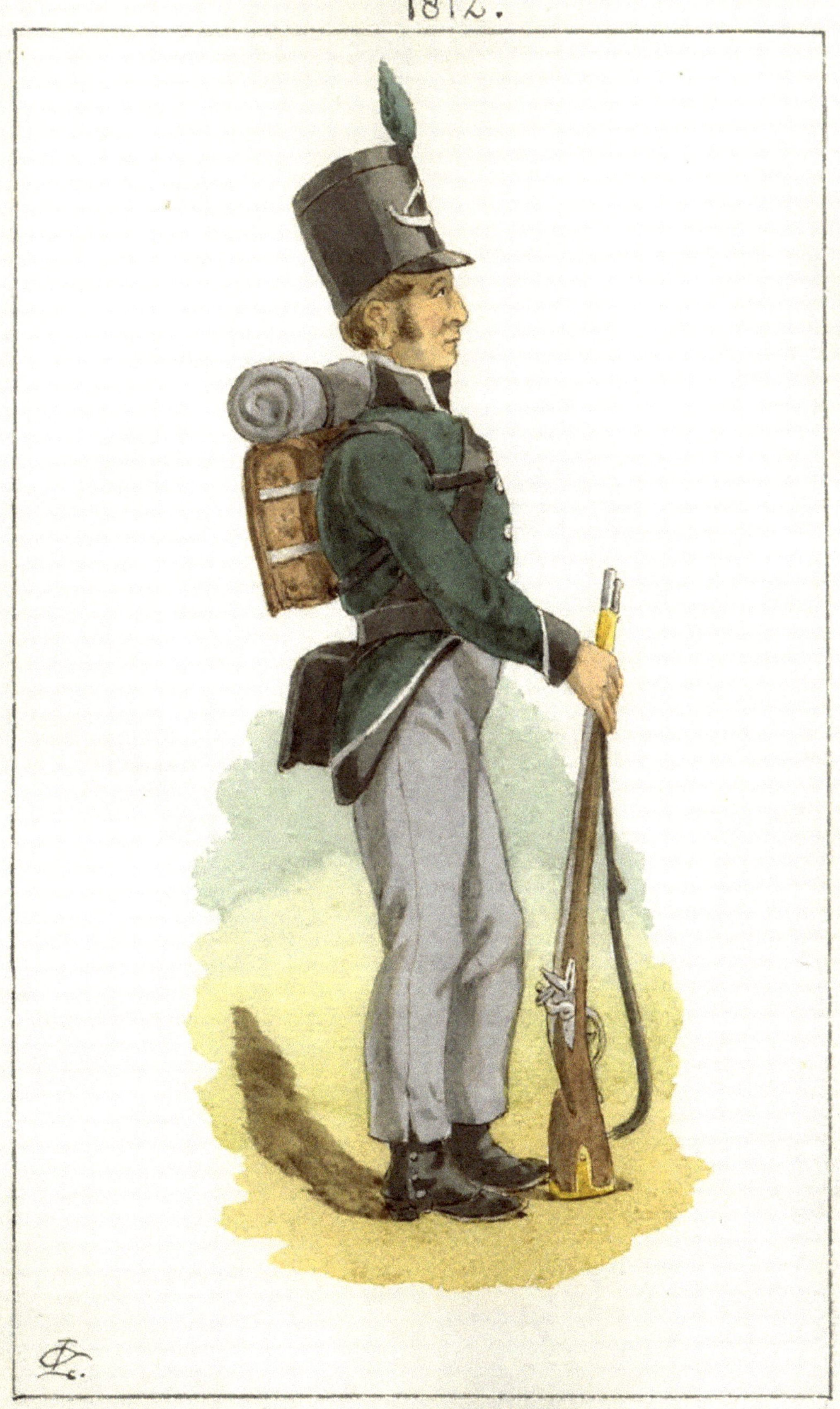

Rifleman. 95th Regt.

120 – 95TH OR RIFLE CORPS, OFFICER 1812

Since the formation of the Rifle Corps in 1800, officers were dressed very much in the style of light dragoons, Charles Lyall's painting of 1812 showing a fur-topped headdress with green plume and turban, tight pantaloons with piping down the front and a dark green pelisse trimmed with black fur. As with the previous plate, the facings are black.

1812.

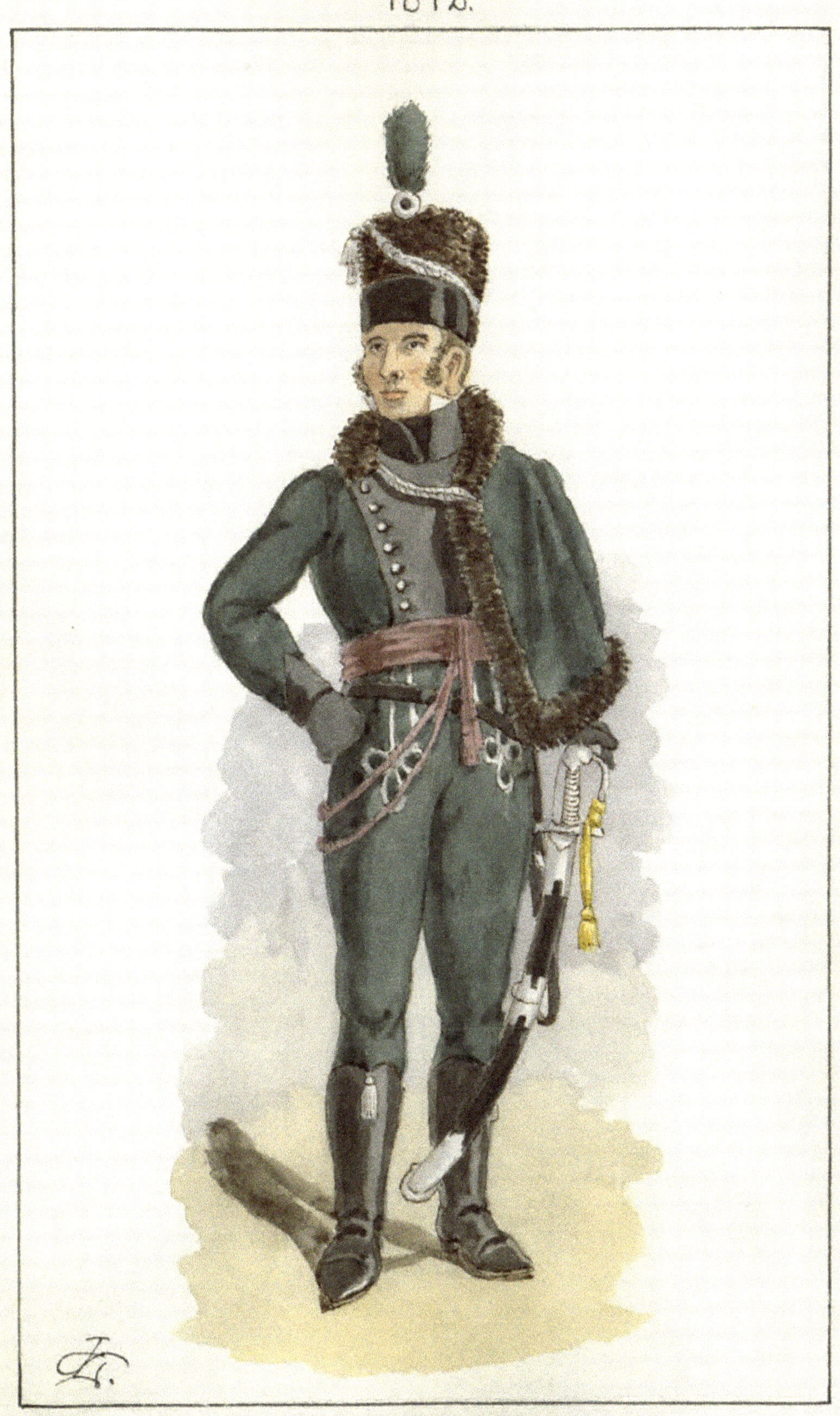

95th. or Rifle Corps.
Officer.

SOURCES OF INFORMATION

Carman, WY, *A Dictionary of Military Uniform*, BT Batsford Ltd, London, 1877.

Carman, WY, Richard Simkin's *Uniforms of the British Army, The Cavalry Regiments*, Webb & Bower, Exeter, 1982.

Carman, WY, Richard Simkin's *Uniforms of the British Army, The Infantry Regiments*, Webb & Bower, Exeter, 1985.

Connolly, TWJ, *The History of the Corps of Royal Sappers and Miner*, Longman, Brown & Green, London, 1855.

Fletcher, Ian, *Wellington's Regiments, The Men and Their Battles 1808-1815*, BCA, London, 1994.

Kipling Arthur L, and Hugh L King, *Head-dress Badges of the British Army Volume 1*, Frederick Muller Ltd, London, 1973.

Lawson, Cecil CP, *A History of the Uniforms of the British Army*, five volumes by several publishers, 1940-1966.

Leslie, NB, *The Succession of Colonels of the British Army From 1660 to the Present Day*, Society for Army Historical Research, 1974.

Parkyn, Major HG, *(Military) Shoulder-Belt Plates and Buttons*, Gale & Polden, Aldershot, 1956.

MacDonald, RJ, *The History of the Dress of the Royal Regiment of Artillery, 1625-1897*, Henry Sotheran & Co, London, 1899.

BELLANGÉS'S SOLDIERS OF THE FRENCH REPUBLIC AND THE EMPIRE 1795-1814

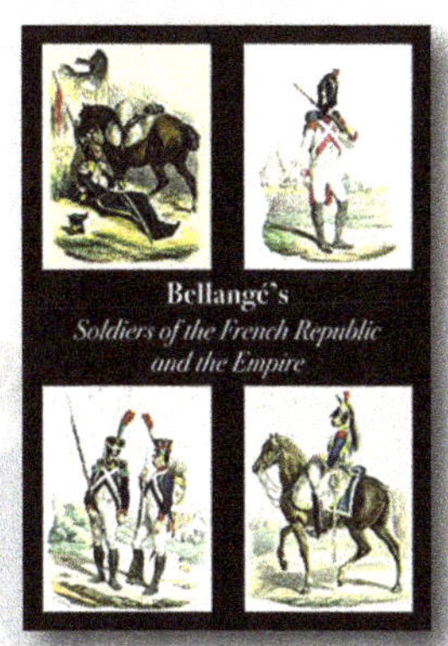

Taken from the first German translation of 'Histoire de l'empereur Napoleon' (1840), that was enlarged for this edition with six new illustrations.

Bellangés's fifty detailed and brightly coloured uniform plates present the soldiers of the different regiments of the French Republic and the Empire in their respective costumes.

9781783318414

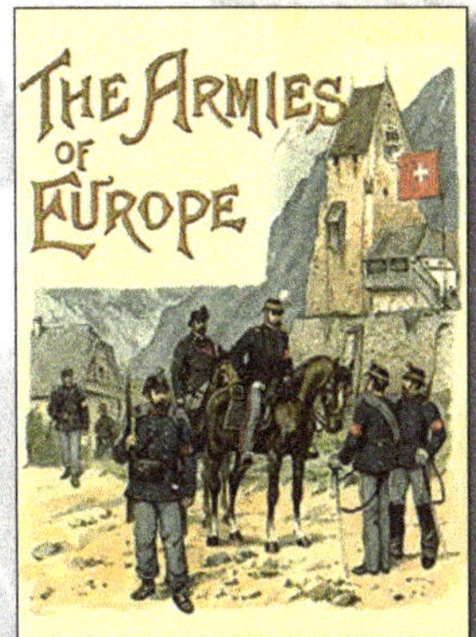

Richard Knötel's ARMIES OF EUROPE ILLUSTRATED (1890)

Classic descriptions complete with colour plates and vignettes by the renowned military artist and pioneer of the study of military uniform Richard Knötel, covering the armies of: The British Empire – The German Army – Austria-Hungary – Italy – France – Russia – Denmark, Sweden and Norway – Spain and Portugal – Switzerland – Holland and Belgium – Turkey and the States of the Balkan Peninsula.

9781783311750

CHARLES HAMILTON SMITH'S COSTUME OF THE ARMY OF THE BRITISH EMPIRE – ACCORDING TO THE 1814 REGULATIONS

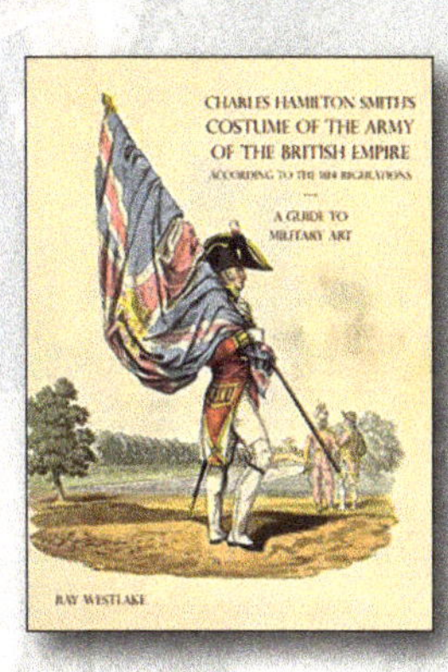

This is a full reissuing of the 60 hand-coloured aquatint plates by I.C. Stadler, after drawings by Smith, originally produced in 1815 for the oldest commercial art gallery in the world, Colnaghi and Co. Paul Colnaghi became the official print-seller to the Prince Regent, and he was asked to organise the Royal Collection, receiving a Royal Warrant when the Prince Regent became George IV. Uniquely, many of Smith's uncoloured original drawings are also included in this edition.

9781783319916

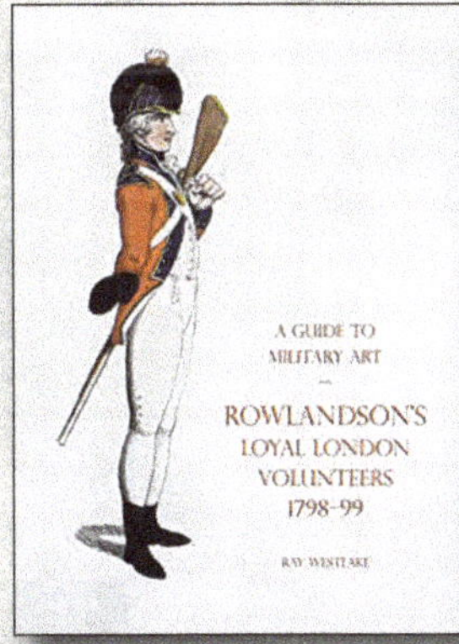

ROWLANDSON'S LOYAL LONDON VOLUNTEERS

The most original set of English military plates from the Napoleonic period – The Loyal Volunteers of London & Environs, Infantry & Cavalry, in their respective uniforms. Representing the whole of the Manual, Platoon & Funeral Exercise in 89 plates. Designed and etched by T. Rowlandson and originally published in London during 1798-99 by Ackermann. Reproduced here from high from an original volume is a full set of Rowlandson's 87 plates, together with an additional two that were to be included in some (even scarcer) bound volumes by the publisher. To accompany each plate, Ackermann prepared a page of letterpress which included details of when the corps had been formed, its uniform and names of officers. That text has been reproduced in full, together with additional notes prepared by Ray Westlake.

9781783318889

www.naval-military-press.com

MAJOR LOVETT'S MILITARY DRESS AND FIELD UNIFORMS OF THE RAJ

During the Years Leading up to the Great War

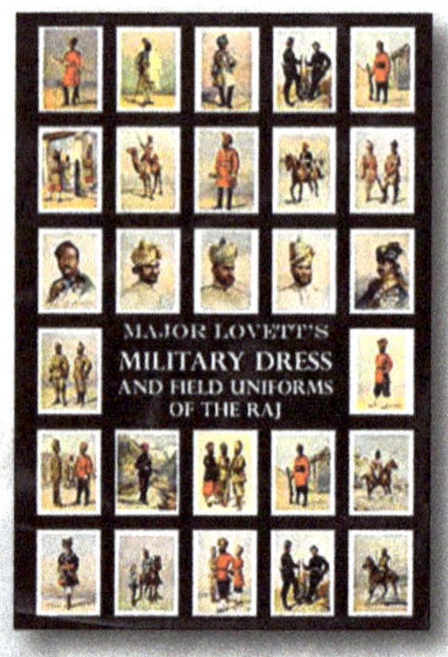

Classic representation of the British Indian Army at the height of the English Age of Empire, in 72 superb uniform plates. This is an invaluable work for anyone interested in the Indian armies and their military uniforms.

9781474536363

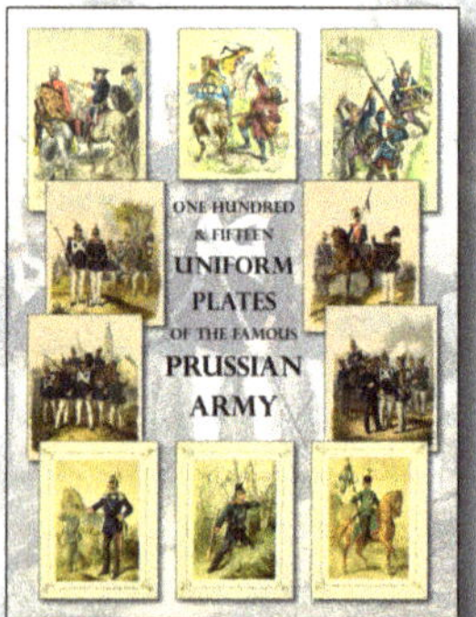

ONE HUNDRED AND FIFTEEN UNIFORM PLATES OF THE FAMOUS PRUSSIAN ARMY UNDER FREDERICK THE GREAT, FREDERICK WILLIAM IV AND PRINCE REGENT WILHELM: OMNIBUS EDITION

This is a compilation omnibus edition of three colourful 19th century military costume plate editions, detailing the Pre-Unification Prussian Army 1751-1855 in accurately hand-coloured facsimile images. Lively commentary from expert Ray Westlake on each plate enhances their historical usefulness.

9781474537551

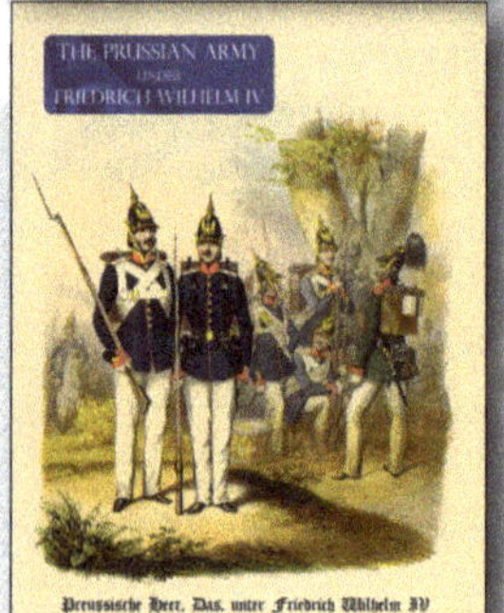

PRUSSIAN ARMY (UNIFORM) UNDER FREDRICH WIHELM IV

PREUSSISCHE HEER, DAS, UNTER FRIEDRICH WILHELM IV

An excellent visual presentation of the Prussian Army and their uniforms under the Kaiser Friedrich Wilhelm IV. Series of 36 facsimile numbered contemporary hand-coloured lithographs. This is a colourful series of military costume plates with over 200 military figures in their 'natural surroundings': camping, in battle, on horseback, on the march, etc.

9781474537582

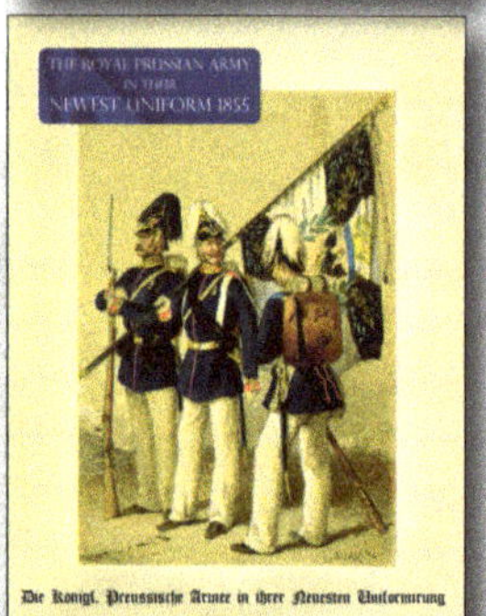

ROYAL PRUSSIAN ARMY IN THEIR NEWEST UNIFORM 1855

DIE KÖNIGL. PREUSSISCHE ARMEE IN IHRER NEUESTEN UNIFORMIRUNG

The beautiful plates depict the various uniforms of the Prussian Army as defined by the 1855 regiment. The work comprises 48 facsimile hand-coloured tinted lithographic plates of military uniforms, each mounted within a lithographed border incorporating the crowned initials of the Prussian king. A small title strip is at the bottom of each leaf, identifying the plate. Mitscher & Röstell, 1859.

9781474537582

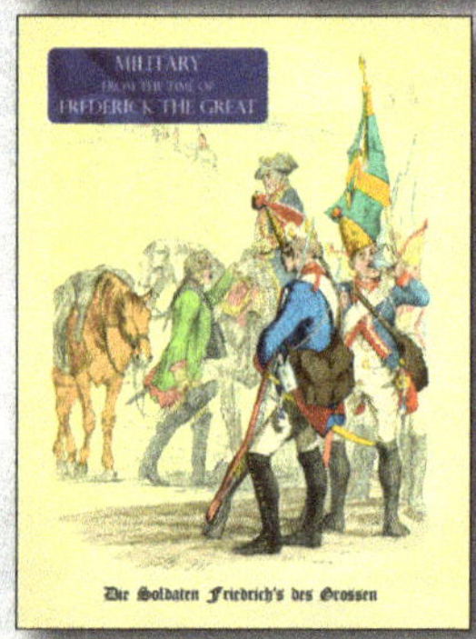

MILITARY (UNIFORM) FROM THE TIME OF FREDERICK THE GREAT

DIE SOLDATEN FRIEDRICH'S DES GROSSEN

Thirty excellent and accurately coloured plates of the uniforms of different Prussian regiments under Frederick the Great by wood engraver Eduard Kretzschmar (1807-1858) and illustrator Adolf von Menzel (1815-1905).

9781474537575

www.naval-military-press.com

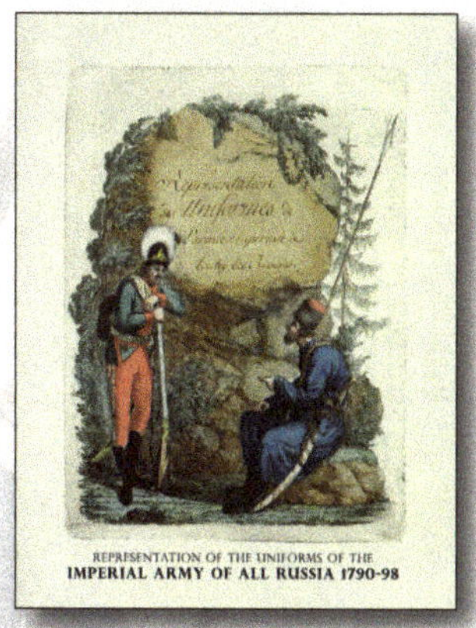

REPRESENTATION OF THE UNIFORMS OF THE IMPERIAL ARMY OF ALL RUSSIA 1790-98

Christian Gottfried Heinrich Geissler, draughtsman and etcher, produced this fine and important series of Russian military costumes when he spent the years 1790 to 1798 serving as the expedition artist with the Prussian zoologist and botanist Peter Simon Pallas, on his travels in the Caucasus and southern Russia.

9781474538275

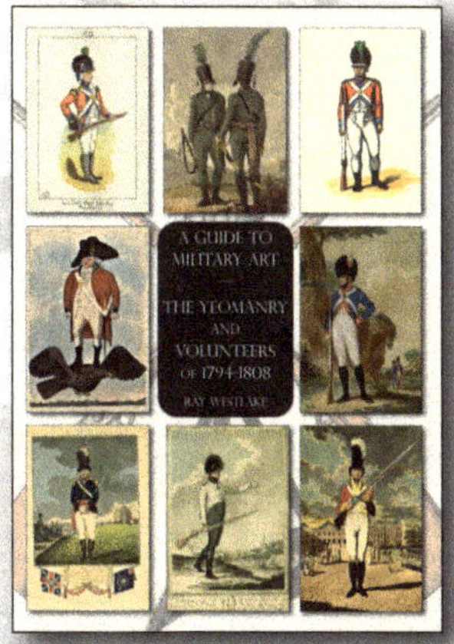

A GUIDE TO MILITARY ART – THE YEOMANRY AND VOLUNTEERS OF 1794-1808

The Volunteer Corps and their mounted component the Yeomanry Cavalry were a voluntary part-time organisation for the purpose of home defence in the event of invasion, during the French Revolutionary and Napoleonic Wars.

The Corps typically drew its members from the propertied classes. Officers were usually members of the gentry and the enlisted ranks tended to be from the lower middle classes. The failed Expédition d'Irlande of 1796 and invasion at Fishguard caused the expansion of the corps, including the formation of workplace units in which the enlisted ranks were filled by the workmen and the officers were drawn from the clerks and foremen. Such units, made up of working-class men, became more common in the late 1790s and early 1800s due to the increased fear of invasion.

9781474538305

A GUIDE TO MILITARY ART – THE VOLUNTEER, 1859-1908

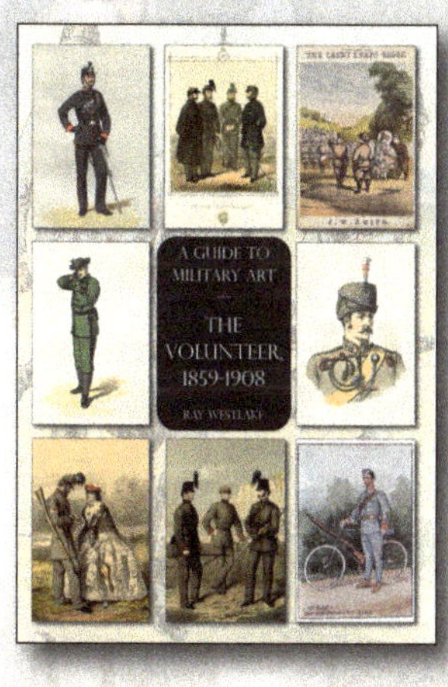

102 manly colour plates taken from various contemporary sources, illustrating the many and varied uniforms of The British Volunteer Force 1859-1908. This part-time military force which came into being to meet the mid-nineteenth century fear of French invasion. It survived and grew for fifty years until in 1908 it was renamed and remodelled as the Territorial Force. Composed initially of middle-class and often middle-aged gentlemen who elected their own officers and paid for their own uniform and equipment, the Volunteer Force soon became youthful and working-class, with appointed middle-class officers, with a Government subsidy, and a minor military role as an adjunct to the Regular Army.

9781474538329

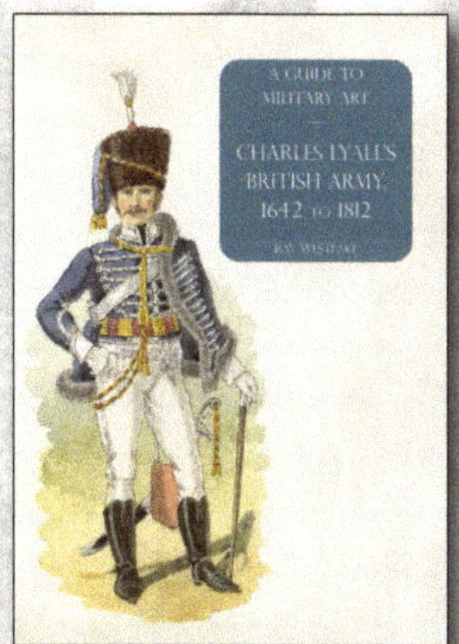

A GUIDE TO MILITARY ART – CHARLES LYALL'S BRITISH ARMY, 1642 TO 1812

One hundred and twenty military figures are shown, and form part of our developing range of books dedicated to Uniformology.

Drawing on the Anne SK Brown Military Collection, Ray has selected a most useful collection of works by Charles Lyall. Covering a broad span of subjects from the 17th, 18th and early 19th century, this series of illustrations is a good reference work for the military modeller and historian, and inspiration for the wargamer who needs to build his army.

9781474538312

www.naval-military-press.com

www.ingramcontent.com/pod-product-compliance
Lightning Source LLC
LaVergne TN
LVHW070408110826
845147LV00017B/973
* 9 7 8 1 4 7 4 5 3 8 3 1 2 *